INTERNET
ACCESS
ESSENTIALS

INTERNET ACCESS ESSENTIALS

ED TITTEL
MARGARET ROBBINS

AP PROFESSIONAL

Boston   San Diego   New York
London   Sydney   Tokyo   Toronto

AP PROFESSIONAL
955 Massachusetts Avenue, Cambridge, MA 02139

An Imprint of ACADEMIC PRESS, INC.
A Division of HARCOURT BRACE & COMPANY

United Kingdom Edition published by
ACADEMIC PRESS LIMITED
24–28 Oval Road, London NW1 7DX

Library of Congress Cataloging-in-Publication Data

Tittel, Ed.
    Internet access essentials / Ed Tittel, Margaret Robbins.
        p.   cm.
    Includes bibliographical references and index.
    ISBN 0-12-691393-5
    1. Internet (Computer network) I. Robbins, Margaret. II. Title.
TK5105.875.I57T58   1995
005.7'13--dc20   94-34444
                                                  CIP

Printed in the United States of America
94 95 96 97 98 IP 9 8 7 6 5 4 3 2 1

Contents

PREFACE   IX

ACKNOWLEDGMENTS   XIII

ABOUT THE AUTHORS   XVII

INTRODUCTION   XIX
Welcome to Internet Access Essentials   xix   •   About This Book   xix   •   How to Use This Book   xx   •   About the Reader   xx   •   How This Book Is Organized   xx   •   Reading the Road Map   xxii

I Introducing the Internet   1

1 WELCOME TO THE INTERNET   5
It's a Dessert Topping—And a Floor Wax!   5   •   A Network of Networks   6   •   Who's On-Line?   7   •   The Internet Culture   10   •   Summary   11

2 A BRIEF HISTORY OF THE INTERNET   13
From Small Things, Big Things Sometimes Come   14   •   Funded by the Advanced Projects Research Administration (ARPA)   17   •   Introducing TCP/IP   24   •   The Birth of the Internet   25   •   The National Science Foundation and Acceptable Usage   27   •   NSF and Acceptable Use Issues   29   •   NREN, the National Research and Education Network   32   •   Summary   32   •   Recommended Reading   33

3 HOW THE INTERNET WORKS 35
*TCP/IP Basics 35 • Understanding TCP/IP's Role in Networking 46 •
Alphabet Soup: IAB, IETF, and RFCs 62 • How the Internet Really Works 65 •
Summary 67 • Recommended Reading 67*

4 HOW TO HOOK UP 71
*What It Means to Be "Connected to the Internet" 71 • Two Types of
Connections 72 • Evaluating Your Needs 73 • What Is Available 80 •
Summary 84*

5 WHO OWNS THE INTERNET? 85
*Who's in Charge Here? 85 • Money and Power 85 • Who Makes It Work 87
• Unofficial Rules 88 • Summary 89*

6 WHAT YOU CAN DO ON THE INTERNET 91
*A Sampler 91 • Mail Call 92 • Library Research in the Privacy of Your
Own Home 92 • Getting Files 93 • The Wonders of Usenet 96 •
Summary 96*

7 CIVICS 101: BEING A GOOD NETIZEN 99
*Electronic Environmentalism 99 • Minimizing Your Impact 99 •
Usenet and E-mail Tips 102 • Summary 105*

8 WHERE IS THE INTERNET GOING? 107
*More Bandwidth 107 • More Services and Service Providers 109 •
More (and Better) Access 110 • More of Everything, Please! 111 •
Summary 112*

II Internet Applications 113

9 INTERNET E-MAIL 117
*What Is E-mail? 117 • How Internet E-mail Works 118 • What You Can Do
with E-mail 120 • Selecting an E-mail Package 120 • How Not to
Drown in E-mail 121 • Exchanging E-mail with Other Networks 122 •
E-mail's Downside 123 • Summary 125*

10 USING USENET 127
*The Central Nervous System of Internet Life 127 • Usenet Basics 128 •
Reading News and Posting Your Own Articles 133 • Usenet Etiquette 136 •
Summary 139*

11 MAILING LISTS 141
*Direct Mail over the Internet 141 • Lists and Newsgroups 142 •
Finding the Mailing Lists 142 • The Mechanics of Mailing Lists 144 •
Mailing List Cautions 145 • Summary 146*

12 GOING INTERACTIVE: TALK AND CHAT   147
*The Art of On-line Conversation   147   •   Using the Talk Command   149   •
What You'll See On-screen   150   •   Internet Relay Chat (IRC)   154   •
Summary   159*

13 FILE TRANSFER PROTOCOL (FTP)   161
*Everything Imaginable Is in a File, Somewhere out There   161   •   What Does
FTP Do?   161   •   Maximizing FTP   172   •   Some Interesting Anonymous
FTP Resources   182   •   Summary   183*

14 TELNET   185
*Why Would You Want To?   185   •   Obtaining a Telnet Connection   186   •
Using Telnet   188   •   Using Anonymous or Service-Based Telnet   191   •
Summary   192*

15 GOING FOR IT: YOUR INTERNET RUNNER   193
*The Famous Rodent   193   •   A Layer of Friendliness   193   •   Getting to
Gopher   194   •   Some Features of Using Gopher   195   •   Summary   197*

16 ARCHIE AND VERONICA   199
*Lost in Riverdale?   199   •   Archie = Archive – V   200   •   Veronica   208   •
Summary   211*

17 WIDE-AREA INFORMATION SERVICE   213
*"We Have WAIS of Making You Talk!"   213   •   Looking for Content?
Use WAIS . . .   214   •   Working with WAIS   216   •   WAIS Commands   218   •
Summary   220*

III Resource Guide   221

18 THE WORLD WIDE WEB   223
*Wonder of the Internet   223   •   From Hypertext to Hypermedia   224   •
Getting the Most the Web Has to Offer   225   •   The Station Wagons of
Web Browsers   226   •   Trying out the Web   227   •   What Is the Web
Good For?   228   •   Summary   229*

19 FINDING OUT WHAT'S OUT THERE   231
The Indexing Problem   231   •   Search Techniques   233   •   Summary   236

20 APPLIED FOLKLORE   237
*Some Things to Avoid   237   •   The Brain Tumor Boy   237   •   My Name Is
Dave Rhodes   238   •   The World Will End Any Day Now   238   •   Worms and
Viruses, or Can I Get Usenet in Jail?   239   •   Summary   239*

21 GOVERNMENT DOCUMENTS   241
*Compiled by Uncle Sam   241   •   Resources   242   •   Send E-mail to an
Elected Official   245   •   Summary   246*

22 FINDING AND MANAGING E-MAIL ADDRESSES 247
Finding People 247 • Ways to Find People 249 • Summary 253

23 GOPHERING FOR GOLD 255
Getting Started 255 • Veronica Search Techniques 256 • Gophering is a Visual Experience 257 • A-Hunting You Should Go! 259 • Summary 260

24 TCP/IP SOFTWARE FOR YOUR PC 261
What to Expect 261 • Shareware/Freeware vs. Commercial Packages 262 • Absolute Basics 264 • Bells, Whistles, and Add-ons 265 • Provider Profiles 265 • Vendor Profiles 266 • Additional Sources of Information 267 • Summary 269

25 BULLETIN BOARD SECRETS 271
Making the Most of Usenet 271 • Finding Things 271 • Controlling the Flood 275 • Summary 276

26 INTERNET IN THE WORKPLACE 277
Where to Begin 277 • User Training 283 • Allocating Resources 284 • Security Rules and Guidelines 285 • Summary 285

27 ACCESS PROVIDERS AND MORE . . . 287
Getting to the Lists 287 • PDIAL 288 • The Public Dialup Internet Access List (PDIAL) 289 • Publications 329

IV **Internet in the Real World   333**

28 Real/Time Communications 335
The Organization 335 • The Network Layout 337 • The Staff 340 • The User Community 341 • RTC's Services and Offerings 342 • Contact Information 343

29 Zilker Internet Park 345
About the Organization 345 • The Zilker Staff 346 • The Network Layout 346 • Zilker's Service Offerings 349 • Zilker's Future Plans 350 • Contact Information 350 • Zilker Publications 351

Appendices

A GLOSSARY OF INTERNET TERMS 353

INDEX 369

PREFACE

INTRODUCING THE *ESSENTIALS* SERIES

Welcome to networking! You may be new to the topic or have some experience with computer networks; either way, we want to help you learn more. In this volume of the series, we tackle the granddaddy—or is it the grandma?—of all networks, known as the *Internet*, and try to provide a useful handbook/tour guide to show you what's out there and how to use it.

Maybe you've already looked for a reference on the Internet and have been overwhelmed by the number of options. According to our own bookstore survey, more than a hundred titles describing the Internet are available today. So why do we, your humble authors, need to write another one? The answer is in the concept behind the series, and in how it informs this book.

The *Essentials* series aims to fill the gap between theory and practice for networking. It offers solid, practical, networking information, without jargon or unnecessary detail. It explains networking topics in clear, concise language, and plainly defines terms that may be unfamiliar. The series is divided into the topics most likely to be of use to network administrators, from setting up a network to finding problems with it, to more specialized topics such as mobile computing and electronic messaging. Each book takes a gentle, lighthearted approach to the material that focuses on the basic principles an administrator needs to know to master the topic, with plenty of tips and proven techniques gleaned from the authors' wealth of practical experience in putting theory into practice.

INTERNET ACCESS ESSENTIALS

Where the Internet is concerned, what makes our book different from some of the others is that we assume little or no foreknowledge of Internet culture, history, or capabilities, and lead you into each one as best we can. In fact, we tried to lay out the materials so there's something for everyone, whether beginner, novice, or seasoned cybernaut.

What makes our book different from some of the other Internet tomes is that we make no attempt to provide an encyclopedic reference to all of the Internet's resources, services, and abilities; our book is designed as much to provide a set of techniques for you to do your own exploration as it is to provide a roadmap to what's out there on the Internet. Finally, our book is designed to provide useful tools and techniques to help you learn for yourself and to supply you with the essential information you'll need to be able to navigate and cope with the Internet's embarrassment of riches.

THE OTHER MEMBERS OF THE ESSENTIALS CAST

Three books in this series will be of interest to anyone operating a local area network. The first, *Network Design Essentials*, covers everything the reader needs to know to put a smoothly running network in place, including the maintenance tasks that will keep it running. The second book, *E-mail Essentials* is intended to be useful to anyone who uses message-based applications over a network or who needs to understand how to design, install, or manage an electronic mail system. A future title, *Network and Systems Management Essentials*, discusses in practical detail how to identify, diagnose, and solve problems on a local area network.

The remaining books in the series are intended to expand on networking topics that should apply to most, but not all, network administrators. This book, the third in the series, responds to the recent explosive growth of that huge network of networks, the Internet, and is designed to help you to tap into the enormous and sometimes overwhelming treasure trove of information that the Internet represents. And if your computing needs extend to large, far-flung networks, you'll definitely want to investigate both *Internetworking Essentials* and *Wide Area Networking Essentials,* which should appear in bookstores in 1995.

Tell Us What You Think

The authors want to hear from you about these books. Please write to us care of the publisher, or contact us through the electronic mail addresses we provide in the About the Authors section. We'd like to hear more about what you liked and didn't like about these books, and on your ideas for other topics or more details that you need for your networking life.

In closing we'd like to say: "Thanks for buying this book." We hope you find it worth the money you've paid for it, and the time it takes to read!

ACKNOWLEDGMENTS

Together, we have lots of people to thank for helping us with this book and for making this series possible. We want to start with Dave Pallai, the editorial director at AP PROFESSIONAL, who has kept us around even after we finished the first two books in this series. We sincerely hope that the project continues to live up to his expectations and that it will repay him handsomely for the time, effort, and attention he has lavished on us. To Karen Pratt, the editorial supervisor: thanks for getting us set up and working so smoothly and quickly! To Reuben Kantor and Mike Lindgren, thanks for working out all of the details with us, for being there when we needed you, and for making this project so easy to finish! If there is anybody else at APP we haven't mentioned, we want to thank them for their help and apologize for omitting their names.

This time, we get to thank a whole host of heroes, sung and unsung, who made the Internet possible. Starting with the original architects and implementers like J. C. R. Licklider, Robert Kahn, Steven Carr, Vinton Cerf, Bob Metcalfe, Steve Crocker, Dave Crocker, Frank Heart, Alex McKenzie, Severo Ornstein, Jon Postel, Larry Roberts, Steve Taylor, and Dave Walden—we have too many people to thank to possibly mention, but we thank them all anyway with vast gratitude and appreciation. Our own particular favorite mentors (in print, anyway) have to include John Davidson, Bill Stallings, Andrew Tanenbaum, Marshall Rose, and Douglas Comer. Ed also particularly wants to thank Robert Zakon for his excellent Internet Timeline, which helped to get his thoughts on Internet history organized and in order!

We also need to thank the newest member of our team. Dawn Isaacks, who's joined us as an editorial assistant, is doing a great job of helping us keep our eyes crossed and our T's dotted! Finally, we'd like to continue our effusive thanks to our production person, closet humorist, graphic artist, and print professional extraordinaire Susan Price, proprietoress of Susan Price and Associates, and still the fastest keyboardist on the planet. We couldn't do this project without you, Susan, especially the typesetting, but also the index, the graphics, and so much more!

ED TITTEL

I'd like to continue my acknowledgments close to home, with effusive thanks to my family. Thanks to each of you, Suzy, Austin and Chelsea, for putting up with all the time I've spent working on this and other books (hard to believe it's my ninth one). Dusty, our seven-year-old Labrador retriever, continues his sterling job of keeping me moving during the daytime and providing regular keyboard breaks.

My special thanks go to Bob LeVitus, who got me started on this strange oddysey with the *Stupid* books, and who taught me how good books get made (titles notwithstanding). Thanks also to Carole McClendan, my agent at Waterside, who was able to package this project and pull it off. And thanks again, Margaret Robbins, for making yet another project so much fun and for singlehandedly meeting our first manuscript deadline. Finally, I'd like to thank my early IP and Internet mentors from the Excelan days—Rich Bohdanowicz, Brian Meek, Duane Murray, Steve Spanier, and Carolyn Rose—for teaching me most of the useful stuff I've learned about networking! You're still the greatest, even after all these years.

All of the good things about this book can probably be attributed to others, especially Margaret. All of the stuff you don't like or can't understand is probably my doing.

MARGARET ROBBINS

My heartfelt thanks go again first to Ed. The time during which we worked together on this book has been a fairly interesting time for both of us; no matter what happens, Ed remains cheerful and unfazed. Another fun project completed, and many more to go. Thanks also to everyone at Waterside, especially Carole and Belinda—they're always patient, helpful, and professional.

Every now and then we get a chance to see just how much we appreciate the support of friends and family. Carolyn, Paula, Stan, Roy, Volker, it just wouldn't be worth it without all those good talks and fun times. Thank you.

ABOUT THE AUTHORS

MARGARET ROBBINS

Ms. Robbins is coauthor of four other books. She wrote the first two, *Networking with Windows for Workgroups* and *Novell's Guide to NetWare 3.12 Networks*, with Cheryl Currid. Her third and fourth books, *Network Design Essentials* and *E-mail Essentials*, are the first two books in the *Essentials* series, of which this book is the third member.

When not writing, Ms. Robbins works as a software developer and has spent over a decade programming software involving various aspects of networking and telecommunications. Most recently, she spent four years at VTEL Corporation helping develop easy and fun user interfaces for its line of video conferencing products. You can reach her on CompuServe at 75730,1451, or via Internet at mrobbins@bga.com.

ED TITTEL

Mr. Tittel is the author of numerous articles for the computer trade press and of several books on computer-related topics, including *NetWare for Dummies* (IDG Press, 1993) and a series of PC shareware books, cowritten with Bob LeVitus. He recently concentrated on computer networking, for which he is best known, and has written extensively on that subject for the likes of *MacWeek, MacUser, ComputerWorld, Byte, WindowsUser,* and other publications.

Most recently, Mr. Tittel worked as director of corporate marketing at Novell, Inc., where he was responsible for technical content of trade shows and Novell-sponsored conferences, which is how he learned about networking. You can reach him on CompuServe at 76376,606 or on the Internet at: etittel@zilker.net.

INTRODUCTION

WELCOME TO INTERNET ACCESS ESSENTIALS

Welcome to the *Essentials* series from AP PROFESSIONAL. *Internet Access Essentials* is the third book in the series and is dedicated to telling you everything you need to know about using the Internet—from obtaining access to its cornucopia of information, to living with the Internet from day to day. Like the rest of the *Essentials* series, this book concentrates on the real-life information any user needs to get up and running on the Internet and to work with it smoothly and efficiently.

ABOUT THIS BOOK

This fourth book in the series will take you through the history and evolution of the Internet and will lay out the many modes of interaction and the many kinds of information it supports. It will also cover the basic capabilities of Internet access software and methods, as well as providing a map of the territory in Cyberspace that the Internet spans. In addition to providing detailed instructions about where to go, what to do, and what software may be worth investigating, *Internet Access Essentials* also includes tips about what to do in special circumstances, including problem situations.

How to Use This Book

We designed this book so that you don't have to read it from cover to cover. If you like, you can just pick it up at any point and start reading or you can begin wherever you find a topic of interest. The cross-references, along with the index and the table of contents, will help you build your own thread through this material in whatever way makes sense for your particular situation. Of course, if you want to read it straight through from front to back, that works too! It's a tool, though, not the "great American novel." We want you to find it valuable enough to carry it with you as you work and hope it ends up dog-eared and stained from constant use.

About the Reader

Is this book for you? We assume that you, our gentle reader, have some familiarity with personal computers—you probably know a little of the jargon and most likely have one on your desk. You are probably not a complete beginner, but just in case, we define most terms so that you can get around without trouble. You know a little bit about the Internet and what it can do for you, and you want to know more.

Here's what we think might be driving you to read this book: perhaps you have a network in your workplace already and have been asked to investigate this "Internet thing", or you have reasons of your own to catch the Internet wave. Or perhaps you have no experience with the Internet at all and need to find out what's up. On the other hand, you may be an old Internet hand, looking for more information to assist your less experienced colleagues or coworkers. Whatever your reason for wanting to learn, *Internet Access Essentials* will supply you with everything you need to know to get onto the Internet, to explore its wealth of resources, to find what you need, and to get the job done!

How This Book Is Organized

This book is divided into four sections. The first section of the book contains orientation information. Scan this introduction, along with the table of contents, to get your bearings about what's in the book and where to find what you need.

Part 1, Introducing E-mail

This part of the book covers all the background you'll need to understand the Internet. We discuss what the Internet is, cover its history, describe what it includes, and how it works. We go over the fundamentals you'll want to apply when you sit down to interact with the Internet, as well as some key concepts to make that process easier. Also, we look at some strategies for getting the most from your time (and money) while using the Internet.

Part 2, Internet Applications

In this part we get into the real nuts and bolts of the software tools and techniques you'll use to interact with the Internet. Here we describe how to use Internet electronic mail, cover the ins and outs of Usenet, and talk about mailing lists. We also cover the basic Internet applications, including those for conducting real-time conversations, transferring files, logging into remote systems, and searching for information from a variety of resources. We include crucial strategies for getting the best from your Internet connection, including mastering the art of proper connections and identifying and working with Internet service providers.

Part 3, Resource Guide

This is your Internet toolbox and learning guide. In this part of the book, we try to teach exploratory techniques for locating and accessing items of potential interest. We also describe the elements of the Internet culture and its rules for behavior (called *netiquette*), to help newcomers learn about the Internet natives, and their sometimes puzzling customs and rituals. In addition, this section also describes how to navigate the government's presence on the Internet, from obtaining electronic copies of all kinds of interesting documents, to sending e-mail to the White House.

From a more workplace-oriented perspective, this is also the part of the book wherein we talk about locating and selecting front-end software for Internet access, about obtaining company connections and services, and more. We conclude with a chapter on Internet resources that covers how to learn more about the Internet itself, including access providers, vendors, publications, and other potential sources of useful information.

Part 4, Case Studies

Here we give you some real-life examples. In this part we look at two different Internet access providers, one small, and one of medium size, to examine their installations in terms of the principles covered in the first three sections of the book. We discuss their configurations and internal operations to help you understand what's on the other end of the relationship when you arrange for Internet access from a service provider. In addition, their setups may point you at some design elements and strategies you might otherwise not have considered. Either way, it represents what we hope is a valuable opportunity to learn from the experience of others!

Reference Materials

Near the very back of the book you'll find a glossary of technical terms where we try to turn computerspeak into something a bit closer to English. Since networkers and the Internet community are so fond of acronyms, we've also tried to explode (or at least expand) them all for your potential edification here, too.

Finally, if you need to look up or cross-reference something, we provided a thorough index at the back of the book to assist your search. Happy hunting!

READING THE ROAD MAP

Remember, there are no rules about how to read this book. Start at the front and go straight through to the back if you like; you'll absorb everything you need to know about the Internet that way. Or, if you have a specific topic you'd like to investigate, start anywhere that interests you. Use the cross-references, along with the index, glossary, and table of contents, to jump to other sections of the book and move through in whatever way makes the most sense for your needs. Each chapter is designed to be complete by itself, so dive right in. Whatever you do, enjoy it!

INTRODUCING THE INTERNET

I

OVERVIEW

Welcome to the fast-growing and exciting electronic world of wonders that is the Internet! This first section of the book covers all the basics about the Internet, from the major concepts to the important roadside attractions, and offers some practical tips to consider before going on-line to the Internet. It also goes over what types of things you can do with the Internet and discusses some features you will want to consider when looking for Internet access software. When you finish reading this section you'll have a good idea what the Internet can do for you, about basic Internet capabilities, services, and resources; and how to make sure you get the most out of your access without too much time wasting or frustration.

The eight chapters in this section fall into three categories. The first three chapters provide an Internet background and description, the next three discuss obtaining access and what the Internet can enable you to do, and the final two chapters in the section cover the basics of proper Internet usage and behavior and talk about what may lie in the Internet's future.

BASIC NETWORKING CONCEPTS

The first three chapters cover the basics. In Chapter 1 we lay the groundwork for understanding the Internet and define some essential terms that you'll be seeing throughout the book. This chapter introduces the user's view of how the Internet works, what holds it all together, and who the key players are. Chapter 2, "A Brief History of the Internet," describes the systems, events, and programs that have led the Internet to what and where it is today. Then in Chapter 3, "How the Internet Works," we look at the Internet's organization and behavior in terms of addressing, network connections, important applications, and discuss how the Internet is governed and managed (or not, as the case may be).

GETTING ONTO (AND INTO) THE INTERNET

In the next three chapters we get onto and into the Internet, at least metaphorically speaking. First, Chapter 4, "How to Hook Up," supplies you with the points you need to consider in obtaining the right kind of Internet connection. Chapter 4 also describes how to locate and obtain Internet access from one of the many commercial providers, some of whom may be operating from a telephone exchange near you. Chapter 5, "Who Owns the Internet?" describes the many constituencies and interest groups with a presence on the Internet, and the ownership of the medium and the messages it carries. Finally, Chapter 6, "What You Can Do on the Internet," takes you through a thrilling sampler of the many activities and resources that might constitute a typical day for an Internet user.

INTERNET USAGE, BEHAVIOR AND DIRECTIONS

In the next two chapters we go on to the rules of the road for that part of the information superhighway covered by the Internet, and take a look at where that road seems to be leading us. Chapter 7, "Civics 101: Being a Good Netizen," covers usage guidelines and other rules of etiquette and considerate behavior that should help you maintain a good image on the Internet. It also deals with some basic do's and don'ts, and provides some useful pointers on the difference between verbal and written communication.

Chapter 8, "Where's the Internet Going?" raises and answers some interesting questions about the impact of increasing bandwidth and ever more powerful software on the kinds of the things the Internet can deliver. It also addresses some important issues about the potential impact of the Internet on how we do business with one another today and how it could change things in the future.

WELCOME TO THE INTERNET

1

IT'S A DESSERT TOPPING—AND A FLOOR WAX!

You've probably been hearing a lot about the Internet lately. Take a quick look through a big city newspaper and you can find a reference to it in every section. In the main section, for instance, you'll find coverage of a political speech in which a government representative talks about the importance of the Internet. Turn to the business section, where a media company announces a new way to take advantage of the Internet. In the human interest pages, you'll see a feature about a user who has found an innovative way to use it. Even characters in comic strips talk about it.

But what is it?

There are a lot of ways to answer this question, and how you choose to answer it is really a matter of how you use it. To some people it's a source of entertainment, to others, a research tool; to others, a disaster-proof defense infrastructure (see the history of the Internet in Chapter 2), and to some, it is a gold mine of money-making opportunities.

The most general definition, however, describes the Internet as a network of networks. Of course, if you're not sure what a network is, that definition won't help much, so we elaborate in a later section. But the fact that there are so many different definitions indicates the real answer to the question—the Internet, in a sense, is anything you want it to be. If you use the Internet to get information about building models of 1950s airplanes, that's what the Internet is to you. Similarly, if you are a legal scholar researching all of the decisions of the U.S. Supreme Court in the last 30 years, then the Internet is your reference library. If you're a travel buff wanting to find out what the weather is like in eastern Mongolia this time of year, the Internet can be your advisor.

Let's back up a bit and explain what we mean by *a network of networks*. Then we go on to discuss in a bit more detail some of the things you can do on the Internet and how its treasures can benefit you.

A NETWORK OF NETWORKS

You're probably familiar with networks already, because you very likely use one in your workplace. In this section we clarify what we mean by the term *network* and explore what it all means to you. We start with some basic definitions and move forward from there.

What Is a Network?

A network is any group of computers connected together to share information resources. If the computers are connected within a single building or similarly sized area, the network is called a *local area network*, or LAN. The number of computers on a LAN could be as few as two or could number in the thousands, though most LANs today connect fewer than 20 computers. These computers are connected via coaxial cable, twisted pair wires, fiber optic cable, or perhaps even radio transmissions. The connection method, however, does not concern us. The only characteristic that makes a network a LAN is that it extends over a relatively small area (compared to the size of cities, for instance, or countries).

When a LAN extends outside a building, it becomes a *wide area network*, or WAN. It's helpful to think of a WAN as a collection of LANs, communicating with each other by telephone, satellite, or some other non-LAN type of connection. A WAN can extend between two adjacent buildings, across a city, or across the world. Because a WAN is really a group of networks, it is also sometimes called an *internetwork*.

The most famous internetwork in the world today, and arguably the largest, is the Internet. This is a network of thousands of different networks from all over the world. Some of these networks have only one or two computers, others have thousands. The number of users, by some estimates, is in the tens of millions, and is growing at an amazing rate. You, too, can be a part of this growth.

Getting Access

Getting access to the Internet is also pretty different from getting access to the local workplace network. Typically, to get onto the office network, you just call up the network administrator and arrange for that person to add an account for you. That person often also handles making sure that you have the correct wiring to your office so that your computer can operate over the network and might even be the same person who makes sure you have a computer in the first place.

Unfortunately, getting onto the Internet is not that easy. There is no network administrator, nor is there any single "right" way of gaining access. To get onto the Internet, you need to know a lot more about it than you do about your office network, including how your computer can connect to the network and how to get an account. The mission of this book is to give you that background and to whet your appetite for all the treats available to you once you get connected.

WHO'S ON-LINE?

To get a better picture of what the Internet is and what it can offer you, let's take a look at some of the types of organizations and individuals who regularly use the Internet and what they do with it—you may get some more ideas for your own use as well.

Universities and Schools

To encourage technology education, the United States federal government has a policy that they will subsidize the Internet connections of educational institutions, but only if the institution in turn makes Internet access available to every student. In the past, only universities could afford to take advantage of this offer, because giving students access meant getting computers for those students to use. As a result, many university students have had the chance to go exploring on the Internet in the last decade or so. Now, with more and more elementary and secondary schools getting on-line, you're just as likely to encounter a fourth-grade student as a college student on the Internet.

What are these students doing? Often they are assigned projects requiring them to do research on-line, to teach them various computing skills. They might take surveys, access historical documents, or sift through weather records. Many use the Internet as a social tool, too, exchanging e-mail with other users and participating in discussions on everything from encryption technology to the Denver underground music scene.

University users are also the graduate students, faculty, and staff of various educational institutions. They might exchange papers with colleagues across the oceans or across the city. They use the Internet to track developments in their fields and keep in touch with professional contacts, as well as to search for data to aid their research projects.

Libraries

Whether university or state run, many libraries have Internet connections. This means that users can log in to the library computer to search for a particular book, article, recording, or other document. Users can not only determine whether the library carries the material they need, they can find out whether the item is currently in stock and what other libraries might have it. In some cases, users can even view the contents of short items such as articles, without ever entering the library building.

U.S. Government Agencies

The United States government is not particularly famous for making all of its information easily accessible to its citizens. However, since most of what the government publishes is not subject to copyright protection, it is possible for network users to rectify the situation by making the information available to themselves. And they have done so with dramatic results.

You can access census data, weather data, and State Department travel advisories from the Internet. Perhaps you want to search the current federal budget for a particular keyword—it's possible via the Internet. If you need information about food labeling regulations and contents, you can get to that too. It is also possible to skim through White House press briefings and send e-mail to the president, vice-president, or your local representative. (It's not particularly likely that they'll answer personally, but it's not unheard of.)

It's a bit unfair to suggest that the government is reticent with its information; it's more a problem of the overwhelming quantity. It has provided access to many public documents in the past few years and continues to add more all the time. Chapter 22 discusses these documents in greater detail.

Governments of Other Countries

While every country has different policies concerning public access to government documents and therefore might not have all of their documents on-line, most countries do recognize the importance of being tied into the global exchange of data and ideas that the Internet is facilitating. As a result, you'll find that most countries in the world have recognized Internet addresses. These addresses might go only to a government office or to the main state university, and they might be full Internet addresses or less-elaborate e-mail-only sites. Whatever type of access, you can now send e-mail to approximately 140 of the 190 or so countries in the world, and that number will probably be higher by the time you read this.

Corporations

Very large corporations have long had a presence on the Internet, which they used to exchange information with remote branches, universities with whom they had partnerships, and other corporations with whom they had joint ventures. Until recently, though, the cost of hooking up was so high, and the benefits so vague, that only a very few smaller companies even bothered. With costs coming down and the benefits becoming more obvious, however, it is now possible for

ABC Computing to have just as much of a voice in on-line discussions and just as much access to new materials and data as IBM.

Nonprofit Organizations

The goal and charter of many nonprofit organizations is changing. Increasingly, they are data-collection operations, and their responsibility is to make that data accessible to the public. Internet access, they are finding, is the ideal mechanism to making their data available to the largest number of people. From environmental groups collecting information about toxic waste dumping to political watchdog organizations presenting campaign finance data, nonprofits are turning to the Internet more and more to help them get their messages out.

Individuals

This is a group of users that is very hard to describe. Such people come to the Internet for a huge variety of reasons and access it in hundreds of different ways. These are people who know that the Internet has a lot to offer them and perhaps have computers at home, at school, or at the office, which they can use to access the Internet. They want to be able to get to research results about topics that interest them, view graphics images of famous paintings, talk with others who share their passion for travel or music, send submissions to magazines, send work to the office, or send mail to a friend. They were unable to pay the massive amounts of money that a connection would have cost them a few years ago, but with the multitude of new providers, that's no longer necessary.

THE INTERNET CULTURE

The Internet is much more than a collection of networks or computers. Its nature is really an agreement by the people who use it and who have used it and created it over the last couple of decades. They have a set of beliefs, values, and ideals, and it's good to have a sense of those values before you go traipsing through the woods. Like someone from the United States traveling to the Middle East and sitting with the soles of his feet pointing toward his host, it is possible to unwittingly offend people on the Internet simply because you don't know the local culture and customs. If you make such a transgression, you could find the results unpleasant.

As with any culture, most miscommunications happen when people interact. So if you spend all your time on the Internet tunneling between ftp sites (see Chapter 13), you run less risk of transgression than if you spent all your time in Usenet newsgroups (Chapter 10). Therefore we go into the cultural aspects of each type of service in the appropriate chapters. Most are common sense matters designed to keep the Net as useful as possible to a large number of people, so you probably won't find any of the local customs to be terribly burdensome.

SUMMARY

All of the riches of the Internet are available to you if you have a computer and a modem. You don't need a high-powered graphics workstation, either—a fairly basic home personal computer can work just fine, as long as it can run the necessary software.

Like your computer, or your electric drill, the Internet is a tool. To drill holes you need understand only how to use your drill, not how it works. To a certain extent, the same is true of the Internet. Your drill, however, has a lot fewer features, and there is only one way (well, maybe two) to pick it up. Not so with the Internet—there are dozens of ways to access it and thousands of uses, so you have to know more about it to use it effectively. This chapter gave you an overview of some of those uses; the rest of the book will give you the background you need to get to them.

A Brief History of the Internet

2

In many ways, the whole Internet phenomenon is the upside of the United States military's involvement in research and academia. At a time when at least one of this book's authors was protesting the military's involvement in activities in Southeast Asia at the Institute for Defense Analysis at Princeton, the same "military–industrial complex" was laying the foundation for an explosion of computer networking and communications technology that has made the Internet what it is today. This same amorphous conglomeration of the military, business, academic, and research institutions has also enabled the realization — or at least the articulation—of concepts like the national or global information infrastructure, worldwide telecommunications, the global satellite network, and much, much more. Given the bounty and blessings that have resulted, it's hard to keep thinking of them as the bad guys.

In fact, were it not for a Department of Defense organization known as the Advanced Research Projects Administration (ARPA), the Internet as we know it today couldn't exist. This organization, and its successors, were instrumental in supplying the funding, the encouragement, and the old-fashioned kind of networking that brings human beings together that made possible the new-fangled kind of networking so necessary to the Internet. In this chapter we take a look at the sequence of events and some of the key players who made this whole thing happen. As we walk down memory lane, we also see why the Internet is as much a community and a mindset as it is any collection of computers and communications links.

FROM SMALL THINGS, BIG THINGS SOMETIMES COME

As one of the biggest buyers of any kind of technology that comes along, the United States government was an early and enthusiastic investor in computing technology. The earliest incarnations of computers—those tube-driven, room-sized monsters with names like ENIAC and MANIAC—were built at the government's behest, to assist with the war effort in World War II. Ever since, the government has been up to its ears in the bleeding edge of computing technology, while maintaining what is probably the largest collection of computing equipment of any organization in the world.

Thus, it should come as no surprise that the government scientists and engineers entrusted with the care and feeding of the earliest computers quickly realized that increasing access to such scarce and expensive beasts would be to everyone's benefit (especially the taxpayers'). They also realized that making it possible for computers to communicate with each other would enable the transfer of information in a much quicker and more useful way than shipping around punch cards, paper tapes, or other forms of information.

Have Your Computer Call My Computer . . .

The earliest methods of getting computers to communicate with one another typically depended on stringing wires between pairs of them and working out the programming details to enable each machine to understand what the other one was saying. The same approach worked pretty well for hooking other devices to computers, such as printers, disk drives, terminals, and other kinds of peripherals. However, the limits of these wires could easily make themselves felt, simply because the strength of a signal is inversely proportional to the length of the wire it has to traverse (think of shouting down a very long hallway—the further down the hall the sound has to travel, the louder you have to yell).

From the beginning, the telephone system helped to provide the wires that could tie together computers that were far apart from one another. This required the development of technology that would let computers, which communicate in signal patterns that stand for ones and zeros (binary digits, or bits), use the phone lines, which are primarily intended to conduct sound rather than binary data.

Devices that modulated the computer signals into audible tones to send across the phone lines and then demodulated them back into computer signals on the other end were developed to let computers use the phone system. Today, we call these devices *modems* (MOdulator/DEModulators), and they are still the primary devices used to let computers communicate via telephone lines.

The voice heritage of the telephone system poses some interesting problems for computer communication, even when the binary to analog conversion issues handled by the modem are solved. For one thing, the human ear can understand a conversation reasonably well when only a small portion of the audible sound spectrum (say only 15% of the range of human hearing) is provided by a phone link. This makes a tolerable vehicle for moving voice, but a very narrow pipe for transporting computer data.

Thus one of the issues in using telephone links between computers always has been (and still remains) the bandwidth, or the "size" of the pipe that a telephone line provides. This remains true even today, when megabit-sized pipes are commercially available, and gigabyte-sized pipes are starting to become possible.

For continuous connections between one computer and another, like those needed for a network connection, the telephone line that links them has to be up and running all the time. Because this means that the line is completely consumed by this use, it's called a *dedicated circuit* in phone lingo, and such connections cost a fair amount of money even today. When they first came into use in the 1960s, they cost a great deal more in today's dollars.

The longer the distance between the computers that need to be linked, the more complicated those connections become. Even in the days when the phone company was one big domestic conglomerate (Ma Bell) in the United States, getting different regional operations to supply dedicated circuits and fail-safe connections became more difficult as the distance increased. Today, with needs for connections as likely to be international as domestic, the problems are magnified by the kinds of distances that are possible and the number of potential carriers involved. On the plus side, though, there's a lot more experience in handling data communications in the carriers than there used to be!

Let's Get Serious About Communications!

By the late 1950s, it became clear that some alternatives to telephone links were desirable, for a host of technical and expense-related reasons. With the number of computers well into the hundreds, the need for real networking was born—that is, the development of technologies to allow many users to run many activities while accessing many shared computers.

This need for manifold access and sharing is what made the telephone unsuitable: when one computer calls another, the connection between them is called a *circuit* based on telephone terminology. While that circuit is active, nobody else can participate in the ongoing conversation. So, although the telephone will theoretically let any two properly equipped computers communicate, it is difficult for more than two to get together this way.

Various kinds of schemes for letting multiple users share a common line or transmission medium, called *multiplexing*, were developed and tried in the 1950s and 1960s. Like radio or television, both of which break their usable frequencies into limited bands or channels, multiplexing lets computers take out regular time slices (called *time-division multiplexing*) or portions of the signal spectrum (called *frequency-division multiplexing*) and use them more or less independently on a common line. This only made the bandwidth problem worse for telephone connections, though, because it took a narrow pipe and subdivided it into even more narrow pieces.

What was needed, unfortunately, was a bigger pipe; one better suited for computer conversations than human ones.

Parceling Plentitudinous Packets Perfectly

By the end of the 1960s, a more suitable approach for handling computer traffic was developed, called *packet switching*. Instead of breaking up the pipe over time (as with time-division multiplexing) or over the bandwidth (as with frequency-division multiplexing), a new approach recognized the possibility of many routes between any two points A and B, and broke up the traffic by route was created. Because this approach requires breaking an arbitrarily long message into equal-sized packages of information, called *packets*, and switching routes depending on the best one available at the time any one packet gets shipped, it is known as *packet switching*.

As long as the resulting packets are properly labeled when a message gets disassembled for shipment, and those labels can be read upon receipt, the individual packets can arrive in any order and can take whatever routes are available. The computers that need to communicate can handle this disassembly/assembly work for themselves, by adding a special set of tags to each packet during disassembly. At a minimum, such tags would include a sender and receiver address, a sequence or identification number, and a variety of data quality-control information that would enable a receiver to make sure that the information had arrived exactly as sent by the transmitter.

All that is required, with this kind of approach, is a set of computers at each link between any two or more lines, to read incoming information from a line and route it onto another line, if appropriate, or to hand off information intended for use at the current location. Of course, each computer must know how to read the destination address in each packet and what routes to use to forward the packet on to that destination. In this approach, the links between computers are called *lines*, and the computers where lines come together are called *nodes*. This lingo comes from the mathematical field of graph theory, where collections of interlinked nodes are known formally as networks. Because this kind of setup lets computers communicate, they are known informally as *networks* to most of us today (but that wasn't always the case).

This kind of environment is called a *packet-switched network* because packets are continually being switched from one line to another by the connecting nodes, as they forward information on from sender to receiver. Packet-switching lets many senders and receivers share a common transmission medium because the labels keep individual transmissions distinct, even as they mingle during the transmission process. It also lets links be chosen preferentially, based on cost or availability, so that the routes through the network can change as nodes enter or leave, and even help relieve congestion by equalizing traffic across alternate routes.

FUNDED BY THE ADVANCED PROJECTS RESEARCH ADMINISTRATION (ARPA)

As it turns out, packet-switching was the technology that made the raw beginnings of the Internet possible. A branch of the Department of Defense, ARPA was chartered with finding more and better ways to network the government's growing collection of expensive computing equipment around the country (and the world). In the late 1960s, ARPA provided funding for a group of academic institutions to build an experimental network to develop and experiment with packet-switching technologies, to see if they could provide a workable solution for using expensive long-distance leased lines to link computers in several states.

Several key ingredients made this experiment particularly significant: First, the initial idea was to connect different kinds of computers at different sites, rather than only linking machines from a single manufacturer. This deliberately made the communications problem more complex, but ensured that the resulting hardware and software would have the broadest applications. Second, the idea was to assist a widely dispersed group of researchers in working together and to learn how to use networks with computers. Therefore, ARPA wanted the resulting network to support a broad range of capabilities, including remote access for users at one site on machines at another site, for exchanging files across the network, and for sharing resources like printers, plotters, or other kinds of specialized output devices. At the time, electronic mail was no part of the design requirements, but its importance quickly made itself known as the earliest users learned that they could just as easily exchange text message files among themselves, as well as programs, data, and more conventional computer information.

More than packet-switching, the requirements for linking heterogeneous computer systems and providing multiple types of communications capabilities are what laid the foundation for the Internet as we know it today. In a way, ARPA's experiment has succeeded beyond anybody's wildest dreams!

Welcome to the ARPAnet

The creation of the ARPAnet, a packet-switched long-haul computer network, was presaged by several significant events and elements. These are depicted in the time-line shown in Figure 2.1, taken from Robert H Zakon's Internet timeline v1.3 (see "Recommended Reading" at the end of this chapter for the details). The first is Paul Baran's seminal paper, "On Distributed Communications Networks," which laid the architectural ground work for ARPAnet. Then in 1967 the main academic computing organization in the United States, the Association for Computing Machinery (ACM), held a symposium on Operating Principles that laid out a plan for building a nationwide packet-switched network. This resulted in a meeting in 1968 at ARPA where several organizations pitched the idea of a long-haul network to the agency in a bid for funding.

Hobbes' Internet Timeline v1.3
by
Robert H'obbes' Zakon
hobbes@hobbes.mitre.org

1956	USSR launches Sputnik, first artificial earth satellite. In response, U.S. forms the Advanced Research Projects Agency (ARPA) within the Department of Defense (DoD) to establish U.S. lead in science and technology applicable to the military. (:amk:)
1962	Paul Baran, RAND: "On Distributed Communications Networks"—Packet-switching networks; no single outage point
1967	ACM Symposium on Operating Principles—Plan presented for a packet-switching network
1968	Network presentation to the Advanced Research Projects Agency (ARPA)
1969	ARPANET commissioned by DoD for research into networking.
1970	ALOHAnet developed by Norman Abramson, U of Hawaii (:sk2:)
	ARPANET hosts start using Network Control Protocol (NCP).
1971	15 nodes (23 hosts): UCLA, SRI, UCSB, U of Utah, BBN, MIT, RAND, SDC, Harvard, Lincoln Lab, Stanford, UIU(C), CWRU, CMU, NASA/Ames
1972	International Conference on Computer Communications with demonstration of ARPANET between 40 machines organized by Bob Kahn.
	Internetworking Working Group (INWG) created to address need for establishing agreed-upon protocols. Chairman: Vinton Cerf.
	Ray Tomlinson of BBN invents e-mail program to send messages across a distributed network. (:amk:)
1973	First international connections to the ARPANET: England and Norway
	Bob Metcalfe's Harvard PhD dissertation outlines idea for Ethernet (:amk:)
1974	Vint Cerf and Bob Kahn publish "A Protocol for Packet Network Internetworking" which specified in detail the design of a Transmission Control Program (TCP). (:amk:)
	BBN opens Telnet, commercial version of ARPANET (:sk2:)
1975	Operational management of Internet transferred to DCA (now DISA)
1976	UUCP (Unix-to-Unix CoPy) developed at AT&T's Bell Labs and distributed with UNIX one year later.
1977	THEORYNET created at U of Wisconsin providing e-mail to more than 100 computer science researchers using UUCP.
1979	Meeting between U of Wisconsin, DARPA, NSF, and computer scientists from many universities to establish a Computer Science Department research computer network.
	USENET established using UUCP between Duke and UNC by Tom Truscott and Steve Bellovin.
1981	BITNET, the "Because It's Time NETwork," started as a cooperative network at the City University of New York. Provides e-mail and listserv servers to distribute information. Unlike USENET, where client software is needed, e-mail is the only tool necessary.

Figure 2.1 *An excerpt from Hobbes' Internet Timeline v1.3 (continued)*

Figure 2.1—continued

1981   Minitel (Teletel) is deployed across France by French Telecom.

1982   INWG establishes the Transmission Control Protocol (TCP) and Internet Protocol (IP), as the protocol suite, commonly known as TCP/IP for ARPANET. This leads to one of the first definitions of an "internet" as a connected set of networks, specifically those using TCP/IP and "Internet" as connected TCP/IP internets.

   DoD declares TCP/IP suite to be standard for DoD (:vgc:)

1983   Name server developed at U of Wisconsin, no longer requiring users to know the exact path to other systems.

   CSNET / ARPANET gateway put in place

   Desktop workstations come into being, many with Berkeley UNIX, which includes IP networking software. Berkeley releases 4.2BSD incorporating TCP/IP (:mpc:)

   EARN (European Academic and Research Network) established. Very similar to BITNET.

   FidoNet developed by Tom Jennings.

1984   JUNET (Japan Unix NETwork) established using UUCP.

1986   NSFNET created (backbone speed of 56Kbps). ARPANET bureaucracy keeps it from being use to interconnect centers; NSFNET comes into being with the aid of NASA and DOE. This allows an explosion of connections, especially from universities.

1987   Number of hosts breaks 10,000; number of BITNET hosts breaks 1,000.

1989   Number of hosts breaks 100,000. NSF backbone upgraded to T1 (1.544 Mbps). First relay between a commercial electronic mail carrier (CompuServe) and the Internet.

1990   ARPANET ceases to exist.

1991   WAIS released by Thinking Machines Corporation; Gopher released by University of Minnesota. U.S. High-Performance Computing Act (Gore1) establishes the National Research and Education Network (NREN)

1992   Internet Society is chartered. World Wide Web released by CERN. Number of hosts breaks 1,000,000. NSFNET backbone upgraded to T3 (44.736 Mbps). First MBONE audio multicast and video multicast.

1993   InterNIC created by NSF to provide specific Internet services:

   Directory and database (AT&T), Registration (Network Solutions, Inc.), Information (General Atomics/CERFnet)

   U.S. White House comes on-line; President Bill Clinton (president@whitehouse.gov)

   United Nations and World Bank come on-line

   Businesses and media really take notice of the Internet

   Mosaic takes the Internet by storm; WWW proliferates at a 341,634% annual growth rate of service traffic. Gopher's growth is 997%.

1994   Communities begin to wire up directly to the Internet

   U.S. Senate and House provide information servers

   Shopping malls and mass junk mailings arrive on the Internet

Figure 2.1 *An excerpt from Hobbes' Internet Timeline v3.1 (© 1993–94 by Robert H Zakon; used by permission)*

Finally, in 1969, the funding came through, and ARPAnet was commissioned by the Department of Defense for research into networking. It used a special set of communications rules, called the *Network Control Protocol* (NCP), to handle network traffic. The packet-switching duties were performed by a set of specially programmed Honeywell minicomputers, called *Interface Messages Processors* (IMPs), built by Bolt, Beranek, and Newman (BB&N), a Boston-area consulting firm.

ARPA also contracted a number of universities, which at first included the University of Utah, the Stanford Research Institute (SRI), and the University of California at Santa Barbara (UCSB) and Los Angeles (UCLA), to help further develop the host-to-host protocols and programs that would let computers and humans use the network. Figure 2.2 shows a crude rendering of what the first four nodes and links on ARPAnet looked like (the links consisted of dedicated telephone links, for which ARPA picked up a substantial monthly bill).

By the end of September 1969, the ARPAnet was up and running, and all four institutions were exchanging information with one another. Over the next ten years, ARPAnet would succeed beyond anybody's projections, as an average of one computer would be connected to that network every 20 days. Figure 2.3 charts the Internet's growth from its inception as the ARPAnet in 1969 through the beginning of 1994. (Note: this information is derived from the output of the Internet address zone program available from SRI at `ftp://ftp.nisc.com/pub/zone`, as prepared by Robert H Zakon in the Hobbes' Internet timeline).

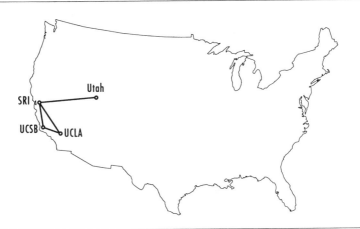

Figure 2.2 *The original ARPAnet linked four nodes*

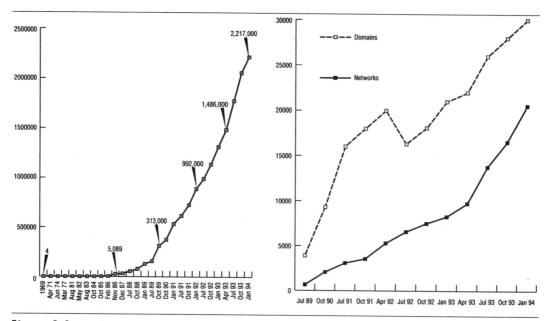

Figure 2.3 *Graphing Internet growth by hosts, networks, and address domains*

Heroes of the Network Revolution, Sung and Unsung

ARPAnet didn't just happen overnight; it was the result of years of research, experiment, and development from individuals in research and academia. Certainly, the group at BB&N deserves a great deal of credit for developing and delivering the initial set of hardware and software needed to make ARPAnet a reality, just as the research and teaching staffs at the various institutions that got involved along the way deserve mention for their subsequent work that made the Internet a reality.

The initial idea of linking computers came from a BB&N staff member named J. C. R. Licklider, while he was researching methods to help the government get better use from its computers. Licklider also participated in the IMP development team, along with Frank Heart, Robert Kahn, Alex McKenzie, Severo Ornstein, Larry Roberts, Steve Taylor, and Dave Walden.

The host-to-host protocol and software development work undertaken at SRI, UCLA, UCSB, and the University of Utah was headed by Steve Crocker, and included a team of 40-odd graduate students, many of whom have gone on to fame, fortune, and notoriety in the networking industry. This group includes luminaries like Steven Carr, Vinton

Cerf, David Crocker, Robert Metcalfe, and Jon Postel, among others. Many, if not most of them, are still active on the Internet—this is a history where many of the prime actors are still involved and still making things happen to this day!

ARPAnet Grows and Grows, Other Nets Follow

Once ARPAnet got started, many other institutions jumped onto the bandwagon. By 1971, MIT, the RAND Corporation, BB&N, Harvard, MIT's Lincoln Laboratories, Stanford, Carnegie-Mellon, Case Western, and the NASA Ames Research Center had joined up, each with its own IMP on campus or somewhere nearby.

In 1972, ARPAnet was the subject of a demonstration of networking technology, involving over 40 machines, orchestrated by Dr. Robert Kahn at the International Conference on Computer Communications in Washington, D.C. This created a tremendous amount of publicity and led to a quickened pace of proliferation and a dramatic increase in interest in networking technologies worldwide.

Later that year, Dr. Vinton Cerf began his work as chairman of the InterNetworking Working Group (INWG) to address the need for definition and use of an agreed-upon set of standard networking protocols. Ultimately, this work would result in the definition of the TCP/IP protocol and applications suite, which provides the technology backbone of today's Internet and which still functions as the Department of Defense standard for networking communications to this day.

In 1973 ARPAnet went international, as England and Norway joined in. By 1975, operation of what had by then become known as the Internet was transferred to the Defense Communications Agency (known today as the Defense Information Systems Agency, the governmental group responsible for analyzing and specifying systems technology on behalf of the United States government and its agencies). In that same year, Bolt, Beranek and Newman opened Telenet, the first commercial implementation of ARPAnet technologies, and a significant step to opening Internet technology beyond the then-normal group of elite government, research, and academic institutions it connected.

The 1970s was also the decade when electronic mail began to come on strong on the Internet, supported in large part by the addition of uucp (unix-to-unix copy) to the UNIX operating system by AT&T Bell Labs in 1976 and the subsequent introduction of THEORYNET at the University of Wisconsin in 1977 (the first large-scale uucp-based e-mail experiment).

By the end of the 1970s, meetings were held involving the University of Wisconsin, DARPA (ARPA, renamed as the Defense Advanced Research Projects Administration), the National Science Foundation, and computer scientists from a broad collection of colleges and universities to discuss the need for a Computer Science research computer network (introduced in 1981 as CSNet, which provided nationwide dial-up access to electronic mail, and an acceptable alternative for many institutions unable to participate directly in ARPAnet).

At the same time, USENET was established using uucp between Duke University and the University of North Carolina at Chapel Hill. Ultimately, all of these efforts would result in additional network capacity being deployed to serve multiple interests groups, all of which added to the scope and reach of the Internet itself. It would also lead to the proliferation of additional research and commercial networks, each of which would ultimately add to the prestige and reach of what would come to be known as the Internet.

INTRODUCING TCP/IP

By 1982, the Internet had grown to accommodate over 200 hosts, across the nation and around the world (over 22 countries had IMPs by then, in addition to some 210 domestic sites). During the time that ARPAnet was growing the government agency responsible for its initial funding was also growing, and was renamed as the Defense Advanced Research Projects Administration. While the computer scientists, researchers, and engineers at its affiliated organizations were growing ARPAnet, DARPA was funding the development of satellite and packet radio-based networks (like ALOHAnet at the campuses of the University of Hawaii) which it also wanted to add to the ARPAnet.

Unfortunately, the networking protocol in use at the time, NCP, was too dependent on the characteristics of the original ARPAnet to accommodate some of these new and radically different technologies. DARPA had also sponsored Vint Cerf's InternetWorking Working Group (INWG), which oversaw the specification and development of a new suite of protocols named the *Transmission Control Protocol/Internet Protocol*, known commonly as TCP/IP (pronounced "tee cee pee eye pee").

Unlike its predecessors, TCP/IP was designed from the ground up to supply networking capabilities to networks made up of different kinds of machines and utilized a broad array of communications technologies that ranged from local-area links, to asynchronous links, to packet radio and satellite links. The best explanation for TCP/IP's continued popularity and use, over 20 years after work began on its design, is its ability to link virtually any kind of computer to any other kind, over almost every conceivable form of networking medium or technology.

THE BIRTH OF THE INTERNET

In field tests, TCP/IP quickly demonstrated technical superiority over its NCP predecessor. (For a technical discussion of TCP/IP, please consult Chapter 3—in this chapter, we skip the Internet's key technology and concentrate on history instead.) Once the testing was complete, there was no more question: TCP/IP was the way to go for future internetworking needs.

By the beginning of 1983, the Defense Communications Agency officially switched the ARPAnet and the related (and classified) Defense Data Network over from NCP to TCP/IP. In the minds of many participants and observers, this changeover marked the real inception of the Internet because it made worldwide networking available to all qualified participants, at a time when nearly any interested business, research, or academic organization could qualify simply by requesting a network address (or range of addresses).

In the minds of other participants and observers, TCP/IP ushered in the Internet simply because it made networking both possible and affordable. Suddenly, networking required no highly proprietary, expensive, and vendor-specific hardware and software, nor was it limited to a particular model or make of computer. TCP/IP made it possible to bring just about any kind of computer on-line, at a cost of $15-20,000 or less. This might keep individual players out of the game, but it couldn't hold back just about any institution with even a modest annual computing budget.

Finally, the set of definitions from the INWG described TCP/IP and first introduced the term *internet*, with a lower-case *i*, to describe a connected set of networks—specifically, those using TCP/IP. The INWG documents also referred to *the Internet*, with an upper-case *I*, to describe the existing set of TCP/IP internets already in place on the ARPAnet and elsewhere.

So, which of these phenomena really explains the emergence of "the Internet"? The truth of the matter is that all three sets of ideas are important, but the real emergence of "the Internet" rests on the widespread deployment of networking technology across the United States and throughout the world. The existence of many individual networks and their continued deployment and proliferation is what made the Internet possible and what has contributed to its explosive growth, which continues to this day (reexamine Figure 2.3 if you want to see some impressive numbers).

From Academia and Research, to the Whole Wide World

In 1983, a number of important developments followed the introduction and widespread adoption of TCP/IP and the adoption of Internet in the networking lexicon. First, a network name server was developed and deployed at the University of Wisconsin, which made it necessary to know only the name of another system, and not necessarily the exact route to reach that system. This greatly simplified network access and made it far easier for users to employ the far-flung resources so widely distributed around the networks they could already reach. By 1984, this would lead to the development of Domain Name Servers, to provide similar functionality for any TCP/IP-based internet.

Second, the Computer Science Network (CSNet) was linked to the ARPAnet, via a gateway that could move traffic (mostly electronic mail) between the two internets. This opened the resources to the entire academic computing community, and involved an entire generation of faculty, staff, and students that would be the nucleus of today's multimillion member Internet community.

Third, 1983 was the year in which the IBM PC was launched. This brought computing power to the desktop and spawned a networking revolution that continues to this day. At the same time, workstation vendors like Sun and Apollo were delivering UNIX-based machines to desktops around the nation and the world, most of which included the TCP/IP-based networking capabilities developed at UC Berkeley under DARPA's aegis (this operating system was known as UNIX 4.2, Berkeley Software Distribution, or BSD).

Finally, 1983 witnessed the widespread proliferation of local-area network technologies, as more affordable computers began the demand for more affordable networks with which to interconnect them. At this point, the Internet focus finally changed from one of seeking to interconnect large, time-sharing machines at widely distributed sites to one of interconnecting local-area networks composed of multiple machines per site. This too, strongly fueled the growth and appetite for Internet capabilities and services.

THE NATIONAL SCIENCE FOUNDATION AND ACCEPTABLE USAGE

In 1986, the National Science Foundation staked out an important role on the Internet, with the creation of NSFNET, which offered a set of high-speed links across the country. NSFNET also provided access to a set of five supercomputing research centers around the United States, to make high-powered computers available for widespread use in the research and academic communities.

At the same time, ARPAnet's administrators (DCA) backed away from supplying the connections between these supercomputing centers, citing an already overwhelming workload and a desire to limit their activities to more strictly government- and defense-related networking needs. This created an opportunity for a broader focus for the Internet and, with funding from NASA and the Department of Energy, led to the creation and delivery of NSFNET.

Up to this point, possessing an ARPAnet connection was a sign of status and ultimately, of having the right political connections to arrange for network access. The introduction of NSFNET made it much easier for organizations, especially those in research or academia, to obtain network connections and led to an explosion of Internet linkups, especially within the academic community.

By 1987, the number of Internet hosts had exceeded 10,000, and the 1,000th design document for TCP/IP had been published. By 1989, the number of hosts would exceed 100,000 and the NFSNET backbone would be upgraded to T-1 lines (1.544 MBps). In the same year, the Europeans formed a TCP/IP research group (RIPE, or Reseaux IP Europeans) to expedite the formation of a multinational internet for the EEC and other participants.

Bye Bye, ARPAnet

By 1990, the ARPAnet ceased to exist as such, having been overtaken and replaced by the NSFNET backbone, with a well-developed set of regional and metropolitan area feeder networks. At this point, the modern shape of the Internet begins to take shape as MCI became the first commercial electronic mail carrier to establish an Internet gateway. This allowed MCI mail users to freely exchange e-mail with the Internet; today, this type of access is typical and available for America Online, CompuServe, BIX, AT&T Mail, and most other major commercial e-mail and on-line services.

In 1991, a Commercial Internet Exchange (CIX) Association was formed by the cooperation of a number of commercial internet service providers, to clearly establish legitimate business uses for the Internet. This organization brought General Atomics, the providers of CERFnet, Performance Systems International, the providers of PSInet, and UUNET Technologies, the providers of AlterNet, together in a nationwide extension to the Internet that was available to anyone who could afford the necessary equipment, account, and usage charges.

In this same year, the Internet got another major boost of a different type with the release of two key technologies, called WAIS and Gopher. The first, the Wide-Area Information Service (WAIS), from Thinking Machines Corporation, supplied a highly automated front-end to the myriad of databases on the Internet, letting users easily access collections of data from across the world based on collections of simple keywords. WAIS eliminated the arcane knowledge required to locate and access each database or news source individually, and let ordinary mortals look for items of interest from a variety of sources without having to master the gory details of Internet navigation (for a full-blown discussion of WAIS, please consult Chapter 17).

The second, Gopher, was a search program developed at the University of Minnesota designed to let users access many of the Internet's information resources in a simple, consistent way. Using Gopher was—and is—just as simple as making selections from a menu. Some of these menus were hierarchical (that is picking a selection produced another menu, which in turn produced yet other menus, and so on). Here again, the arcana required to obtain additional menus or the items they represented were handled by the software, thereby shielding users from the intimate details of locating the actual information source over the Internet, making a connection, and obtaining the requested data (for complete Gopher coverage, please consult Chapter 15).

These tools represented a major step in improving the usability of the information available from the Internet, and in making it accessible to casual users. They were the first signs of an increasingly sophisticated use of automation to deliver the Internet as a collection of abstract resources, rather than as a loose federation of interlinked computers. Much of the rest of this book will be devoted to investigating the tools that make this possible, and the underlying capabilities that deliver on users' requests for information and services.

Moving into the Present—and Beyond

By 1992, the number of Internet hosts exceeded 1 million. The full-scale deployment and use of Internet technology was evident from coverage on television, newspapers, as well as the computer trade press and related media. Buzzwords like the *National Information Infrastructure* and *Global Information Infrastructure* became a part of political, as well as technical, rhetoric.

In 1993, the Internet Network Information Center (InterNIC) was created to provide specific Internet services to a burgeoning community of commercial and public service providers, and to an even larger and ever-growing user community. For the entire Internet community, AT&T took on the role of providing directory and database services, Network Solutions took on registration and access information services, while General Atomics/CERFnet took on supplying information services.

In the same year, the White House went on-line, with direct e-mail access to key administration figures. This year, 1994, witnessed numerous communities and school systems wiring up to the Internet, with both the United States Senate and the State of California offering on-line access to information servers via the Internet.

The wave of Internet access and use continues to grow, even as we write this chapter. For a peek at what the future could bring, please consult Chapter 8. For the time being, we've arrived at the present, and this is where the history of the Internet ends. Right now, over 2.5 million hosts are on the Internet, over 35,000 networks, and over 50,000 Internet domains. By the time you read this, these numbers will probably be off by 50%. The show never stops, and the Internet just keeps growing!

NSF AND ACCEPTABLE USE ISSUES

Starting as early as the late 1970s, in the heyday of ARPAnet, but most clearly from the mid-1980s and onward, the issue of "acceptable use" or "appropriate use" of Internet facilities has been a thorny issue. On the one hand, it's always been desirable to have a mix of government, research, academic, and business users on the Internet. On the other hand, certain parts of this network are completely owned and subsidized by the taxpayers (including all of us).

In the earliest days, only those organizations were allowed to connect that had something to contribute to the development and deployment of the Internet, typically with needs or abilities that related to United States defense or related research. Admittedly, the interpretation of what was "related" was sometimes stretched, but the idea was soon formulated that exchange of information was completely acceptable, but outright commercial activities, like advertising, billing, or sales-related information, was not.

The charter of the NSFNET Backbone helps to clarify matters somewhat, because it clearly states that its role is to support educational and research activity, and to carry traffic related to those things. Nobody is censoring each e-mail message to make sure that these guidelines are honored, but the intent of this document is clear, as Figure 2.4 should indicate.

Here's the bottom line: if you're not sure whether or not what you're sending over the Internet will traverse the NSFNET backbone, the safest course of action is to honor these guidelines, no matter what you're doing. It is also wise to be wary of blatantly commercial activity of any kind on the Internet—particularly advertising—as reading through this book should indicate (especially Chapters 7, 10, and 20). As you'll learn, sins of omission provoke far fewer firestorms than do the ones of commission!

Commercial Internets

Given that some organizations wanted to use the Internet for activities that didn't meet the NSFNET acceptable use policies, it was inevitable that purely commercial implementations would follow. In 1991, the foundation of CIX (Commercial Internet Exchange) helped to propel a new era of fully commercialized Internet use. Since its formation, other networks have joined the CIX, as a new generation of network providers has arisen to meet burgeoning needs for commercial internet access. Today, CIX includes organizations like Sprint, whose SprintLink network thereby gains Internet access, along with a variety of Internet access providers of many sizes and business orientations.

Curiously, though, the Internet culture remains remarkably consistent—commercial or otherwise, the unwritten rules about acceptable use still provide excellent rules for how best to behave on-line.

NSFNET Backbone Acceptable Use Policy

1. NSFNET backbone services are provided to support open research and education in and among United States research and instructional institutions, plus research arms of for-profit firms when in engaged in open scholarly communication and research. Use for other purposes is not acceptable.

Specifically Acceptable Uses:

2. Communication with foreign researchers and educators in connection with research or instruction, as long as any network that the foreign user employs for such communication provides reciprocal access to United States researchers and educators.

3. Communication and exchange for professional development, to maintain currency, or to debate issues in a field or subfield of knowledge.

4. Use for disciplinary-society, university-association, government-advisory, or standards activities related to the user's research and instructional activities.

5. Use in applying for or administering grants or contracts for research or instruction, but not for other fund-raising or public-relations activities.

6. Any other administrative communications or activities in direct support of research and instruction.

7. Announcements of new products or services for use in research or instruction, but not advertising of any kind.

8. Any traffic originating from a network of another member agency of the Federal Networking Council if the traffic meets the acceptable use policy of that agency.

9. Communication incidental to otherwise acceptable use, except for illegal or specifically unacceptable uses.

Unacceptable Uses:

10. Use of for-profit activities (consulting for pay, sales or administration of campus stores, sales of tickets to sports events, and so on) or use by for-profit institutions unless covered by the General Principle or as specifically acceptable use.

11. Extensive use for private or personal business. This statement applies to use of the NSFNET backbone only. NSF expects that connecting networks will formulate their own use policies. The NSF Division of Networking and Communications Research and Infrastructure will resolve any questions about this Policy or its interpretation.

Figure 2.4 *NSFNET Backbone acceptable use policy*

NREN, the National Research And Education Network

Vice-President Al Gore has championed the concept of a National Information Infrastructure. To help provide the electronic analog of the physical highways that made economic growth so powerful in the United States after World War II, he has also championed the idea of an "information superhighway," which will be to computers and their users what the highway system was to the cars and trucks that transported economic prosperity into the 1950s in the United States.

A key concept in this superhighway has been the introduction of legislation to support the creation of a National Research and Education Network. The government is working to provide seed money and to encourage business to build a high-speed, fiber-optic network that can expand existing Internet capabilities by several orders of magnitude. The idea is that this network will enable the formation of new economies and business opportunities for the next millennium, while it helps the United States to maintain its technology lead.

The reality is that building such an infrastructure will take several decades, as existing wire-based communications systems get upgraded, and new technologies emerge to replace them. The vice-president has helped to supply a much-needed vision of where our infrastructure needs to take us, but it will be up to the same community that helped to build today's Internet to help migrate to tomorrow's.

In the meantime, NREN should provide much-needed funding and support for the research and development efforts needed to build an information superhighway. It's too early to tell, but we hope not too much to hope, that this new initiative proves as powerful and positive as that undertaken by the (Defense) Advanced Research Projects Administration, starting over 25 years ago.

SUMMARY

In this chapter we followed the tracks of a global internetwork that started from the simple idea that it would be a good idea to improve access to scarce and expensive computing resources. As this humble concept was refined, it resulted in the biggest global agglomeration of communications, computing, and information resources the world has ever seen. Along the way, it also proved how powerful and productive the ability to bring people together in more effective ways could be. As we move into the next century, and a new millennium, the seeds sown that have resulted in the Internet we know today should take us to a new concept of information access and communication that will help to define the world of tomorrow.

RECOMMENDED READING

There are lots of good resources on the Internet available (over 100 titles are currently in print, according to our subject search in *Books in Print*). The problem, therefore, is to not in providing references, but in selecting those that are of the best use. When it comes to Internet history, here are our top picks:

Bernard Adoba, "How the Internet Came to Be" (as told by Vinton Cerf), *The Online User's Encyclopedia*, Addison-Wesley, Reading, MA, 1993. List price: $49.95. Words of wisdom and personal experience from one of the movers and shakers of the Internet.

Daniel P. Dern, *The Internet Guide for New Users*, McGraw-Hill, New York, 1994. List price: $27.95. A good overview of Internet chronology and events.

Brendan Kehoe, *Zen and the Art of the Internet*, 2nd edition, Prentice-Hall, Englewood Cliffs, NJ, 1993. List price: $22.00. The first edition is widely available as a text file on the Internet (ZENART.ZIP is the usual filename). Good, but brief, discussion of Internet inception and evolution.

Ed Krol, *The Whole Internet User's Guide and Catalog*, O'Reilly & Associates, Sebastopol, CA, 1992. List price: $24.95. One of the best all-around books on the Internet, it's equally good at the historical side.

Andrew S. Tanenbaum, *Computer Networks*, 2nd edition, Prentice-Hall, Englewood Cliffs, NJ, 1988. List price: $50.00 (hardback). Tanenbaum includes useful information on early ARPAnet, ALOHAnet, and more, with useful information on the Internet throughout.

Robert H Zakon, *Hobbes' Internet Timeline*, electronically published on the Internet, copyright 1993–1994. This document is available by sending an Internet e-mail to:

timeline@hobbes.mitre.org.

At the time we wrote this chapter, the current version was v1.3. This document provides a brief but relatively complete Internet history timeline and a useful summary of Internet growth and evolution. It's also a good compendium of even more resources, if the history of technology is your thing!

HOW THE INTERNET WORKS

3

At its very heart, the Internet is a vast network of networks, able to move traffic around the world. In this chapter you'll learn about the networking technologies and conventions that make this possible, as we examine the key ingredients that make the Internet work. Along the way, you'll also cover the intricacies of how messages find their way around a network like the Internet, as we discuss network addressing, network names, and their domains. You'll also learn how the capabilities of the Internet are standardized and managed, which helps to explain how Internet capabilities very often come to exist.

TCP/IP BASICS

There are those who believe—the authors of this book are among them—that the Internet simply couldn't have taken the form and importance it enjoys today without the advent of the networking protocols that make it run. It was no accident that we singled out the introduction and adoption of TCP/IP as the official Department of Defense (and Internet) protocol in 1983 as one of the most significant milestones in the history of the Internet in Chapter 2.

In this section we try to explain what's so magical about this TCP/IP stuff, and why it has remained such a key ingredient for networking in general, and the Internet in particular, over the past decade. But first, we have to take a detour to examine a well-known networking communications model, so that everyone can share a common understanding of what is involved. Once we put that behind us, we examine TCP/IP in terms of this model and explain the pieces and parts of which it's made. If you want to learn more on the subject, be sure to consult the Recommended Reading section at the end of this chapter.

The OSI Reference Model

The International Standards Organization (ISO) has been involved in networking for a long time, but its most powerful contribution to the subject lies in a model for networking called the *Open Systems Interconnect Reference Model* (or OSI Reference Model for short). This model breaks the functionality inherent in networking into seven layers, as shown in Figure 3.1.

The beauty of the OSI Reference Model is that it separates distinct levels of networking activity from one another, thereby allowing specific types of connectivity issues to be solved separately, rather than all at once. This lets the issues of physical connectivity (the kinds of wires or connections needed to hook up to the network) be separated from the formats of the messages that the network can conduct. It takes a "divide and conquer" approach to networking, which not only separates the hardware from the software required, but also separates how applications communicate from how messages traverse a networking medium.

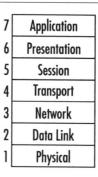

Figure 3.1 *The OSI Reference Model*

The Physical Layer

Starting at the bottom and working our way to the top of this multilay-ered diagram, which is often called a *stack*, we find the physical layer. Here, the problems of connecting to the networking medium are han-dled, as are the electrical or other physical properties of the signals that travel over the medium. This includes the type and shape of the con-nectors, pin arrangements, transmission speed limits, and all the other details needed to transmit and receive bits across a wire, a fiber, or a broadcast medium of some kind. At this layer, information consists of a series of signals moving through the medium, off a transmitter, or into a receiver.

The Data Link Layer

The second layer in the stack is called the *data link layer*. It handles the conversion from digital data native to the computer to signals when passing data down to the physical layer, and vice-versa when passing data up from the physical layer. On the other side (looking up to layer 3), it handles special packages of data and puts an envelope around them when data are passed down from the network layer or strips off this envelope when data goes the other way. Information at the data link layer is packaged in generic units called *frames*.

   In some interpretations of the model, layer 2 is broken into two sub-layers. The upper sublayer is called the *logical link control* (LLC) sublay-er and is concerned with the packaging of frames, while the lower sub-layer is called the *media access control* (MAC) sublayer and is concerned with managing the translation from signals into bits or vice-versa. We make little use of this terminology in our discussion, but it is important to understand that dealing with the media (MAC sublayer) is some-times separated from dealing with logical network access (LLC sublay-er) in many networking discussions and explanations.

The Network Layer

The network layer is third in the stack. It handles moving information around a network, including specifying the route that a particular mes-sage will take, either explicitly by providing a particular destination address and route or implicitly by requesting service from specialized network devices called *routers* that can handle directing this kind of traffic to another router or to the destination device that will ultimately receive the message.

At the network layer, information is contained in units, generally called *packets*, representing the basic form for all kinds of messages as mandated by the particular protocol in use for that layer. Because TCP/IP began its life primarily in a packet-switching network environment, this layer is particularly important in its design and implementation. Half of the TCP/IP acronym comes from the Internet protocol (IP) used at the network layer in TCP/IP networking.

The Transport Layer

Above the network layer, we find the transport layer. Here, peers cooperate in moving or transporting messages around the network. The transport layer is responsible for breaking messages into movable chunks for the network layer when sending and for reassembling those chunks into their proper sequence when receiving. This layer also commonly handles the data integrity of such messages, including error checking and techniques for verifying the delivering and accuracy of messages sent and received by cooperating peers, if reliable, guaranteed service is needed.

Here again, TCP/IP's origins make the transport layer also highly important to its design and implementation. The other half of the TCP/IP acronym comes from the transmission control protocol, which provides a reliable delivery mechanism for moving data around the network (and is therefore located at the transport layer in the OSI model).

The Session Layer

The next layer in the stack is called the *session layer*. It is responsible for setting up and breaking down ongoing communications between machines on a network and for managing the dialog between machines while a connection exists. This is the first layer where communications occur above the message level—that is, based on sequences of packets, rather than individual packets)—and is also the first layer at which individual users or processes get recognized, rather than addresses for source or destination machines.

The Presentation Layer

The sixth layer in the reference model is called the *presentation layer*. It manages data conversion between the forms needed to ship information across the network and the specific environment from which the information is sent or by which it will be received. This is the layer at which data formats specific to particular systems are handled so that information can be presented to a consumer in intelligible form or passed from a producer over the network in a generic form.

The Application Layer

The final layer is called the *application layer*. It is where a user interacts with applications that access the network, but the primary concern is the services provided by the application and the access to information, be it local or from across the network. The application layer is the window for all data that a user sees and also the focus of where the "real work" happens as far as most users are concerned. From a TCP/IP perspective, it also provides some specific networking capabilities, as you'll see a little later on in this chapter.

TCP/IP Addressing

On a network, interfaces send and receive information based on a physical address, which corresponds to a unique number that identifies the interface vis-á-vis all the other similar kinds of interfaces of that type. Ethernet interfaces, for example, have a special identifier embedded in the media access controller chip by the manufacturer that virtually guarantees that no duplicate exists in the world (that is why this kind of address is often called a *MAC-layer address*). Using unique MAC-layer addresses has the desirable effect of keeping the network from getting confused and delivering information to the wrong receiver or attributing it to the wrong sender.

TCP/IP was built to interconnect many different types of networks and therefore uses a separate, logical address that is intended to guarantee that a host machine on the network has a unique address no matter what kind of physical network it's attached to, who manufactured it, or any other kind of distinguishing physical characteristics. To make TCP/IP run on a particular kind of network technology or medium, the issues of translating between physical, MAC-layer addresses and logical, network-layer addresses must be solved.

TCP/IP Address Layout and Format

A TCP/IP address is a 32-bit number that must be unique on an entire internetwork, for the network to behave properly (duplicate addresses usually cause all the nodes that share a common address to mysteriously vanish from the network). Every network host and router—that is, each device that needs a network connection—must have its own TCP/IP address to participate in sending and receiving information. In fact, devices (like routers) with more than one network connection must have a different address for each distinct connection. Because the TCP/IP address operates at Layer 3 of the reference model, and IP is the protocol that primarily passes such addresses, these addresses are most often referred to as *IP addresses* rather than as the more formally correct *TCP/IP address*.

Because IP addresses are logical, they do not necessarily indicate geographic location (although some address domains may be deliberately set up this way). Given an IP address, all you can identify is the class of network involved and the authority responsible for managing it. Unlike the telephone system, which supports geographical area codes and branch exchanges, IP addresses are more difficult to categorize and discriminate among.

The 32-bit IP address consists of two parts: a network number followed by a host identifier. Because network numbers can belong to one of three classes currently in use and each class is identified by a sequence of proscribed "class bits," an IP address always has less than 32 bits' worth of useful information. Nevertheless, those class bits should always be included when referencing an IP address, for both completeness and accuracy. Table 3.1 describes the way these bits are organized.

A quick check on the mathematics will show that the number of available addresses is less than the number that binary arithmetic predicts. This is because the first and last values in the first two series is reserved for special use and legal values above the ceiling for Class "C" are currently reserved and not available for general use.

Class Name	Network IDs		Host IDs		Bits	
	Max IDs	# Bits	Max IDs	# Bits	Usable	Required Start
A	126	7	16,777,214	24	31	0
B	16,382	14	65,534	16	30	10
C	2,097,150	21	254	8	29	110

Table 3.1 *IP address classes currently in use*

IP addresses are commonly expressed as a sequence of four numbers, each separated by a period. For example, 198.252.182.200 is the IP address of the UNIX server operated by Zilker Internet Park to which Ed must attach to obtain his electronic mail. These numbers are commonly expressed as shown, in the form of four decimal numbers, but these numbers are sometimes shown in octal (base 8) or hexadecimal (base 16) notation. Be sure to read the documentation for any TCP/IP configurations you might get involved in—just because you understand the address doesn't always mean the software you're using will!

Table 3.2 illustrates a quick way to determine the class of any IP address you might encounter, based on the initial values in the address. Any number that falls within the usable address range for a class belongs to that class (depending on the class, you'll have to check the first, second, and/or third digits in the IP address).

Although the number of individual network/host IP address combinations for each address class is quite large, there is already a dearth of IP addresses available for new networks today. A severe shortage is forecast for 1995 or 1996, when the available addresses are expected to run out, so the governing body of the Internet is investigating ways to extend IP to 64-bit addresses without requiring replacement of the existing 32-bit ones.

Who Keeps Track of All These IP Addresses?

Given that everybody on the Internet has to have a unique IP address for the host through which they connect, there is a definite method to managing and allocating addresses. To obtain an IP address to operate on the Internet, it is necessary to contact the IP address registry managed by the Internet Assigned Numbers Authority (IANA). This authority is part of the Internet Network Information Center, known as the InterNIC, which operates out of Chantilly, Virginia. The InterNIC operates on behalf of the Internet Activities Board (IAB), which is the governing body for the entire Internet, including IP address management, TCP/IP protocols and standards, and more.

Class	Usable Range	Number of Digits to Check
A	1–126	1
B	128.1–191.259	2
C	192.0.1–223.255.254	3

Table 3.2 *Recognizing addresses classes by value*

The InterNIC allocates and manages all IP addresses, which are assigned, not chosen, by organizations, businesses, or individuals seeking to establish nodes that can access the Internet directly. Obtaining an IP address or a range of IP addresses (which most larger organizations will need) is time consuming and requires that assignees agree to shoulder certain management tasks as a part of their responsibilities, should any requests be granted. It then becomes the responsibility of the assignee to make sure the addresses handed out are unique within the range it has obtained; if not, only its networks will be affected (which is exactly what the IAB wants).

Because of the time, effort, and expense required to obtain a registered IP address, we strongly recommend that all individuals and most organizations at least consider obtaining access through a commercial service provider, rather than trying to obtain one's own address. Given the current scarcity of available addresses, this could be considered a form of conservation for a precious Internet resource.

Who Should Apply to Register an IP Address?

While at least some voices within the Internet community recommend that all TCP/IP users should register with the InterNIC for their own IP addresses, we prefer a more rigid set of recommendations, taking into account the total lack of available Class A addresses, the consumption of over 70% of Class B addresses, and the pressure on Class C:

- Any organization that connects to the Internet directly anywhere worldwide must request a registered address. This includes research, academic, or other institutions that require communications via Internet with the United States government.
- Any organization that wishes to communicate with a United States parent or affiliate that is already registered on the Internet is advised to request a registered address. This will help to avoid the problems that accidental duplicates with the already registered group can cause.
- Any large multinational organization that wants to use the Internet for internal communications but does not wish to tackle the complexity or expense of operating a private network should also consider registering.

Because all the Class A addresses are taken, and those from Class B hard to get, larger organizations may have to settle for ranges of Class C addresses to get the number of connections they need.

Unless their requirements for Internet access are pressing, these organizations might be better served by waiting until the address congestion gets relieved when the IAB delivers a working method to expand the addresses available. Because a 64-bit address—a likely candidate for new formats being proposed—would square the address space, this would result in more than a quintillion separate addresses or over a trillion addresses for every occupant of planet Earth. No matter how the IAB decides to carve this up between network and host IDs, waiting should certainly open up a lot of possibilities!

Domains and Domain Names

Just to make life on the Internet even more interesting, users will seldom concern themselves with the numeric form of IP addresses, except when installing or maintaining IP communications software. Users tend to interact with the network in terms of symbolic names, rather than numbers. Nowhere is this as common as it is for Internet e-mail addresses.

Internet e-mail uses the well-known Internet naming scheme, which can be represented in one of the following ways (and others as well, which we omit in the interests of brevity):

```
username@organization.extension
username@country-code.organization.extension
username@organizational-unit.organization.extension
username@server.country-code.organization.extension
```

where the terminology should be understood as follows (here, square brackets indicate optional naming elements):

- `username` is the e-mail name of either the sender or recipient of the message. As the format section later indicates, this is seldom the same as the full name of either party.
- [`server`] is the optional name of the messaging server (SMTP host) from which the message originated. This information can be handy for larger organizations that typically have multiple sites and a multitude of messaging servers.
- [`country-code`] is only optional in the United States, where the older form of internet address shown in the first of the three representations preceding it is still the most common form used. The country codes are formally called *international domain names*.
- `organization` is the name of the organization to which the sender or recipient belongs

- [organizational unit] is the optional name of an organizational unit to which sender or recipient belongs. Like the server field (also optional) it can help to more precisely locate a user in an organization with multiple e-mail servers.
- [extension] indicates the type of organization named in the address. Extension names are formally called *old-style United States domain names*.

With more than 10 million Internet e-mail users online, and more joining the party daily, the breadth and scope of this naming scheme is unquestioned (the availability of TCP/IP addresses for all these users is another matter entirely, but we hope will be resolved before all the addresses are taken!)

The structure of the Internet is most visible in that part of a symbolic address to the right of the @ sign. This is where the number of levels in an organization might show up: Larger, more hierarchical organizations will have more names here than flatter, less hierarchical ones. In general, the more to the right a name occurs in this part of the address, the higher the level or more significant its meaning.

The rightmost name in a symbolic address is often called the *domain name*. In the United States, there are different classifications of domains, to indicate what type of organization is providing the Internet connection. Table 3.3 shows the most common domain names used today; outside the United States, a country code supplies the top-level domain name.

Name Resolution and Name Services

Of course, possession of a symbolic name is not the same thing as possession of an actual numeric IP address. To get from a name to a numeric address, the TCP/IP environment offers a number of solu-

Name	Explanation
.com	Commercial institution or service provider
.edu	Educational institution
.gov	Government institution or agency
.mil	United States military
.net	Network service provider
.org	Nonprofit organization

Table 3.3 *A brief list of top-level domain names used in the United States*

tions, some of which require configuration information, others of which rely on name resolution services of one kind or another. A domain name allows a network node that is registered to the Internet to be identified by that name no matter where it may be located, provided that a way to translate the name into its equivalent IP address is available.

The most simple-minded approach is to supply a list of equivalencies, usually called a *host table,* that lists symbolic names and equates them with their related numeric IP addresses. While this approach is certainly workable, it's completely static and does not let a user address any hosts not included in the table. Once upon a time, host tables were the main tool for name to address resolution but today, most TCP/IP setups use only the name and address information for certain key servers, like a user's login host and local name server.

All other name to address resolution will typically be handled by a name service, which will usually be one of the following:

- *Domain name system (DNS)* is a standard TCP/IP application that is most frequently used on the Internet to provide name to address translations. Typical TCP/IP end-user configurations will require only the IP address and name of the local DNS host be supplied; all other address services will be handled through this connection. DNS can handle two-way translation (from name to address and vice-versa) and can also identify the applications available on a particular machine to prospective users. It can also identify network gateways (machines that link multiple networks together) and indicate which nodes can supply e-mail forwarding to which other networks, if available.

- *Network information services (NIS)* is a TCP/IP name and resource lookup service developed by Sun Microsystems for use with their implementations of UNIX and TCP/IP. It is also quite common and provides the same capabilities as DNS, but includes a broader method for finding local or remote resources (like files systems, printers, or database servers) and for controlling access to those resources.

- *General directory services* have been implemented for directories based on the OSI X.500 specification; some of these are capable of resolving IP names and numeric addresses as well. In most cases, TCP/IP environments will use one of the two IP-based services just mentioned, but over time this will migrate to more generalized services like those provided by X.500 implementations, which typically include both white pages (name lookup) and yellow pages (lookup by category or type of service desired) services.

Knowing the name and address of a name server is crucial to proper Internet access; name services is one of the most important functions that needs to be supplied, whether from a service provider or an in-house network management group. It's like knowing the number for Information at the phone company—given that number you can always find a way to contact people whose numbers are listed and available.

Understanding TCP/IP's
Role in Networking

At this point, we have supplied sufficient background material to help you understand some of the issues that have to be handled by TCP/IP to provide a reasonable collection of networking services for the Internet and for others using its considerable capabilities. In this section of the chapter we return to the protocols and services that TCP/IP provides. We start by explaining how TCP/IP fits into the OSI reference model.

Mapping TCP/IP into the OSI Model

From a formal perspective, the OSI reference model is a great way to understand how networks work and to categorize the operations that must be performed to get the job of networking done. Unfortunately, not every networking implementation corresponds exactly to the OSI model, especially one like TCP/IP, which was constructed before the OSI model was invented. However, the model is a great aid to understanding the subject and particular implementation, which is why we use it as a tool for discussion here.

The difference between the model and an implementation is primarily that the layers describe certain concerns, which may have specific activities to match them, whereas actual implementations are usually built in the form of distinct message formats, called *protocols*, that both sending and receiving computers must understand identically to be able to communicate with one another.

From one perspective, we have examined the model as a set of activities that perform certain tasks independent of one another. But throughout, the idea is that information is being segmented and broken into smaller pieces as it moves down the stack, starting from within an application, to be transmitted across the networking medium. Then, when the information is received it gets unsegmented and reassembled on the other side, to be delivered to an application in a form as identical to the original as the differences between sender and receiver will permit.

Figure 3.2 shows that as information moves down the stack, it gets broken up and carefully labeled at each stage down the receiver's stack, so that this information can be used to put the same information together on the other side, as it moves up the receiver's stack. A useful metaphor here is to think of the process involved as taking a large piece of information and breaking it into smaller chunks, which are stuffed into special envelopes to be sent across the network. When these envelopes are received on the other end, the information on them permits reassembly of the original information and is then discarded.

TCP/IP Protocols: Suites and Stacks

Continuing the metaphor, each of the specific formats for creating and addressing envelopes is handled by a specific set of rules called a *protocol*. Because the TCP/IP implementation—and almost every other networking environment as well—is broken up into a collection of named

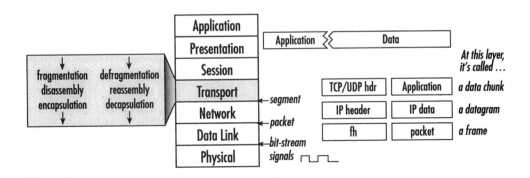

Figure 3.2 *Data moving through the protocol stack*

protocols, known as a *protocol suite*. Because this collection is organized into a set of related and layered protocols, it is also called a *protocol stack*.

Thus, even though only two of its constituent protocols, the Internet protocol at the network layer, and the transmission control protocol at the transport layer, give the TCP/IP environment its name, not all there is to the functionality and capabilities that TCP/IP supplies. Figure 3.3 shows a simplified layout of the TCP/IP protocols, including all of the important ones and a few of the others, that maps into the OSI reference model. In the following subsections, we explore each individually and try to explain what role it plays. After this discussion, you should be well-equipped to understand why TCP and IP play such pivotal roles and why they alone are not enough to carry the whole Internet on their shoulders.

Physical and Data Link Protocols

Although TCP/IP was initially developed for packet-switched networks, like those supplied by the Bolt, Beranek, and Newman interface message processors (IMPs), which later became known as *packet switching nodes* (PSNs), today it can be used on many, if not most, kinds of networking topologies and technologies.

These include the major local-area technologies like Ethernet, Token-Ring, ARCnet, and FDDI, as well as wide-area technologies like X.25

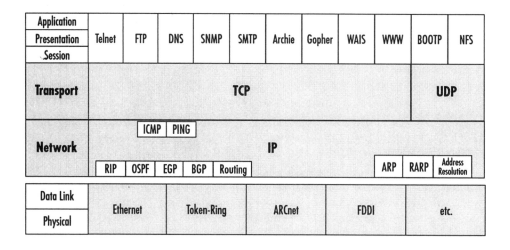

Figure 3.3 *The TCP/IP protocol suite, abridged version*

and X.21, SMDS, and serial line protocols like SLIP (serial link interface protocol) and PPP (point-to-point protocol) among others. Currently neither frame relay nor asynchronous transfer mode (ATM) is officially supported by TCP/IP, but both are in the process of having such support designed and built, with delivery expected in 1995 or thereabouts (for a description of how this process works, please consult the section entitled "IAB, IETF, and RFCs" later in this chapter).

Address Resolution Protocol (ARP)

ARP operates at the network layer of the reference model. Its job is to correlate a physical network address with a logical network address, so that network interfaces that are active on the network can recognize which frames are addressed to them and respond appropriately.

ARP is used to make sure that the TCP/IP traffic directed to a particular network can be forwarded to the right node on that network. It is used only to identify and reach nodes on the same cable segment as the node making an ARP request. Basically, an ARP sends a message saying "Here's an IP address. What's the corresponding MAC-layer address?" to which an ARP server replies with the proper information.

ARP works only on broadcast media (like Ethernet). Because ARP is a MAC-layer service, ARP traffic is limited to a single cable segment and won't be passed on by any routers. This is a useful behavior, because it stops ARP traffic from passing over networks that cannot possibly supply the requested information.

Reverse Address Resolution Protocol (RARP)

RARP, also referred to as reverse ARP, provides the inverse function to ARP; that is, it responds with a node's IP address for which a MAC-layer address is supplied. This is useful in two ways: First, it lets a node obtain its own IP address (because the MAC-layer address, if available, usually comes from firmware, it can be used to obtain that node's IP address from a server rather than forcing the address to be stored somewhere on the node itself). Second, it lets a network interface establish a correspondence between the MAC-layer addresses it sees in traffic passing by and related IP addresses, if any.

Like ARP, RARP also works only on broadcast media; similarly, it too is purely local and will not pass through routers. RARP's capabilities are somewhat limited and have largely been supplanted by BOOTP, which can provide services in addition to address resolution (see the section on BOOTP for more information).

Internet Protocol (IP)

IP is the foundation protocol for the whole TCP/IP stack. IP provides the network component for TCP/IP, delivering functions for transferring information between a sender and a receiver across any combination of intermediate networks. The basic functions of IP are concerned with delivering data to the correct node on the proper physical network, from the sender to the receiver. In other words, IP handles the routing of information across the network between the parties involved in sending and receiving.

In formal networking jargon, IP is called a *connectionless datagram service*. In English, this means that it transfers packages of information, called *datagrams*, that might be designated for one, many, or every node on the network. It also means that IP has no requirement for a datagram's recipient (or recipients) to acknowledge the receipt of the packages that are sent, nor is any error correction applied at this level of communications, so that the reliability of the datagram delivery is defined by the underlying network technologies in use. IP is called *connectionless* because it does not require a call or virtual circuit be established before communications can commence; each datagram contains all of the information needed to reach its intended recipient without requiring a connection to be established in advance.

Connectionless also means that each IP datagram stands on its own. There is no concept of sequence, so that a collection of datagrams is regarded as comprising the contents of some message or other type of formatted communication. Also, no specific route between sender and receiver needs to be defined within the datagram, leaving the establishment of a route up to the devices that direct this traffic along the way.

A major function of IP is to insulate the higher layer protocols from any knowledge of the underlying networking technologies in use. IP provides a boundary layer between the physical layer below it and the transport layer above it. Thus, IP's major functions are

1. To handle network addressing at the logical IP level, to uniquely identify sender and receiver. We have already covered this in our discussion of numeric IP addresses.
2. To manage fragmentation and reassembly of arbitrarily long messages into the maximum transfer unit size dictated by the intervening media for sending and to restore the original format upon receipt when reassembling.
3. To manage and manipulate the type of service (TOS) established between sender and receiver, where the types supported are low

delay, high throughput, high reliability, and low cost. When an application sets the TOS flags to particular settings, the routers that operate at the IP layer are expected to supply the right kinds of connections to deliver what has been requested or to provide error information (via ICMP) as to what prevents such delivery.

IP is ideally suited for a mixture of networking technologies, but especially so for a packet-switched environment (as you might expect, knowing the Internet's origins).

Internet Control Message Protocol (ICMP)

As discussed, IP itself is a datagram service that offers no guarantee of information delivery. Nevertheless, ICMP is provided within IP to deliver error messages and to supply diagnostics about network operation.

ICMP error messages are generated when a node recognizes that there is a transmission problem and ships the message to the node that initiated the offending traffic. Since ICMP traffic is carried within IP datagrams, it may fail to arrive for the same reasons that any IP traffic fails. For the same reason, no additional reporting on ICMP transmission or reception errors is added to the overhead traffic that the protocol creates. ICMP is used to deliver information about failed deliveries, network timeouts, as a way of delivering network addresses for dial-up connections, and more.

The most common use of ICMP, by far, is to echo traffic across the net for a TCP/IP utility program called *PING*. PING is used to check the availability of an IP address (or rather, the node at that address) by sending an ICMP packet to the target address that provokes an echo of what was sent. Any response indicates that the node is reachable; measuring roundtrip time for the response gives an indication of the quality of the connection between the sender and receiver.

Transmission Control Protocol (TCP)

As the other stalwart member of the TCP/IP protocol suite, TCP's primary job is to provide a robust and reliable delivery service for information across the network. TCP provides a connection-oriented service, which means that it works like a circuit that connects two nodes on the network. While no broadcast or multicast service currently is supported by TCP, it has all the bells and whistles it needs to provide a reliable transport between two systems, including guaranteed delivery and error recovery. TCP is also the protocol responsible for segmenting messages into the right-sized pieces to be efficiently transmitted across the network for sending and resequencing and restoring those pieces into the original message on the receiving end.

Reliability and robustness come at a price, however. TCP perforce imposes a fair amount of overhead to handle acknowledgments, to manage flow control, and to handle timers and connection management facilities. All TCP packets received are acknowledged with a short "got it" message called an *ACK* if the information came through unscathed or a *NAK*, or negative acknowledgment, if the information didn't get through correctly or at all. TCP is also capable of recognizing congestion on a link by monitoring roundtrip time for acknowledgments and other ongoing overhead traffic and of slowing down or momentarily halting communications in response to user commands or to wait for conditions to improve. Finally, TCP includes the ability to negotiate, set up, maintain, and tear down active connections across the network to support the requirements inherent in supplying a connection-oriented service.

TCP also includes a simple but powerful error correction mechanism. If an acknowledgment has not been received for any particular packet of information within a certain timeout interval (another case where its built-in timers are called upon), the packet is automatically resent. NAKs also trigger retransmission.

Finally, TCP manages the disassembly and reassembly of arbitrarily long messages into a maximum segment size suitable for the underlying network media in use. It adds sequence numbers and data integrity checks to each segment, so that individuals can be properly identified and resequenced upon arrival, and checked to make sure that the data received agrees with the data sent. This mechanism is particularly important to reliable delivery, since it helps to ensure that sender and receiver maintain an identical view of the information they are trying to share.

User Datagram Protocol (UDP)

UDP is another TCP/IP transport protocol, but it is specifically designed to be a lightweight alternative to TCP. That is, UDP is a connectionless protocol that adds only some modest header information to that already supplied by the underlying IP: namely, a method of identifying the sending and receiving processes on the source and destination machines, a count of the length of the datagram, and a checksum computed to provide modest data integrity checking on the datagram's contents.

Whereas TCP was designed to provide reliable, guaranteed delivery suitable for use over a variety of networks, with no presumption that the underlying networks were error-free or even reasonably efficient, UDP was designed with the opposite concept in mind. It assumes that the underlying network is relatively error free and relatively efficient as well and decides not to add the overhead that TCP's mechanisms impose.

UDP was intended to provide a mechanism to let applications send datagrams to other applications, so it includes a special additional identifier called a *protocol port* to uniquely identify the sending and receiving processes on the source and destination machines. This lets the right applications talk to each other, as well as the right machines.

UDP includes no acknowledgments, sequencing mechanisms, or flow control mechanisms like those described for TCP. Any application program that uses UDP has to provide its own services to ensure reliability, including datagram loss, duplication, or out-of-sequence delivery, and to handle loss of the connection between sender and receiver. That's why the local use of UDP is far more common than on a large, multisite TCP/IP internet.

TCP/IP Routing Protocols

The TCP/IP suite includes many more than we cover here, but those that handle internetwork routing deserve at least brief mention (if we had included them in Figure 3.3, they would all be situated within IP at Layer 3 of the diagram). These routing protocols are

- *Exterior gateway protocol (EGP)* is designed to let independent networks advertise to the core gateways that interlink the Internet the networks what it wants the outside world to see. EGP is the communications tool that lets organizations proffer servers and services to the world at large without opening the doors to their entire networks. The border gateway protocol (BGP) is emerging as a second-generation replacement for EGP today, but is not yet widely available in commercial implementations.
- *Routing information protocol (RIP)* is a simple, old-fashioned routing protocol that maintains tables of networks and the routers that

link them together. It uses a very simple-minded metric, called *hop count* (the number of routers between a source and destination) to pick routes. It can use only a single route between any two networks and has no way of correlating hop count with delivery time (two or more fast links will often outperform a single slow one, but RIP will choose the latter every time). RIP uses a broadcast advertisement of the network topology at regular intervals, which leads to constant overhead traffic. Although still widely used, RIP is no longer regarded as a capable Internet protocol (most experts advice that RIP be used purely on a local-area basis, if at all).

* *Open shortest path first (OSPF)* is a more modern routing protocol than either EGP or RIP. It takes into account the status of connections to a network, including performance aspects when deciding which routes to assign. OSPF takes a number of innovative steps to reduce routing traffic overhead, including limiting the number of routers that have to maintain a map of the active network topology and a route advertisement mechanism designed to support compact, infrequent map updates rather than constant ones.

TCP/IP Applications and Services

As a quick glance back at Figure 3.3 will attest, an interesting point of confusion creeps into our discussion as we move into the next layer of the TCP/IP protocols. This confusion arises because each of the named elements corresponds not just to the name of a networking protocol, but also to the name of an application (or at least a set of defined capabilities) that relate to a protocol.

In other words, the file transfer protocol is more than just a set of rules for how to transfer files across a network; it is also a set of commands or operations for logging into a remote host, manipulating local and remote file systems, and transferring files to and from the remote host. The best advice we can give you at this layer of the stack is to say that each element involves a specific protocol or set of protocols to do its job, but also includes direct end-user access to the capabilities that the protocol is supposed to provide.

Today's computing world is primarily a graphical user interface (GUI) world, so the command-line approach that is the minimal requirement for these TCP/IP applications has been supplanted by a point and click equivalent by most commercial vendors. However, the command line hasn't vanished completely, as you'll see in the chapters that cover these applications in detail. All we want to accomplish in this part of the book is a quick introduction to some of the most basic and essential TCP/IP applications and their related protocols; we save the details for Part II, and vendor information for Part III (Chapters 28 and 29).

PING

As we mentioned in the section on ICMP, PING actually uses a specially formatted ICMP echo request datagram to send a message to a target IP address. If received, it will simply be returned to the sender. This lets PING do its job—namely, indicating whether or not the station being PINGed is up and running. PING also measures the roundtrip time for the echo packet to return; given some prior performance information on the link, this can also indicate how well the connection between sender and receiver is behaving.

Also, PING has the smarts to use a name service to look up the numeric IP address for a host name. This means it is not necessary to include the hosts you want to PING in your hosts table, or to manually enter the numeric address. (PING will use DNS to obtain the numeric IP addresses your requests need.)

Finger

The Finger application provides information about users on a designated host. The information provided includes the users' login name, full name, home directory, his or her login shell, time of current login (if applicable) or the last time logged in (if not currently online). Finger also supplies information about the last time a user received mail, the last time he or she read mail, and some other details about idle time and host configuration.

Here's what Finger does that is worthwhile:

- Finger is smart enough to use name services to locate a host from a symbolic name, so it can be used as a kind of PING for nodes for which a numeric IP address is not available (provided the node has a Finger server running).
- Finger can identify users on specific hosts and indicate whether they are logged in or not. This can be useful to check if a user's available for an interactive chat, to see if the user has read mail, or simply to find out who is using a particular machine.

As utilities go, Finger can be useful for IP detective work, especially to locate other users or to check if your e-mail has been read.

Simple Mail Transfer Protocol (SMTP)

SMTP is the foundation for Internet e-mail, which has proven to be a powerful glue in linking the far-flung and loosely coupled Internet community. Usually e-mail is quicker than the Postal Service (known as *snail mail* among the cognoscenti), and mail systems are easy to extend so that mailing lists, adding attachments, and handling registered e-mail are customary features of most e-mail systems, whether on or off the Internet.

SMTP, and mail applications, have fostered the elaboration and growth of TCP/IP and related technologies by providing a mechanism for the free distribution of information around the Internet, including proposals, specifications, and strictly informative documents.

SMTP is a network service that lets multiple mail applications exchange messages with one another. As the name is meant to suggest, it is a simple protocol, based on a set of simple ASCII commands from the client to the mail server and an equally basic set of alphanumeric responses. Few users ever get exposed to this interaction—it's the job of the e-mail software in use to capture and format this information to make more sense to human beings.

To ensure delivery, SMTP uses TCP as its transport protocol, establishing a connection between the sending and receiving hosts to transfer the message from sender to receiver. SMTP is not sophisticated about expanding distribution lists: more modern e-mail protocols explicitly address issues like fan-out and delivery to multiple servers; SMTP requires that each target server get its own copy, even if one copy has to pass through other target servers along the way.

Simple Network Management Protocol (SNMP)

SNMP was developed specifically for use in the TCP/IP environment, but was based on the OSI definitions for network management. Even though SNMP is technically the name of the protocol used to carry management information, it really refers to the whole set of management databases, operations, and agents needed to control a network. Like the TCP/IP e-mail protocol, SNMP is called *simple*, not because it has only elementary capabilities (which is untrue) but because it passes information in the form of simple text-based messages, using TCP as its transport protocol and IP as its network protocol.

SNMP's justification is that the increasing proliferation of networks and their growing individual complexity, makes it imperative for administrative personnel to be able to monitor and control the network and the elements of which it is composed by using the network, rather than by physically interacting with each element directly. Because the technology for network management has been developed primarily for large and widespread internets, it has tended to be operated in large-scale business, government, and research environments, not as a general-purpose set of utilities that anyone would use.

Today, the tide is turning: More and more components are being made manageable, more management tools are being built, and management technology is becoming vastly more affordable. The result is a proliferation of management agents and tools popping up all over the place. SNMP is emerging as the protocol of choice, since it combines the strength of the OSI's beautiful technical models with the hard-won practical experience gained in over ten years of experience with the Internet.

Even so, the science of network management is just in its infancy. Today, although SNMP management agents and corresponding tools are widespread, they are capable mostly of gathering and displaying statistics (about traffic levels, error rates, processes in use, etc.) but really have gained little capability to help administrators understand what the statistics and trends they gather can really mean. Nevertheless, we expect SNMP to continue to play an important role as next-generation management systems start to emerge, and network management becomes a proactive control function, rather than a reactive statistics display.

Remote Utilities (Sometimes Called R-utils or R commands)

The "r" commands are basically a set of UNIX commands that have been implemented for use across the network rather than on a local host. Because they were basically built as a set of UNIX-to-UNIX tools and because they offer no real security controls (anyone with a valid account name for the target machine can run programs, execute a shell, copy files, or login across the network), these tools have fallen into disfavor in the Internet community.

The four most common r utilities are shown in Table 3.3. All of these remote utilities are lightweight in terms of the level of negotiation and service that they deliver; most of them make default assumptions about the type of terminal to be emulated or service to be delivered. The real

Command	Explanation (Remote Command)
`rlogin`	Supports connection to a remote computer (remote login)
`rsh`	Allows a shell command to be executed on a remote computer (remote shell)
`rexec`	Allows a program to be executed on a remote computer (remote exec)
`rcp`	Allows files to be copied between remote computers (remote copy)

Table 3.3 *The TCP/IP remote utilities (R-Utils)*

intention of these commands was to give power users an easy way to jump across the network to spawn a task, run a program, or move files around. For heavy-duty use we recommend investigating the more powerful TCP/IP applications that follow, where Telnet would typically be used instead of rlogin, rsh, or rexec, and FTP instead of rcp.

File Transfer Protocol (FTP)

FTP is an application created to deal with the problems inherent in moving large files across a network, between dissimilar machines. Using TCP for transport takes care of reliability and robustness for the information crossing the network, but FTP's job is to make sure that the files delivered from one system to another are as readable on the target system as they were on the originating one.

Because different kinds of computers store information in different formats—an extreme example of which is the use of ASCII for character data on most computers nowadays, but IBM's use of EBCDIC for character data on mainframes and some older minis—FTP has to be able to translate among the different kinds of formats used for character data, binary data, and record-formatted files.

In addition, FTP also has to be able to overcome the differences among multiple operating systems when it comes to navigating file systems, to change and list directories, to create, delete, and rename files, and the like. In its command-line form, FTP is a crude but powerful tool for managing files across the network and copying files to or from remote systems. In keeping with the GUI tendencies of modern software, many vendors have greatly improved on FTP's interface, making it possible to do away with arcane commands and use point-and-click methods to work within remote file systems across the network. Whether old fashioned or new fangled, FTP is a workhorse application on the Internet and is both widely and heavily used.

FTP also has a lightweight cousin, called the *trivial file transfer protocol* (TFTP). TFTP uses UDP instead of TCP for transport and is intended mainly as a convenience for forgetful Telnet users on DOS or Windows PCs (or other single-tasking systems). TFTP is most commonly used when you have started a remote session on a host on the network and suddenly realize that you have to transfer a file to or from your local machine. You could run FTP on the remote host, but that would mean losing your GUI interface (assuming you've got one); more dire, it would mean mastering the syntax and commands for navigating the file system on that machine. TFTP lets you bypass the intricacies of the remote host's operating system (typically, UNIX) and use an interface both local and more familiar. Maybe that's why they call it trivial! The other major use of TFTP is as part of a bootstrapping protocol, to let diskless computers or embedded systems transfer boot-up files over the network at startup time.

In Chapter 13 we cover both trivial and nontrivial flavors of FTP in excruciating detail. For the time being, if you think "file transfer" when you see or hear FTP, you're more than halfway to mastering its capabilities.

Telnet (Terminal Emulation over a Network)

In the earliest days of computers, personal computers were unheard of (given their cost at the time, the concept would have sounded like wasteful arrogance or blasphemy). Users wishing to interact with a computer would either submit a batch job using paper tape, magnetic tape, or punched cards, or if they were really lucky or well-connected, might use a CRT (cathode-ray terminal) or teletype device to input their information to the computer directly through a keyboard and see the responses on their display or as hard copy output. This was the basis for so-called interactive computing.

Telnet was designed to let users attach to a remote computer across the network, as if they were terminals directly attached to that computer. Then, the remote host would appear just as if it were a local host, subject only to the additional delays caused by the quality and character of the links between user and remote host.

Telnet is a terminal access application interface, but for standalone computers it must also include a terminal emulation application. In reality, dumb terminals must use the CPU power of a terminal server or a local host to manage the local end of the connection with the remote host, just as a PC emulating a terminal has to run the emulation software to be able to act "just like a dumb terminal."

Telnet supplies terminal-level access to remote hosts, so that those hosts "see" the device that connects to them as if it were just another terminal. Telnet users must therefore log in and be authenticated (supply a valid account name and password) to gain entry to the remote host. Then, they must indicate what type of terminal they are going to act like, so the host machine will know exactly how to communicate.

Telnet uses TCP as its transport protocol and, to provide the most optimal terminal-like response, packages each keystroke as a separate packet to be sent from the user to the remote host. Each packet is acknowledged and echoed from the remote host so that the user knows that the remote host is getting exactly what is being sent. Telnet uses special control characters to manage communication between terminal and remote host and is capable of supporting highly sophisticated emulations (high-resolution vector or raster graphics, for instance).

Like FTP, Telnet is one of the real TCP/IP workhorse applications. It also is both widely and heavily used on the Internet (and in other TCP/IP environments as well). Chapter 14 will cover Telnet in detail.

Line Printer Services (lpr, lpq, lprm, lpc, lpd)

TCP/IP line printer services let users manage print jobs on remote hosts. Known also as *LPS*, line printer services allows users to access shared printers controlled by a remote host (if printing is the only service that such a host supplies, it will often be called a print server).

LPS permits print output to be redirected across the network from one computer to another. LPS includes two main processes: lpr, the client side, and lpd, the server side. Lpd handles print jobs sent to it through lpr and directs the output to a print queue, which is basically a holding area on the print server (either in RAM or on disk) where the information will reside until its turn to be printed, when it will be sent to the selected printer. Remote print commands do not typically work from within applications (so that selecting Print from inside your word processor would automatically invoke an LPS command), but most network environments offer reasonable alternatives to meet this kind of need.

The lpr/lpd protocol uses TCP as its transport to guarantee accurate delivery of the files to be printed. LPS also includes a set of basic print job management utilities, as covered in Table 3.4.

Command	Explanation (Remote Command)
lpr	Assign output to a remote print queue (line print remote)
lpq	Display contents of remote print queue (line print queue)
lprm	Remove a job from a remote print queue (line print remove)
lpc	Control output queue (line print control; for system administrators only)

Table 3.4 *The line printer services utilities*

Network File System (NFS)

As with TCP/IP, NFS actually delivers more functionality than its name might imply. Although NFS was developed by Sun Microsystems, it has released specifications for most of its important components into the public domain, so that many vendors today offer NFS implementations that can interoperate with one another. Consequently, NFS has become part of the TCP/IP protocol suite and is very commonly used on IP-based networks.

NFS provides a good way to interconnect PCs, minicomputers, and mainframes. It allows files to be stored at globally available locations, for those files to be shared among dissimilar computers, and supports remote print services. NFS acts to provide virtual disks across an internetwork, so that remote file systems appear as nothing more than extensions of the local file system. When NFS works as it's supposed to, users gain access to more disk space and print services without necessarily realizing that these services are being delivered by the network.

NFS provides disassembly and sequencing and desequencing and reassembly services for file transfers at upper layers in the application (above the transport layer), so it uses UDP as its transport protocol. Other components of the environment can use either UDP or TCP, as appropriate (typically UDP for local, and TCP for wide-area communications) for the operations being performed.

This concludes our discussion of the elements of the TCP/IP protocol suite. Believe it or not, we really just scratched the tip of a very large iceberg. Even so, what we covered is probably more than you actually need to know to be a capable Internet user. If you're still curious or have to know more to administer an Internet connection, please consult the TCP/IP references included in the Recommended Reading list at the end of this chapter.

ALPHABET SOUP: IAB, IETF, AND RFCs

Having been exposed to the collection of protocols and services that TCP/IP represents, and the need to control and manage IP addresses on the Internet, you might be tempted to ask: "Who's responsible for all this stuff?" The answer to that question can be found in a bowl of alphabet soup, as we look into the governing bodies for the Internet and TCP/IP, and encounter a multitude of interesting acronyms.

Where TCP/IP is concerned, the architectural standards and the United States Internet are governed by the Internet Architecture Board (IAB), previously known as the Internet Activities Board. The IAB delegates its responsibilities for development, operation, and management of the Internet and related protocols and services to various subcommittees, working groups, and suborganizations that it controls and to other commercial companies specializing in communications, computing and various types of consulting (like the combination of AT&T, General Atomics, and Network Solutions that provide key services and support for the InterNIC, as discussed in Chapter 2).

The subgroup chartered with protocol development and implementation is the Internet Engineering Task Force (IETF). It comprises a steering committee, which reports to the IAB, and a collection of working groups, each of which is responsible for various protocols and services under development or in maintenance mode. The bulk of Internet protocol development and standardization activity is handled by the working groups within the IETF.

A companion group, the Internet Research Task Force (IRTF), is responsible for tracking emerging technologies and developing and pursuing new protocols and communications tools that could extend or enhance the capabilities of the Internet and that might someday be considered for standardization. This group rides the cutting edge of networking research and development, on the lookout for promising or interesting items for further research or consideration.

The Standards-Making Process

Not all protocols or services are destined to become standards; those that ultimately qualify as such must go through a series of defined developmental stages to qualify, as shown in Table 3.5. Protocols and services are typically delivered to the IETF in the form of a detailed specification, sometimes with a prototype implementation as well.

"Interesting" submissions will often attain the status of experimental protocol, just so IETF members and their affiliate organizations can try them out. Sometimes, proposed protocols may be assigned to the experimental level, if the IETF decides that it is not yet ready for standardization. At this point, the protocol is no longer on the standards track, but may be resubmitted later for further consideration.

The transition from proposed standard to draft standard can result only from a decision by the IESG to advance its status to that level, and then only after the protocol has been a proposed standard for at least six months. Going from draft standard to standard (or "official standard" as it is sometimes called) also requires a decision by the IESG to advance its status, and then only after at least four months as a draft standard. Also, during the draft standard period at least two implementations of the protocol or service from the specification must be developed, and then demonstrated to interoperate with one another.

Once a protocol or service becomes a standard, it will be assigned a status. A required standard is one that must be included in any TCP/IP implementation to meet Department of Defense requirements for minimum functionality. An elective standard is one that implementers are free to include or not, at their own discretion. Finally, a recommended standard is one that is not absolutely required, but that most implementers will include because it is either in wide use, high demand, or provides meaningful new functionality for TCP/IP implementations. Two other possible status designations are "limited use," which means that the protocols or services are for use only in special, proscribed

Standard Level	Definition
experimental	Defined and implemented for experimental purposes
proposed	Defined and submitted for consideration by IETF
draft	Accepted as draft by IESG, proposed for 6+ months
standard	Accepted as std by IESG, draft for 4+ months
required	Must be included to meet government standards
elective	Inclusion/exclusion at developer's discretion
recommended	Inclusion not required, but recommended
historic	Obsolete or outmoded protocol no longer in use
information	Instructions, documentation, information on standards process

Table 3.5 *Levels of Internet standards*

circumstances, and "not recommended," that means they are not intended or suggested for general use. These last two status designations occur rarely.

RFCs: Documenting TCP/IP Standards

The documents that specify and describe TCP/IP protocols and services are called *requests for comment*, otherwise known as RFCs. RFCs are assigned in numeric order by the IETF and are referred to by number. The document that describes the Internet Official Protocol Standards is RFC 1600, which is near the top end of the range of numbers assigned thus far.

Even though *request for comment* sounds more like a question to solicit feedback on an idea (which is how the bulk of RFCs actually function), standard RFCs have the weight of law (or at least, decree) in the Internet and TCP/IP communities. These documents represent only a fraction of the total collection of RFCs, but they literally dictate how protocols behave and what functions they must perform. Failure to conform to these definitions—especially for required or recommended protocols—can cost a vendor the opportunity of doing business with the United States government and all the other bodies and agencies that adhere to its guidelines (of which there are many, both inside and outside the United States). In matters of dispute or in questions regarding the protocols, the RFCs are the final authority, and the IETF the final source of resolution.

Obtaining RFCs for Perusal

RFCs may be obtained from the Internet host named DS.INTERNIC.NET via FTP, WAIS, and electronic mail. Using FTP, RFCs are stored as rfc/rfcnnnn.txt or rfc/rfcnnnn.ps where *nnnn* is the RFC number, and *.txt* is the ASCII version, and *.ps* the PostScript version of the file (for the details on using FTP, please consult Chapter 13).

To use FTP to get these documents, login to DS.INTERNET.NET as 'anonymous' and supply your e-mail address as the password (to keep track of who is downloading what). Using WAIS, use either your own local client or Telnet to DS.INTERNET.NET and login as "wais"—no

Command	Explanation (Remote Command)
`document-by-name rfcnnnn`	'nnnn' is the RFC number. The text version is always sent.
`file /ftp/rfc/rfcnnnn.yyy`	'nnnn' is the RFC number. If 'yyy' = '.txt' the text version is
	sent; if 'yyy' = '.ps' the PostScript version is sent.
`help`	Sends a text file on how to use the InterNIC mail server

Table 3.6 *Ordering RFCs for e-mail delivery*

password is required—to access a remote WAIS client. Help information and a tutorial on using the program are available online. The database to search for the documents is named *rfcs* (for the details on using WAIS, please consult Chapter 17).

AT&T Directory and Database Services also provides a mail server interface to the RFC documents. Send a mail message to mailserv@ds.internic.net and include any of the commands in Table 3.6 to obtain the requested RFC file or files (a single message can include multiple requests). At the very least, we recommend that you download RFC 1600 and examine its comprehensive list of the standards-related RFCs currently in force for TCP/IP and the Internet. For the details on using Internet e-mail, please consult Chapter 9 (or see our companion volume, *E-mail Essentials*).

How the Internet *Really* Works

Now that you have been exposed to some of the intricacies of the TCP/IP protocols, of domain names and name servers, and of the governing and standards-making bodies for the Internet, you're ready to understand how the Internet actually works. After all the ground we covered, it will probably seem anticlimactic. Remember this, though: It is pretty amazing that an internetwork composed of hundreds of thousands of individual networks and millions of users that spans the entire globe actually works at all!

The Internet is composed of a vast collection of smaller regional internetworks, which together form the complex web of connections that the Internet represents. A good analogy is a modern system of roadways: at the highest level, cities and continents are linked by superhighways. From these large, high-speed links, smaller freeways, and lesser limited access roads reach out to connect smaller cities and towns. Within urban areas, lots of local links exist to tie individual locations together; the further you get from population centers, the sparser and smaller the roads become. Yet anyone armed with a map can find his or her way from just about any point of departure to any conceivable destination.

The superhighway for the Internet is its high-speed backbone, previously known as ARPAnet and NSFnet and now operated for the IAB by ANS (a cooperative venture that involves Merit Network, Inc., IBM, and MCI as partners in establishing and maintaining the nationwide backbone and multiple international link-ups). In the United States this backbone uses T-3 technology, which can move data at speeds up to 45 MBps over long-haul connections. The regional networks and service providers, like CERFnet, BITNET, PSI, and others, connect to the backbone; they generally use T-1 technology, which moves data at speeds up 1.544 MBps. Private and institutional networks feed into these nets, using links that may be as fast as T-1, but which often run at 56 KBps or slower (especially for modem-based connections), even though they are coming off of local-area networks that typically run at speeds of 4 MBps or faster.

It is important to note that there is no central clearinghouse computer through which all traffic must pass, or any centralized authority for administering the Internet as a whole. Other than the InterNIC, which handles address registration and provides a registered domain name service, there is hardly anything about the Internet that happens at all, except for the coordinated efforts of many network administrators and communications providers everywhere.

This decentralization, especially when coupled with the Internet's far-flung and widely distributed information resources and services, helps to explain why TCP/IP and the RFC mechanism controlled by the IAB are so important to the workability of the overall environment. They define a set of shared understandings and expectations, along with an open set of standards for networking, that brings the whole conglomeration together and makes it work.

Thus, from a technical perspective, what makes the Internet work is the existence of a network distribution structure much like the road system, that can direct local traffic across the intervening regional and global data highways to take information from source to destination or sender to receiver. More than the links and connections, this requires the protocols and services that can carry the traffic reliably and that can effortlessly navigate a potentially confusing network maze. But from a practical perspective, what makes the Internet really work is the uncountable hours of toil and effort that have gone into the standards process of providing clear definitions and reference implementations for all the pieces and parts involved. Likewise crucial is the tacit agreement throughout the networking community to make things as easy as possible and play by the resulting set of shared networking rules and conventions.

In the final analysis, the Internet works only because so many individual operators and contributors really want it to!

SUMMARY

In this chapter we peeled back the covering of the Internet and have looked at the communications capabilities—both between computers and among humans—that make it work. Along the way, you learned about the TCP/IP protocol suite, about network domain names and addresses, and about the standards-making process that brings the development and implementation of the Internet's myriad of capabilities together and keeps them under control. We hope, the magnitude of the task is clear; likewise, the miracle that the Internet represents should also be obvious.

From this point on in the book, we dig further into the details, as we first explore how to get connected and what kinds of things you can do with the Internet and then move on to investigate the tools and techniques you'll use to go exploring.

RECOMMENDED READING

For this chapter we include both TCP/IP references and some additional Internet reference materials as well. Don't forget to go exploring on the Internet itself for more information on both subjects. Remember, too, that any of the RFCs is easily obtained via FTP, WAIS, or e-mail—if you're really keen on the details, these are the ultimate reference!

TCP/IP Resources

Of the books listed below, we recommend the newer ones over the older ones, almost every time. The sole exception remains John Davidson's excellent introductory book that, despite its age, is still a very good place for a complete beginner to start. The most exhaustive and detailed references are by Douglas Comer and the two volumes that involve W. Richard Stevens—these are probably best-suited for someone who really needs as much detail as possible. The others are all good general TCP/IP references (we particularly like the Washburn and Evans book).

Arick, Martin R.: *The TCP/IP Companion*, QED Publishing Group, Wellesley, MA, 1993. List price: $24.95

Comer, Douglas E.: *Internetworking with TCP/IP*, Volumes 1–3 Prentice-Hall, Englewood Cliffs, NJ, 1991 (Vols. 1 & 2), 1993 (Vol. 3). All volumes have a list price of $50.00.

Davidson, John: *An Introduction to TCP/IP*, Springer Verlag, New York, NY 1988. List price: $19.95.

Stallings, William: *Handbook of Computer Communications Standards, Vol. 3: Department of Defense (DoD) Protocol Standards*, Macmillan Publishing Company, New York, NY 1988. List price: $39.95

Stevens, W. Richard: *TCP/IP Illustrated*, Vol. 1, Addison-Wesley, Reading, MA, 1993. List price: $47.50

Washburn, K. and J. T. Evans: *TCP/IP: Running a Successful Network* Addison-Wesley, Wokingham, England, 1993. List price: $48.50

Wright, Gary, and W. Richard Stevens: *TCP/IP Illustrated*, Vol. 2 Addison-Wesley, Reading, MA, 1994. List price: $52.75.

More Internet References

Here is a short list of more Internet materials, both of which are available from the Internet itself, for the cost of the necessary file transfers and printing.

Gaffin, Adam: *Everybody's Guide to the Internet*, MIT Press, Cambridge, MA, 1994. List price: $14.95
Download instructions for the electronic version:
FTP host: ftp.eff.org
file directory: **/pub/Net_info/EFF_Net_Guide**
file name: **netguide.eff**
Gopher host: **gopher.eff.org**
database: **1/Net_info/EFF_Net_Guide**
file name: **netguide.eff**
WWW info:
http://www.eff.org/pub/Net_info/EFF_Net_Guide/netguide.eff

Kehoe, Brendan: *Zen and the Art of the Internet: A Beginner's Guide* Prentice-Hall, Englewood Cliffs, NJ, 1992. List price: $22.00.
Download instructions:
FTP host: **ftp.cs.widener.edu**
file directory: **/pub/zen**
file name: **zen-1.0.dvi** (device-independent TeX version)
file name: **zen-1.0.ps** (PostScript version)

How to
Hook Up

4

What It Means to Be
"Connected to the Internet"

Many people who work in any moderately sized company are able to receive and send Internet e-mail and conclude, therefore, that they are connected to the Internet. This is not really accurate. In most cases they are getting that e-mail through a gateway, which is a computer running software that translates the format of their local e-mail messages into the Internet message format and translates incoming Internet e-mail messages back to the local format. So while these people are able to take advantage of a very useful and important feature of the Internet, they are not connected to it.

A number of people have the access to both Internet e-mail and the Usenet bulletin boards. They might have this access via a service that allows them to access these two services, which is the most flexible means, or their access to Usenet groups might be limited to posting through e-mail. Although these folks have even more of the power of the Internet at their command, they are still not connected to it.

Actually, to be able to say that your computer is connected to the Internet, you must be able to read news, send and receive e-mail, participate in "chat" sessions, use telnet to log in to other connected computers, and generally use all of the features of the Internet, all from your own computer. Not only that, but other people can log in to your computer and access data on it as well. For this world of delights you need a TCP/IP connection.

There is another way. If you can dial up a computer connected to the Internet and, using your own computer as a terminal to the Internet-connected one, do all of the same things that the user with a "real" connection can do, then it is accurate to say that you are "connected to the Internet." (Some purists—or snobs—might quibble with you on this one, but it is a generally accepted usage of the term.) Your computer is still not connected, however, and in this chapter we help you decide whether that matters to you.

There are a number of different ways to connect to the Internet, all with various pros and cons. We look first at a basic division between types of connections—on-line versus off-line usage. Thinking about these two types of usage will help you pinpoint what general types of capability you expect from your Internet connection.

Next, we discuss capabilities in more detail, by examining most of the basic types of things people do on the Internet. Think of this section as a checklist that you can use to decide what features you need and what features you can live without, at least for the time being.

Finally, we take a look at the types of service you are most likely to find, so you can match your requirements to what's available. Of course, service providers are constantly expanding and responding to the changing market, so if you don't see quite what you need in the categories described here, ask anyway. By the time you read this, the exact service you desire may be available.

Two Types of Connections

One way to look at Internet connections is in terms of the constancy of the connection—whether you are always connected to the Net or only occasionally, when you need to do something. The cost of your connection will vary greatly depending on which type of access you need, so let's look at these in more detail.

Accessing the Internet in Batches

If you need to connect to the Internet only to read your e-mail, or perhaps to read Usenet news, batch usage is probably your better choice.

This means that you dial up to your provider, perform whatever chores you need to, and log off. The most cost effective solutions are yours to sift through.

This type of service does not limit you to e-mail and news, though. With the right service provider you can just as easily run file transfers, converse with hundreds of people in a chat session and explore the wonders of the World Wide Web sites. This just means that you are not connected to the Internet 24 hours per day.

Constant Access

If, on the other hand, you need to know about new e-mail as soon as it arrives, or you need to provide access to your computer so that other people can log in to it and access your data, or if you have a large number of people using your connection, who might need it any time of the day or night, then you should consider getting a dedicated connection. With it, you are assured that you can get to the Internet anytime, and you never have to worry about busy signals. This type of connection costs a lot more, but depending on your requirements it may be worth it.

EVALUATING YOUR NEEDS

Let's crank the microscope in another notch and look closely at how you plan to use your Internet connection by going over several of the most popular and useful Internet services. Each of the services we examine in this section is discussed in more detail later in the book. This section is designed to give you an idea of the types of services you might want and the impact they will have on your connection type. We also go over some other matters you should consider, including the number of people using the connection and how much you can afford to spend.

Things You Can Do on the Internet

In this section we look at several common Internet tasks and give you some guidelines for determining whether you need the service and how demanding it will be on your connection.

Internet E-mail

Ah, ubiquitous e-mail. If you have only one Internet service, this is likely to be the one. Converse with people all over the world as easily as with a coworker across the hall. Write books, develop architectural plans, make dinner dates, all by sending messages via e-mail.

The nicest thing about e-mail, from a connectivity point of view, is that it is typically composed mainly of text messages and therefore usually relatively small in volume. Text files are usually much smaller than data files that contain sound recordings, for example. So even if you get 50 e-mail messages per day (typical for a medium to heavy e-mail user), you can retrieve those messages easily in a short time, and storing them does not present a significant space problem (as long as you keep your storage area tidy and purge old messages regularly).

Usenet News

Another very popular Internet service is access to the hundreds of interactive forums that make up the Usenet. Each forum is called a *newsgroup,* and within each newsgroup you will often find multiple conversations in progress. These conversations are called *threads.*

If you want to receive all of the Usenet news that appears every day, you need to plan on having about 50 MB (megabytes) of free disk storage for each day's news. With that sort of volume, you might well wonder why we consider news to be a low-volume application! Well, it depends on how you use it. If you are getting news only for yourself, you do not want to receive all 50 MB everyday—for one thing, you couldn't possibly read it all. Fortunately, it's not too difficult to pick and choose what news you receive, and once you isolate only the newsgroups in which you are interested, you can easily trim that 50 MB down to a manageable 20 K (kilobytes) or less.

If, however, you are managing a site and your users need access to all of the newsgroups, your Usenet activity falls firmly on the side of "heavy usage," and you have lots to do in terms of making sure you always have enough disk space. You also will need a much higher speed connection than someone who reads only a handful of newsgroups—with a slow modem, you would be unable to download all of the news in a day!

File Transfers

This is another Internet application whose volume and usage patterns depend heavily on who is using it. A casual user transfers a moderately sized file (one or two megabytes) every week or so, while a heavy user might transfer several 20 MB files every day.

To give you some idea about whether these transfers are important to you, consider some of the types of files people send over the Internet:

Book chapters—Many publishers allow authors to transfer completed text electronically over the Internet. Which saves everyone time and overnight delivery charges. These files can run from 10 or 20 K to several hundred.

Software—A large amount of software is available in the public domain at various sites on the Internet. This means that when you hear about a nifty new e-mail reading program, you can go get it and download it to your own machine. These files can be several megabytes in size, though you will often find them compressed.

Research data—Perhaps you work for a university, and you need to send your many hundreds of megabytes of data to a nearby super-computing center. The Internet is the natural choice.

Photographs—Some things are much easier to show than to explain. If someone asks you what your hometown skyline looks like, it's probably much easier to send a digital image. Such images can get rather large; one with a high resolution might take up 750 K of storage.

Sound and Graphics

Suppose you want to take your Internet activity a step beyond simply sending graphics files via one of the file transfer mechanisms. It is possible to send messages that incorporate sound and graphics as well as text and for the recipient to view the graphics, listen to your recording, and respond in kind.

Clearly these features are more sophisticated than the ones we've been discussing, and that advancement comes at a price. Not only do you have to equip your workstation with the necessary viewing and audio hardware, you may have to upgrade your disk drive and network connection if you send or receive a lot of these types of files. As we noted, graphics and sound files are considerably larger than text files, and this size becomes apparent both in terms of storage space and the speed of your connection.

Video and Sound

Among the newest applications of the Internet are those involving live video and sound transmissions. A musical group might wish to send you a recording of their latest effort, for instance, and with the right audio equipment you can listen to it as you receive it off the Net. Similarly, you can now see and talk to someone over the Net, if you have the equipment to decode and display the transmitted video and audio data.

Applications such as these are extremely demanding of network and computing resources. In the case of video, for instance, it is necessary to see about 30 frames per second for the video to look smooth and natural. At rates less than that, the movement will appear jerky or choppy. The digital images necessary to present you with a full 30 pictures per second demand prohibitively expensive transmission speeds (for most applications), so typically these images are compressed, which leads to other problems. It takes a very powerful computer to compress 30 frames every second and send them out over the link, while at the same time decoding the incoming 30 frames from the other side. Therefore when you see video over the Net it is usually at rates more in the area of 10–15 frames per second, which are still very demanding of network resources.

The same principles apply to audio. While compression and other techniques reduce the amount of bandwidth these applications require, they are still extremely resource intensive, especially when compared to low-impact applications such as e-mail. If you require video or audio capabilities from your Internet feed, you need a relatively fast link. If you plan to store any of these sound or video clips, make sure you have a large disk drive—they take up a lot of space!

Making Data Available to Others

Perhaps you have a set of graphics files of your vacation photos, demonstrating beyond a doubt that the Loch Ness monster does exist. Now you want to set yourself up as an ftp site so that anyone who wishes to do so can log in to your machine and collect copies of these photo images. Or perhaps you are the president of a nonprofit agency devoted to tracking the destruction of the rainforests, and you want to make your data available to reporters and other researchers. If you need to make any data available to other people on demand, your best bet may be to set yourself up as a true Internet site.

In this case, a dial-up connection, whether using your computer as a terminal or via a SLIP or PPP connection, may not work for you. To provide access to your data files on demand, you need to make your computer available all the time, and you need a fixed address that you can publish. Therefore you need to investigate dedicated links to the Internet and get yourself a permanent IP address.

There is another way to get your data out to the world, though. Instead of making these files available via ftp or other file transfer methods, you could simply publish your e-mail address and maintain a dial-up account. When the reporters, researchers, or curious monster seekers want to access your data repository, they can simply send you e-mail, and you can in return send the requested files. You can send the files either by e-mail or by uploading them from your home computer to your dial-up system and from there send them to the requester.

This approach has a couple of advantages. For instance, you avoid the expense and maintenance overhead of managing your own full-blown Internet site. Plus, the small effort involved in sending you a message might discourage the idly curious, so you can screen for serious inquiries. On the other hand, though, you will be unable to present your files in any of the Internet file indexes (such as archie indexes), and you have the overhead of handling every request yourself.

Again, volume will be the determinant. You might want to start out with the e-mail approach, and if the number of requests gets too large, you can switch to another method later.

Who's the User?

In addition to evaluating the sorts of tasks for which you plan to use the Internet, you also need to consider who will be using the connection. If it is just for your home computer, and only you and a couple of family members will be using it for e-mail and Usenet news, a low-speed dial-up link will serve you just fine. If, on the other hand, your entire company of 300 people will be using the link for their Internet mail, the previously low-impact application of e-mail becomes a relatively high-volume one. If you have a large number of people you need a higher speed link, even if individually they are all fairly light users.

Keep in mind, too, that your needs will change. At first, only about 10% of those 300 people might use e-mail very seriously. As more and more of them discover what they can do with the link, though, usage will increase. Then a few people will need file transfer capabilities or access to Usenet. This growth is a sign of success, so be sure to plan for it.

A List of Costs

In this section we list the basic charges that you need to keep in mind as you budget for your Internet connection. Not all of these charges will apply to every type of connection. This list is to help you ensure that you don't forget anything in your initial accounting.

Modem

If you are dialing into an analog line, you will need a modem. While it is possible to dial up at very low speeds (2400 baud or less), we recommend spending a little bit more and getting a modem with a speed of at least 14.4 Kbps. As prices continue to drop on modems, the cost of these faster modems is quite reasonable.

Line Interface Unit

If you opt for a more expensive and typically higher volume digital line, you will need not a modem, but a device called a CSU/DSU. Chapters 29 and 30 offer more information.

Phone Lines

If you dial into the Internet from your home and spend more than a few hours per week on-line, you might want to consider installing a separate telephone line from your home voice line. In some areas this is a simple matter, and you can do it at any time, but in other areas it might be quite difficult. Check with your local telephone company.

Long Distance Charges

If you have to dial in to a server that is not in your local area or if your telephone service is metered (so that local calls accumulate charges just like long distance calls), be sure to allow for the cost of each phone call when you create your budget. Coupled with on-line charges, an apparent savings at the site of a remote provider might prove to be less of a bargain than paying a relatively high fixed rate to a provider who offers a toll-free number, for instance. Again, a lot of this balancing act depends on your expected usage.

Charges for a Dedicated Line

If you have determined that you need a dedicated connection, be sure to factor in the cost of the dedicated line. Such lines typically have fairly high installation fees (on the order of several hundred dollars in the United States) and higher monthly fees than ordinary telephone lines. Unfortunately, such lines might not be available in every area; again, check with your local telephone company. Your Internet provider should be able to provide you with some information here as well.

Cost of the Internet Connection

Of course, you also have to pay your provider for your Internet access. Every provider has a different pricing scheme, so it can be difficult to compare prices. Some charge an hourly connect fee, for instance, while others charge a flat rate per month. Many charge a monthly rate *plus* an hourly rate. Most charge a fee to set up your account. Some charge for support—if you think you need a lot of help setting up your connection, these might not be the best value for you. In many cases, providers charge more for higher speed connections, and most have peak and off-peak rates. Ask lots of questions before you select your provider.

Graphics and Video Equipment

If you need to transmit or receive video or audio data, be sure to budget the cost of the encoding and decoding equipment. Frequently all you need is speakers and a set of boards to put in your computer, but this equipment is still rather expensive.

How to Decide

Now that you have clarified your thoughts about who will be using your equipment, what they will be using it for, and what items go into your budget, you need to weigh your needs for speed, power, and even reliability against cost. You might find, for example, that you can get a very cheap connection, but it might not be particularly reliable. We know of a provider, for instance, who offers unlimited dial-up access with full Internet capability for $10 per month, or $75 per year (U.S. dollars). The catch is that they lack enough staff to keep things running smoothly, and the lines are often busy as demand has overwhelmed their resources.

If you plan to use your Internet connection for recreation, this trade-off might be very attractive. Business users, however, will probably require something more reliable and stable and be willing to pay more for it.

Again, keep in mind that your usage is likely to increase. Will your provider be able to keep up? Ask about their expansion plans and ask what options you will have if you someday decide to upgrade your dial-up account to a PPP account. It can be expensive to move to a new provider, in part because you have to send out address changes to all of your correspondents and associates. Think of your Internet address as a residence and, if possible, select your provider with an eye on the future.

WHAT IS AVAILABLE

Now that you have a better idea what types of things you can do on the Internet, you may have decided, for the time being at least, that you don't need a full Internet connection at all. If that's your case, you'll be interested in the following discussion of partial service providers.

If you need more than just a few services, but think a dedicated connection is a bit excessive, take a look at the discussion of various types of dial-up connections. This section should give you the information to decide whether you can be happy using your home computer as a terminal or you need the extra power that a SLIP or PPP connection provides.

Finally, if your analysis of your needs suggests that you need a dedicated connection to the Internet, we discuss some of the considerations to help you determine whether that is the most appropriate connection for you.

Dial-up Connections

We use the term *dial-up connection* to refer to any connection from your home computer to an Internet-connected computer. For this type of connection you need a home computer, of course, and a modem. The computer you dial into is probably running the UNIX operating system. This is not a problem, it simply means that if your home computer runs something else (such as DOS or the Macintosh operating system), you may have to go through some extra steps to transfer data between the systems.

With this type of connection, your home computer acts as a terminal to the Internet-connected computer. To do this you need terminal emulation software and communications software, both of which often come with modems.

The key feature of the dial-up connection is the gap between your computer and the Internet. You can log into your provider computer and perform all sorts of Internet tasks, such as gophering, ftp-ing, and so on, and retrieve files from all over the world to that Internet-connected computer, but another step is required before you can use that file on your home computer. You have to download it from the Internet-connected computer to your own. This is often called *double downloading*, and some people find it quite inconvenient. For limited requirements, though, the advantages outweigh the drawbacks.

Pros and Cons
The biggest advantage of these types of connections is the price. They are typically the cheapest option for getting connected to the Internet, and for limited use they are quite convenient.

Of course, there are also disadvantages. The speeds of these types of connections are limited to the speed of your modem, which might be rather slow. If the provider is offering a particularly good price, you might find that your bargain connection is impossible to use because the modems are always busy. Ask prospective providers for figures showing modem capacity and accessibility before you sign up. Another potential disadvantage is that your options of user interface may be limited—you might be restricted to a simple character interface rather than a sophisticated full-screen graphical display. And finally, the burden of the double download might be a drawback if you do a large number of file transfers.

The Double Download Issue
Suppose you see a message in a newsgroup asking if anyone knows the radio alphabet (where A is pronounced alpha, B is bravo, C is charlie, etc.). You have extensive experience as a radio operator and just hap-

pen to have a file on your DOS PC that lists this alphabet. How do you get it to the requester?

First you have to upload the file from your home computer to your Internet account; you do this using a transfer program such as kermit or zmodem. The same software that allows you to connect to your Internet account will often have a file transfer mechanism built in; check the software documentation. But there's a catch—since the target machine is running UNIX (probably) and the file is a DOS file, you have to perform a format conversion on the file, because UNIX and DOS handle line feeds and carriage returns at the end of lines different-ly. Again, check with your communications software for instructions.

Once you have transferred the file to your Internet account, you can then send it via e-mail or, if you deem it to be of general interest, post it to the newsgroup in response to the request.

To get files from the Internet to your home computer, you simply reverse the process. This double downloading process is not particular-ly burdensome once you get the hang of it, but it is something you have to remember. If you do a large number of file transfers, though, the hassle might make a "real" connection more and more attractive.

Dial-up Variations: Partial Service Providers

If all you need to do is get Internet e-mail and perhaps Usenet news, a number of reasonably priced options are available to you. CompuServe, for instance, has a gateway to Internet e-mail (but they charge extra for each piece of mail) and has plans to add access to Usenet newsgroups soon. The same is true of Prodigy, another popular bulletin board service.

Note that most providers are constantly adding new capabilities, and by the time you read this, they might well have many more services available. Again, ask a lot of questions and shop around. The Resource Guide in the back of the book gives access information for several of these providers.

SLIP and PPP Access

Technically, SLIP and PPP connections are also dial-up connections, because you dial into the Internet-connected computer when you want to perform an Internet task. But, with these types of connections, your home computer is running TCP/IP software, and the connection is via an IP link. In this case you are truly connected to the Internet for the time you are on-line. Among other things, this means that you have eliminated the need for double downloads.

When you have an IP connection, all of your Internet applications such as e-mail, World Wide Web browsing, and newsreading run on your home computer rather than your provider's computer. When you get a file using ftp, you retrieve it straight to the disk of your home computer. In some cases (that is, with some providers), you might even get your own domain name and address. Others use dynamic addressing, so your address is valid only for the duration of your connection. Furthermore, these types of connections usually allow multiple simultaneous sessions, so you can start a Gopher search and let it run while you look through your e-mail.

This convenience is quite attractive, but it naturally comes at a price. SLIP and PPP connections are sometimes as much as ten times as expensive as dial-up connections. They are also a lot more complicated to configure and get running, and because of the likely higher volume of network traffic, you will probably need a faster modem than a simple dial-up connection requires. Still, if the advantages are important to you, an IP connection might be the way to go.

The Luxury Connection: A Dedicated Line

If none of these solutions is sufficient for your needs, it's time to look at installing a dedicated line. These types of connections are generally cost effective only for groups of users—a company that needs Internet access for all its employees, for instance.

The advantages of dedicated connections, of course, are that they are always available—no worries about busy signals when you want to get to your Internet provider. They also handle much higher volumes than dial-up connections, so they can support both larger and more frequent data transfers and larger numbers of users.

On the down side, dedicated connections are very expensive and can be quite a lot of work to set up. It's really best to have someone around whose job it is to deal with the connection, the administration of the site, and the security issues. In most companies this job falls to whomever is already managing the LAN.

A note about security—once you have a dedicated connection and become an Internet site, you not only have the ability to explore the

Internet from your site, but other Internet users have the potential ability to explore your site as well. Whether this constitutes a security risk or not depends on what you store on your Internet connected computers, and how you manage access to your site. The services of an experienced administrator are invaluable in coordinating and managing these matters.

SUMMARY

With the information in this chapter, you now know how to evaluate your Internet connection needs. In upcoming chapters we discuss some more background issues and describe how you can get the most out of your Internet connection while minimizing your impact on other users. If you want to get right to the nuts and bolts of calling providers and working with them, turn to Chapters 28–30 for a rundown of some of the available options.

WHO OWNS THE INTERNET?

5

WHO'S IN CHARGE HERE?

One of the first questions new Internet users always ask is who owns the Internet, who pays for it, and who runs it. From our discussion of connecting to the Internet in Chapter 4, you probably have some idea who pays for it: you do. So do all the other people and institutions who have connections to it. But this doesn't really answer the question.

Sometimes people regret asking this question, because the answer is far from clear. No one runs the Internet, for instance, but there are standards boards that determine how it runs. Similarly, no one agency or board owns it, but every network attached to the Internet has its own governing body, usage policies, and owners. In this chapter we elaborate on these ideas, to help you get closer to the elusive answer to that seemingly simple question.

MONEY AND POWER

In many instances, if you want to find out who has power over something, find out who pays for it. To a certain extent this rule applies to the Internet as well, as long as you remember that it's paid for by thousands of different organizations. Well, that probably doesn't help much, but in this section we attempt to describe who pays for the Internet and what that means to you.

Every Net Pays Its Way

Every network attached to the Internet is owned by its governing organization. Thus the National Science Foundation owns the portion of the Net known as NSFNET, and your company owns the LAN that it operates and has attached to the Internet. Universities, corporations, and governments all have their own internal networks, and they also have policies governing their use. Sometimes these policies vary widely between networks, so it might behoove you to be aware of the rules—your provider should be able to give you a summary of what you can and cannot do.

Universities, corporations, and individuals must also pay for the cost of connecting to a national Internet service provider on top of the costs of their own networks. Depending on how they connect to the Internet, they might be subject to different usage guidelines. Let's look at some examples.

The Folks with the Money Make the Rules

Every organization that has a network has guidelines about its use. Your company, for instance, may not allow you to send personal e-mail over its network. It may figure that since it owns the network and the equipment, as well as its paying you for your time, it has the right to determine what you do with its equipment and on what it considers to be its time.

Similarly, government agencies have rules about what can travel over their networks. These rules are based on fair use principles, as we will describe. And, of course, every Internet provider has a set of rules. These are usually designed to keep any one user from having a negative impact on the performance of the network for other users.

Acceptable Use Policy (AUP)

There's still a bit of confusion over this policy and what it means. It originally came into existence when the United States government funded the creation of the NSFNET. That funding was contingent on the premise that the network was used only for educational and research related-transfers. Nobody quibbled over the occasional personal e-mail, but openly commercial activity was strictly forbidden.

Because of this, several commercial networks sprung up in the late 1980s and early 1990s, and in 1991 they were linked together, creating a widespread alternative to NSFNET and its cousins and freeing users from the restrictions of the AUP. This group of networks is called the *Commercial Internet Exchange* (CIX).

So someone who tells you that commercial activity is not allowed over the Internet is operating from old information. True, any traffic that passes through the NSF backbone is still restricted by the rules of the AUP, but if the message takes another route, it can to belong to a company or even contain advertising.

Commercial Providers and Their Rules

Because your provider owns the equipment and the business that provides access to you and others, it has a stake in protecting both the business and equipment, and so probably it has rules and guidelines that you must agree to in order to get an account. Read through the contract before you sign and make sure you are not agreeing to anything that you find troublesome.

Most providers inform you, for instance, that you are not allowed to send materials that are illegal or obscene. This is important to the provider who could be held liable for material that passes through its systems (a controversial matter in itself). It also typically states that it will cancel your access if you engage in activities that negatively affect its or others' systems. (We look at what this means in Chapter 21.) Some providers have been known to go as far as to read and censor users' e-mail, something you might want to check on before you sign up. Also, if you will need to send commercial materials over your link, check with your provider and make sure that is allowed (that it is not directly connected to NSFNET, for instance).

WHO MAKES IT WORK

A better way of thinking about who "runs" the Internet is to look at who determines how it works, a network that does not operate in the same way as the rest of the Internet will not be able to communicate with it—a form of control, you might say. Luckily for us, the folks who make these rules are well-organized and even have a name, the Internet Society (ISOC).

The ISOC and the IAB

The ISOC meets regularly to discuss changes to the way the Internet works, and these meetings sometimes lead to meetings of the IAB (Internet Architectural Board). These two groups discuss details of the network operation, from how addresses are assigned to individual sites to how bits are interpreted in network packets. If a network adheres to the guidelines created by the IAB and presented by the ISOC, and that network wants to connect to the Internet, then that network is "on" the Internet. Otherwise, it's not, since it cannot talk to anyone who is.

So at the technical level, the question of who runs the Internet is fairly straightforward!

UNOFFICIAL RULES

There is another governing body on the Internet, one much harder to define or describe than even the "owners" of the Internet. This group is strongly opinionated and seldom in agreement on many matters. As a whole it is independent and resistant to external control but has created a set of guidelines to which most of members adhere. They are the Internet users, and they form a strong community. Its mouthpiece could be said to be Usenet news—via that medium they discuss community issues, spread information about interesting new services, welcome new users (and correct them when they make mistakes), and convey the rules that keep everything running smoothly.

World's Largest Anarchy

Some Usenet users like to call the Internet an anarchy, since it has no central administrator or rule-making body. Others disagree, which demonstrates a key feature of Usenet—everything is hotly debated and few opinions go uncontested. Any time a new software package comes out, or a natural disaster strikes, or someone flagrantly violates the rules of the community, or just about anything else you can think of, on-line conversations immediately spring up to discuss the background, implications, and ramifications of the event.

Breaking the Rules

If you transgress against the rules of the community, the consequences can be as minor as someone sending you a very testy e-mail message (or several) or as dire as losing your Internet access. Recall that your provider requires you to agree to some rules—if you violate them or enough people complain about your behavior to your system administrator, he or she will very likely reprimand you and could go so far as to cancel your account. This has happened, many times. Intermediate expressions of disapproval might include flames (insulting or inflammatory messages about you posted to relevant newsgroups) and mail bombing (that's when someone sends you several hundred e-mail messages protesting your behavior).

Don't worry. In Chapter 7 we give you all the information you need to keep from unwittingly infuriating the entire Internet community. Just use some common sense and good manners and you're unlikely to run into trouble. If you want some examples of what not to do and the results, turn to Chapter 21.

SUMMARY

From this chapter you have probably gathered that the answer to the question "Who owns the Internet?" is "Nobody and everybody" and to "Who runs the Internet?" is "It depends on what you mean." If you want to know who decides how the Net operates, look to the standards committees and the administrative newsgroups. But if you want to know who makes the rules for your access, check with your Internet provider, because the rules vary depending on whose access network you use and how its Internet feed gets routed. Admittedly this is all rather vague and complicated, but for the most part you won't have to worry about it.

WHAT YOU CAN DO ON THE INTERNET

6

A SAMPLER

In previous chapters we alluded to things you can do on the Internet, tossing around phrases like "check your e-mail" and "converse with people from all over the world." If you've done some work in networked environments you probably have a general idea what we mean but might be wondering what all this really looks like in operation.

Therefore in this chapter we walk through a fictional sample session on the Internet. We check our e-mail, stop in on some conversations, search for some books, and retrieve a file. We opt for some of the simpler software, all of which has user interfaces that are strictly character based rather than graphically based, because these are the ones you are most likely to encounter first. By the end of the book you will know how to find fancier software and instructions on installing it if you're interested.

These sessions are not intended to explain the indicated services in detail, but rather to whet your appetite. We provide the detailed information in Part II of the book—think of this as an orientation tour. Enjoy!

```
Mailbox is '/var/mail/mrobbins' with 6 messages [ELM 2.4 PL23]
N 1   Oct 21   ENAM@utx.dp.edu        (17)   Re: traveling Algeria
N 2   Oct 20   lehman@aol.com         (32)   van Gogh research
N 3   Oct 20   tsmith@vh.com          (31)   Hallo, it's been ages
  4   Oct 20   Jherm                  (23)   Re:screen blanking and downloads
  5   Oct 19   jmack@casbah.imm.edu      (11)     Re: List of newsgroups

You can use any of the following commands by pressing the first
character;  d)elete or u)ndelete mail,  m)ail a message,  r)eply or
f)orward mail,  q)uit
To read a message, press <return>. j = move down, k = move up,
? = help

Command:
```

Figure 6.1 *Three new e-mail messages, and two old ones*

MAIL CALL

One of the first things most people do when they get home is check the day's mail to see if anything interesting arrived. This is often the first thing Internet users do when they log in to their accounts, too. Many systems have an announcement feature that informs you as soon as you log in if you have any unread e-mail, so you don't have to bother to look otherwise. In our example, we have three new messages—the mailbox list is shown in Figure 6.1.

Good news. We have a response to a question we asked on the rec.travel newsgroup about traveling in Algeria, a response to an ongoing discussion about the works of van Gogh, and a note from an old friend. We also have two messages from previous sessions that we have saved, one an answer to a computer question, the other information on where to find a list of all the Usenet newsgroups. Let's look the first one, shown in Figure 6.2.

Okay, this gives us all the information we hoped to find. First, let's answer the request for the name of the book, since we know we can find that easily.

LIBRARY RESEARCH IN THE PRIVACY OF YOUR OWN HOME

We just happen to know that our local university has its library catalog accessible via the Internet—all we have to do is telnet to their catalog

```
Message 1/5  From ENAM@utx.dp.edu           Oct 21, 94 02:31:39 pm
cst

Date: Fri, 21 Oct 94 14:31:39 cst
Subject: Re: traveling in Algeria

> I read your posting in rec.travel saying that you just got back from
> Algeria. I will be going there next month and was wondering if you
> had any experience getting to the ruins at Tipasa. Is it possible to
> get there by bus? Thanks very much.

Yes, you can certainly go by bus. Take the one to Oran, it leaves from
the main station in Algiers. And while you're there, go to El Bahdja,
they
make the best shakshuka you'll find anywhere. Have a great trip!

Message 2/5  From lehman@aol.com            Oct 20, 94 11:07:17 am mst

Date: Thu, 20 Oct 94 11:07:17 mst
Subject: van Gogh research

Could you please refresh my memory—what was that book you found by
Gaugin about van Gogh's -Sunflowers-? I've lost the reference somewhere.
Thx.

     5   Oct 19 jmack@casbah.imm.edu (11)   Re: List of newsgroups

Message 5/5  From jmack@casbah.imm.edu       Oct 19, 94 05:14:56 pm est

Date: Wed, 19 Oct 94 17:14;56 est
Subject: Re: list of newsgroups

The full list of newsgroups is stored at ftp.uu.net. You can get it
```

Figure 6.2 *Reading the e-mail messages*

server and start our search. Figure 6.3 shows our progress. From here, the system takes us by the hand, prompting us for the author, search topic, or other information on which we could base our search. Every such system has a different set of screens and commands, so they usually offer instructions as well.

After a few minutes of looking around, we find the title we need, log off, and return to our list of tasks (making a mental note to send e-mail with the title to our friend who requested it).

GETTING FILES

Next on our list of things to do is to go get the list of all available newsgroups, because we want to brush up on current events and issues in

```
% telnet utcat.utexas.edu
Trying 128.83.186.104...
Connected to utcat.utexas.edu.
Escape character is '^]'.

ENTER TERMINAL TYPE: vt100
 utcat
                    The University of Texas at Austin
                          General Libraries
                       Online Information System

                                                 NEED HELP...
        To begin using the          ***      ..using the system through the
        system, type UTCAT           * *     Computation Center network?
        then press ENTER.           ** **    Call 471-3241.
                                     *   *
                                     *   *    ...using the system through the
        To log off, type STOP        *   *    Administrative Data Processing
        then press ENTER.            *   *    network?  Call 471-8800.
                                     *   *
                                     *   *    ..formulating a search or
                                     *   *    interpreting results?  Call the
                                     *****    library at 471-3813.
    If you logon to this computer system, you agree to comply with applica-
ble laws and policies governing computer security at The University of
Texas at Austin.

    WELCOME TO THE "UTCAT PLUS" CAMPUS INFORMATION SYSTEM
========================================================================
      Article texts now in Academic Periodical Index, extended PCL hours,
      Electronic Info classes, ClariNET news texts, UTCAT V2 ... select #5
=======================================================================++=======
        1  UTCAT (library catalog, reserve lists, U-Renew)
        2  Encyclopedia
        3  Indexes to periodical articles
        4  Library hours
        5  News
        6  Material Safety Data Sheets
        7  UT Austin information (directory, jobs, policies, equipment)
        8  Log Off now

     Type the number of your choice, then press ENTER.

  -> 1
```

Figure 6.3 *Logging in to the local card catalog*

Algeria before we go there. We know that there is a culture newsgroup devoted to issues relating to the area, but we don't know what the name is.

There are two things we could do here. We could post a message to a Usenet group (news.newusers.questions is a popular choice) asking if anyone can give us the name of the newsgroup that relates to Algeria. But why bother thousands of people when we can find the answer just as easily ourselves? Now that our friend at casbah.imm.edu has told us where to find the list of newsgroups, we can go get it and search within it for the newsgroup we need. Figure 6.4 shows what happens when we do just that.

Great! With a bit of creativity we were able to find the group we needed. As an added bonus, we now have the newsgroup list handy, so we can search it again the next time a similar question comes up. Now let's go see what the newsgroup has to offer.

```
% ftp ftp.uu.net
Connected to ftp.uu.net.

220 ftp.UU.NET FTP server (Version wu-2.4(1) Thu Apr 14 15:45:10 EDT
1994) read.
Name (ftp.uu.net:mrobbins): anonymous
331 Guest login ok, send your complete e-mail address as password.
Password:
Remote system type is UNIX.
Using binary mode to transfer files.
ftp> cd networking/news/config
250 CWD command successful.
ftp> ls
200 PORT command successful.
150 Opening ASCII mode data connection for /bin/ls.
total 803

-rw-r-r-    1 34        archive     102823 Apr 21 19:03 active.Z
-rw-r-r-    1 34        archive      84248 Apr 21 19:04 active.gz
-rw-r-r-    1 34        archive     179512 Apr 21 19:05 newsgroups.Z
-rw-r-r-    1 34        archive     132523 Apr 21 19:05 newsgroups.gz
-rw-r-r-    1 34        archive     149894 Apr 21 19:03 sys.Z
-rw-r-r-    1 34        archive     111993 Apr 21 19:03 sys.gz
226 Transfer complete.
ftp> get newsgroups.Z
200 PORT command successful.
150 Opening BINARY mode data connection for newsgroups.Z (179512 bytes).
226 Transfer complete.
179512 bytes received in 11 seconds (16 Kbytes/s)
ftp> quit
221 Goodbye.

% uncompress newsgroups.Z
% grep algeria newsgroups
grep: no match.
% grep africa newsgroups
soc.culture.maghreb      North African society and culture.
```

Figure 6.4 *Retrieving a file with FTP, then searching through it*

```
% trn
== 357 unread articles in rec.travel—read now? [+ynq] go
soc.culture.maghreb
== 50 unread articles in soc.culture.maghreb—read now? [+ynq] +
Getting overview file.
a    2   Maghribi people and family ???
b    1   >Moroccan Status
c    1   FIS Parliamentary Delegation Bureau Communique
d    6   >MOROCCAN SOCCER: WEEK 15 TABLE(Belated Release)
e    1   NORTH AFRICA: ALGERIA, LIBYA, BOSNIA TO BE RAISED AT MAGHREB MEET
f    1   JOBS in MOROCCO
g    4   Belly Dancing !!
h    1   Le 20 avril 1980 (Renaissence de la berberite)
i    1   Le printemp Berbere ( ces revendications )
j    1   Arab-American Media Sources (tiny survey)
k    2   MOROCCAN SITE...
l    1   Le temoignage des victimes de la torture
m    1   We are right you are wrong
n    6   AIDS STATISTICS IN Africa
o    1   14 ans de naissence du Mouvement Berbere.

— Select threads (date order)—Bot [z>] —
```

Figure 6.5 *Skimming a newsgroup with TRN*

THE WONDERS OF USENET

Now let's go into our newsreader and look at what this newsgroup contains. See Figure 6.5.

It looks like by reading this group for a while before our trip we can get a good idea about what social and cultural issues are on people's minds in this area. (It also appears that we need to study up on our French.) Not all of the articles are of interest, of course, so most news-readers allow us to pick and choose among the topics we find useful.

We use TRN in this example, but there are other newsreaders. All offer guides to their commands, usually when you type **h**, **help**, or **?**. Check with your provider to find out which newsreaders are available to you.

SUMMARY

This concludes our whirlwind tour of a small part of the Internet. We hope this whetted your appetite to learn more and at the same time gave you a more solid idea about what you can do and what some of these terms mean.

Before you jump in, though, we urge you to remember that exploring the Internet is a bit like traveling to another country (some might say another planet). As every traveler knows, it's important to apprise yourself of the local customs and etiquette before you start your trip, so Chapter 7 gives you a rundown on how to be a responsible Internet trekker.

CIVICS 101
BEING A GOOD NETIZEN

7

ELECTRONIC ENVIRONMENTALISM

The Internet is a huge and growing resource, but it is not unlimited. Your activities can have a significant negative impact on the performance of the network if you are not careful, so in this chapter we give you some guidelines to help you minimize your impact. Think of it as electronic environmentalism: walking lightly on the Net.

In addition, there are some language and practicality issues that apply to all forms of electronic communication, and they can really impair your understanding if you're not aware of them, so the second section of this chapter will clue you in. Enjoy!

MINIMIZING YOUR IMPACT

Just as it's considered bad form to send a 500-page listing to the one laser printer in the office at 10 in the morning, so should you do whatever you can to avoid burdening Internet resources with unnecessary or ill-timed traffic. Of course, if you urgently need to deliver that 30 MB data set that demonstrates the cure for cancer to the lab, by all means do it. But if you're spending the morning retrieving 30 MB of graphics images of the seven wonders of the world so that you can create posters to decorate your office, it might be time to think about the impact of your activities. (You might in that case also want to consider how your employer would view your activities—people get fired over less!)

Of course, these types of things are rarely so clear-cut, so the real point of this section is to help you become aware of what sorts of activities affect the network and what you can do to minimize that effect. With that information and some good judgment, you can merge gracefully into traffic without affecting the flow of information around you.

File Transfers

One of the greatest benefits of the Internet is the wealth of data available. You can help ensure that it remains available by observing some simple guidelines. If possible, make your transfers during low peak times—usually evenings and weekends. This gets more complicated, of course, if you live in the United States and are retrieving a file from a computer in Japan. Low peak times on one end might be the times of heaviest usage on the other end. Again, use your best judgment.

Lest you dismiss this strategy as simply altruistic and therefore not worth the effort, keep in mind that your transfer is likely to complete much more quickly when other traffic on the network is down. If you pay for the connection time, the savings can be significant.

Sometimes you have to download information to your local computer and sift through it before you know whether you can use it, and this is perfectly reasonable. Other times, though, people download an entire directory full of data so that they can decide later whether any of it is interesting or useful to them. This type of use can easily overwhelm a server. In fact, we know of cases where people made large and unique data publicly available, and so many people logged into those servers and downloaded the entire data sets that the servers were overwhelmed with the traffic and were forced to remove the data sets from public access. To prevent this, most file servers on the Internet offer files called README or something similar. Read through these files first—they can save you a lot of time and effort.

Searches and Queries

In Part II we discuss some of the amazingly powerful tools available for data searches, such as Archie, Gopher, and the World Wide Web. All of these programs are powerful tools to help you find information that you know is out there but can't find or that you hope is out there but don't know where to begin looking.

These powerful programs use limited resources, though, so again, if at all possible, consider exploring them during low peak times. In some cases it's even possible to issue search requests via e-mail. When you log in the next day, the results of your search can be waiting for you in your mailbox. See Chapter 16 for more information about e-mail queries.

Working Off-line

Folks whose Internet access comes with their jobs or university affiliations usually don't think twice about performing all of their Internet activities in live sessions. After all, the account is free, and they don't have to pay for connection time. Those of us who have to pay by the hour for our Internet access, however, are always looking for ways to minimize that time on-line. Luckily, we're not the first ones to think of it, and lots of software is available to help us do just that.

These software packages generally work as follows. You log in to your Internet account, download packets containing your e-mail or selected Usenet newsgroup messages, and log off. Now you can read your e-mail with your off-line e-mail reader, responding to some messages, storing others, and deleting the rest. The reader stores your responses and sends them the next time you log in to your Internet account. Similarly, you can use your off-line newsreader to read your favorite newsgroups, creating follow-up postings or e-mail messages if you wish. The next time you log in, it sends your responses out to the network at large. Much of this software is available in the public domain.

We discuss off-line mail readers in more detail in Chapter 9, and off-line newsreaders in Chapter 10, and give you some suggestions on where to get the software.

Malicious Acts

You've probably heard of computer viruses and worms, programs that replicate themselves and damage data or cause infected computers to behave erratically (or stop behaving altogether). Perhaps you've also heard of the Internet worm, a particularly infamous incident in which a student created a program that could replicate itself and spread to other computers. It spread, in fact, to many hundreds of computers, and the perpetrator was eventually jailed.

Now, we know that 99.99% of you have absolutely no inclination to try anything like this, but before you skip to the next section, consider this caution. An employee of a large computer firm made the news a few years ago by starting a similar chain of events, but did so unwittingly. This person created a mail message that sent a holiday greeting to a set of e-mail correspondents. A nice way to wish everyone a happy new year, perhaps, but the message didn't stop there. It then read through the recipient's mailbox and sent the same message to everyone to whom the recipient had sent mail recently. When the message arrived in those mailboxes, it did it again, and so on . . . The creator of the message vastly underestimated the power of networking, apparently. The computer company's continentwide network became so clogged with messages that it was unusable, and the company had to take the network off-line to clean up. (We don't know how they disciplined the employee.)

The moral is to make sure you know what you're doing before you try something new and clever. For information on how to protect your system from such intrusions, see Chapter 28.

Usenet and E-mail Tips

Electronic communication is a new medium with a unique set of risks and peculiarities. Since it's so easy to send, people send lots of it, copy it and send it on to others, and send it quickly without always thinking carefully about their wording. The results of all this fast-moving, quickly created messaging can be other than what you might have intended, so in this section we offer some tips to protect yourself and help you make the most of your e-mail and Usenet messages.

Don't Shout, We Can Hear You

Avoid writing in all capital letters—it's the electronic equivalent of SHOUTING, and is also harder to read than mixed case.

Use That Subject Line

Imagine opening up your e-mail and finding 36 new messages, all with a subject line saying either "Note" or "Question." You have no idea which messages contain announcements of the company softball game and which ones contain the three-step plan to end world hunger.

Help your readers deal efficiently with the flow of information my always including a meaningful subject line in your message, both in e-mail messages and Usenet postings. With some creativity, you can often pack a lot of information into even the smallest subject lines. "Free tickets to Europe!" for instance, has a very different meaning from "Free tickets to Europe?"

Avoid Flaming

In the electronic world, it's sometimes easy to forget that another human being is on the other end of the message. When you write a message in the heat of annoyance or anger it's called a *flame*, and such a message can be a lot more cutting than the same words spoken aloud. Think very carefully before you send a message; once it's sent, it can haunt you forever.

Don't Get Personal!

Because it's so easy to copy and send, e-mail moves fast and goes everywhere. We heard about a meeting where some people harshly criticized an absent colleague. The notes about the meeting went from one party to another, were copied around all over the region, and within a day ended up by accident in the colleague's mailbox.

Believe us, this is not uncommon. Our advice is this: send nothing you wouldn't want your best friend, your boss, or your mother to see. Assume that the message will go instantly to the worst possible recipient and act accordingly. You could save yourself a lot of grief.

Sarcasm and Smileys

Sarcasm and irony don't always translate terribly well into electronic form. In face-to-face interaction you have shrugs, grins, and raised eye-

;-)   :-(

Figure 7.1 *Winking smiley and frowning smiley*

brows to indicate that you're not serious, and even over the phone the inflection of your voice conveys a range of emotions. But on the screen these signals are lost, so smileys were invented to take their place.

Some people hate smileys, insisting that one should be able to convey any emotion with words alone. Dissenters argue that not everyone is a brilliant writer and that misunderstandings are a common feature of human interaction. Just as someone might take offense at a remark that your best friends would recognize as your style of joke, smiley defenders maintain, so can the spirit of sarcasm or teasing get lost in the cold electronic world.

Smileys can transmit a wink, a grin, an expression of dismay, and much more with just a few well-placed punctuation marks. Figure 7.1 shows two examples, one a wink and the other an unhappy face. You don't see them? Turn the page sideways.

Abbreviations

The use of abbreviations is another cultural feature of electronic communication. We're all familiar with abbreviations such as ASAP and FYI—here are some others that you are likely to encounter on the Internet.

ASAP	as soon as possible
BTW	by the way
DWIM	do what I mean (usually directed at a computer)
FWIW	for what it's worth
FYI	for your information
IM(H)O	in my (humble) opinion
OTOH	on the other hand
ROTFL	rolling on the floor laughing (sometimes spelled ROFL)

SUMMARY

As in any community, certain rules and customs evolve to enable everyone to get along and share the local resources without negatively effecting each other. In this chapter we described some of these customs that relate to the Internet and helped you ensure that your entry into that community is as smooth and graceful as possible.

WHERE IS THE INTERNET GOING?

8

While prognostication is always fraught with peril—at best, of being inaccurate; at worst, of being proven out of touch with reality—we nonetheless like to run these risks and take a stab at pointing toward some future trends and directions for the Internet. Rather than wild guesses, ours are of the more educated variety, based on ongoing research and development work with the protocols, technologies, and services that help to make the Internet the fabulous communication tool and information resource that it is today.

In this chapter we examine several trends that could greatly extend the capabilities of the Internet of today. As we look at some of the more interesting possibilities, we try to indicate where they could lead, and what the current barriers to deployment might be. Ideally, this will give you a sense of where the Internet is going or, at least, where it might go as we rush headlong into the twenty-first century.

MORE BANDWIDTH

One of the lessons that emerges from our history of the Internet is that no amount of bandwidth is ever too much. Its corollary, unfortunately, is that whatever bandwidth is available is probably not enough. But some significant moves are afoot to try to remedy this.

Many of the conventional networking technologies are being augmented by special switching technology. For example, switched Ethernet makes it possible for multiple pairs of communicating machines to grab most of Ethernet's usable bandwidth (about 5.6 MBps), by cleverly isolating pathways in use from one another. Similar work is underway for Token-Ring. The advantages here are that existing equipment and protocols can continue to be used, while nevertheless improving the amount of bandwidth available to individual nodes on a network. This is one of the most appealing methods to improve throughput to the desktop today and is sufficient to support current needs for multimedia, animation, and other demanding applications.

Also, high-speed networking technologies like 100 MBps Ethernet, the Fiber Distributed Data Interface (FDDI), and a variety of 100 MBps technologies (like the Thomas-Conrad networking system, TCNS) are starting to proliferate. Because of expense and the need for special media, these technologies are more likely to be found on network backbones than on users' desktops today. For the time being, this will improve overall throughput only for entire networks, which is not quite as dramatic as pumping up the volume of traffic available for each user.

However, more widespread use of these high-speed technologies, and more and more installations of fiber-optic cable, will introduce further economies of scale and make it possible to bring bigger pipes to the desktop. At that point, effective use of network video conferencing, long-distance hypermedia, and other high-bandwidth applications will become possible. At this point—we guess it will happen somewhere around the turn of the century—widespread usage of such applications will be commonplace on the Internet.

From a wide-area networking perspective, which is perhaps of greatest interest to the Internet community, the coming technologies include things like asynchronous transfer mode (ATM), frame relay, and integrated services digital networks (ISDN). These are basically drop-in replacements for existing packet-switching technologies which are fully digital and will broaden the pipes for the Internet backbone and, ultimately, for individual users as well. These technologies are starting to be widely deployed today and should result in bandwidth improvements for the "average Internet user" in the next two to four years.

The cutting edge in the search for more bandwidth is focused on so-called gigabit technologies, which promise to expand current top-of-the-line capabilities by at least an order of magnitude. Today, these technologies more or less require fiber optic media and are prohibitively expensive, but technological advances and more ubiquitous fiber and other high-bandwidth services promise to deliver usable goods in this realm by the first decade of the next century.

At that point, networks will be able to deliver full-motion, full-screen, high-resolution video (better than broadcast quality), and they will also be able to provide interfaces to so-called virtual realities, where the user interacts with an artificial world of information and input. We can expect to see experimental or small-scale applications that use these capabilities in the next five years somewhere on the Internet, but widespread availability is at least ten years away. When such applications arrive, they will enable an explosion of access and services that should dwarf the already staggering capabilities and resources provided by today's Internet. We will all indeed be living in interesting times by that point!

More Services and Service Providers

The advent of the Commercial Internet Exchange (CIX) in the early 1990s presaged a rush of straightforward business activity and participation outside the traditional Internet community. For the past four years, much of the bulk of the Internet's explosive growth has been fueled by the business community, creating a whole new business sector for companies that need access.

This burgeoning opportunity has created a new line of business for many traditional communications and information providers and has spawned many completely new businesses as well. The Internet domain designation ".net" covers an organization in the business of supplying network (mostly Internet) access to others, and the proliferation of .net addresses on the Internet attests to the serious frenzy of newfound participation that is now underway. We expect to see a continued flurry of entries into the service provider marketplace, followed by a shakeout as commodity access and pricing drives out weaker players (see Chapters 28 and 29 for some case studies). Notwithstanding such shakeouts, people looking for Internet connections should continue to have more options than ever before.

During the same time frame, many of the communications giants have begun to ponder further their involvement with the Internet. Companies involved in long-haul communications (AT&T, Sprint, MCI, WilTel, etc.) have begun to take steps to get plugged in. Likewise, the regional bell operating companies (Southwestern Bell, PacTel, Nynex,

BellSouth, etc.) are also looking into more significant interaction with the Internet as well. This could have significant impacts on the way the Internet works, simply because these players have significant amounts of long-haul infrastructure already in place—at the very least, their increased involvement could expand the carrying capacity of the Internet manifold.

Finally, we are starting to see a proliferation of business services and activities on-line on the Internet. In 1994, Robert Zakon singles out the arrival of florists taking orders via the Internet and the startup of on-line shopping malls there as well as indicative of a growing trend to do business via Internet. We agree wholeheartedly and expect to see opportunities to shop for all kinds of services and merchandise on-line, but also to be able to inquire about and pay one's bills, to handle business correspondence via e-mail, and a host of other capabilities as well. By the turn of the century, it may already be more commonplace to do business by e-mail than by telephone!

More (and Better) Access

Today, the voice telephone system provides the basic technology for most Internet links, except for those organizations with enough budget, clout, or connections to obtain data-grade lines or even higher bandwidth communications. But some emerging technologies may change all of that.

Today, cable access television (CATV) providers—probably known to you as the *cable company*—are looking into providing sophisticated network connections over the same cable that brings you 100-plus stations already. For them, bandwidth is significantly less problematic than for the telephone, because they already have plenty of it and because they are already able to support many varieties of multiplexing needed to supply a multichannel signal for the numerous outputs they already supply. In some cities, it's possible to obtain FM hookups for your radio via cable, as well as television signals, and CATV providers are hungry for additional revenue opportunities. This makes the Internet quite appealing to them.

Because a normal television channel provides over 100 MHz of bandwidth, it's already comparable to technologies like ATM, frame relay, and even T-1 telephone lines. Even more important, because cable TV serves over 40% of the households in the United States already, it's a natural conduit for advanced communications services.

Likewise, the development of small, compact short-range dish receivers is emerging as a wireless alternative to cable. This market is newer, less well-established, more expensive than current cable, and hence, even hungrier to participate in new market opportunities. Whereas many households may balk at spending several hundred to a thousand dollars to get more channels for their TV set (and monthly service besides), many businesses would jump at the chance to get a good-sized pipe onto the Internet for the same money.

Finally, wireless technologies of all kinds are starting to make themselves felt in the marketplace. While they too are currently oriented at voice traffic for cellular telephones and equivalent systems, the potential of the data communications market hasn't eluded these players, either. They, too, will try to stake a claim on a possible Internet bonanza by providing at least mobile services, if not also high-bandwidth in-office services.

What does all this mean to you, the consumer? On the one hand, it means an even more dizzying array of technology and equipment to choose from. If you think things are complicated now, it will only get worse! But on the other hand, the more options you have—and the more outfits competing for your communications dollar—the more positive will be the impact on cost, access, and options. This is a typical technology "good news, bad news" scenario: the good news is, you should be able to afford to get a bigger, better pipe to the Internet; the bad news is, you'll have to make some tough choices. Worse still, think of all the salespeople pushing their choices that you'll have to contend with! Nevertheless, we think the net results overall will be to everybody's benefit.

MORE OF EVERYTHING, PLEASE!

The things that will add the most to the Internet are probably those that we know nothing about. Think of the old labor statistic we've all been reeling from in this age of information and technology—"30 years from now, over half of the jobs that people will do for a living don't even exist yet." We believe that the same is true of the Internet: over half the things that people will be using it for by the turn of the century, and beyond, aren't available on-line today, in any way, shape, or form.

Rather than speculating about what might lie ahead, we prefer to think that the Internet will become the focus of more business, government, research, and industry than it ever has before. We firmly assert that all of these organizations will feel compelled to investigate and then to use the Internet as a part of their daily lives. This will create opportunities for the formation of virtual organizations, information utilities, data brokers, and information wizards the like of which we can't even begin to guess at right now.

In essence, this idea is what underlies Al Gore's vision of the Information Infrastructure: Whether national or global, this edifice will enable new economies and developments that otherwise couldn't happen. From our point of view, the only safe guess is that the Internet will be heavily involved and that it could even be the backbone for the whole thing, whatever it may actually be.

SUMMARY

In this chapter we blew the lid off our normally staid outlook on the Internet. We tried to examine some business, technology, and networking trends that might have a profound effect on the Internet's future. By extension, we hypothesized that this could have an even more profound impact on the way in which all of us work and live, as we grope our way into the next century and a new millennium.

INTERNET APPLICATIONS

II

OVERVIEW

In Part I we mapped out the history, background, and underlying technologies that support the Internet. In this second part of the book, we try to turn your connection to the Internet into a valuable pipeline for information right onto your desktop. We start out by looking at electronic mail, and look at how Usenet and mailing lists have turned e-mail into an astonishingly rich form of information exchange. We move from there into using the Internet to talk with friends and colleagues, and explore Internet Relay Chat, an ongoing "conversation area" where the fun and information never stops! Then we take a look at the workhorse Internet applications, File Transfer Protocol (FTP) and Telnet, which bring users and remote sources of information and compute power closer together. Finally, we wrap up with an examination of several second-generation Internet tools, including Gopher, archie and VERONICA, the Wide-Area Information Service, and the World Wide Web.

E-MAIL AND MORE . . .

In the first few chapters of this section, we examine the power of a simple idea: make the Internet support the free exchange of mail messages between individuals, and they'll use the heck out of it!

In Chapter 9 we explore the fundamentals of Internet e-mail, including the software you'll use to read it, the way in which addresses work, and examine a variety of tools to let you interact with mail messages in the privacy of your own desktop machine. We also cover how to send and receive messages, what to do with them when you get them, and how to separate the wheat from the chaff.

In Chapter 10 we look at Usenet, which is one of the most heavily-used media of information exchange in use on the Internet (and anywhere else in the world, for that matter). We guide you through a sampler of potential topics, point out some of the most useful places to get information, and try to arm you to go out and find what really interests you the most. We also try to pass on some useful rules of behavior—or netiquette, as it's called on the Internet—so that you can avoid becoming the unwitting target of someone's ire.

Finally in Chapter 11 we explore the power of mailing lists for information exchange. After comparing them to a newsgroup and exploring their relationship with Usenet, we cover the basics of how to find out about and join mailing lists, as well as some additional related points of netiquette.

THE ART OF CONVERSATION—ON-LINE

Chapter 12 is devoted to the two most popular methods to interactively exchange information with colleagues, coworkers, and random passers-by using the Internet. If you can handle using your keyboard to "talk" to others instead of your mouth (or if you're the beneficiary of the latest and greatest in voice recognition technology) this topic's for you!

MOVING FILES AND REMOTE COMPUTING

Chapters 13 and 14 cover the two real workhorse applications used on the Internet. Chapter 13 covers FTP, which lets you copy files across the Internet. Since this is the major medium of information access, particularly for software and longer documents, it's a critical component of most users' on-line lives on the Internet. We also cover Anonymous FTP as a major source for the oceans of "stuff" that makes the Internet so attractive, but also so overwhelming. Along the way, we cover what happens when files move across dissimilar systems, and try to arm you to deal with archived, compressed, and encoded files of many different types.

Then, in Chapter 14 we introduce you to Telnet, which lets you turn an expensive workstation or PC into a dumb terminal that's the slave of a master computer elsewhere on the network. In reality, this is a tool that will let you access all kinds of information resources, and to take advantage of specialized applications and supercomputer power elsewhere on the Internet, all from your very own desktop.

A NAVIGATOR REALLY HELPS, WHEN CROSSING TRACKLESS WASTELANDS

The final chapters in Part 2 are devoted to the material and content navigation software that's emerged in the last half-dozen years or so, to help people make sense of the staggering amount of information that's available on the Internet. Chapter 15 introduces Gopher, which can "go for" whatever you tell it to across the network (under the hood, it uses FTP and Telnet, but that just means you don't have to).

Chapter 16 moves on to examine some information management tools called Archie and Veronica. Archie is a program that lets you search FTP archives from all around the world to locate particular files that you might want to obtain. Veronica, on the other hand, helps to get you oriented in Gopherspace, by providing a systematic tool for searching Gopher servers all over the place for keywords that might occur in menus or document names. Basically, what both of these programs represent are powerful shortcuts for searching through huge volumes of information to help you locate items that you need.

In Chapters 17 and 18 we look at tools that can help Internauts (the folks who travel on the Internet) examine the content of what's out there, both for their perusal and also for their edification. In Chapter 17 you'll learn about a database search tool that can look inside documents and materials on the Internet, and make use of powerful search tools, to help you locate things that might interest you when you know the topic you're after, but not necessarily what materials exist that relate to it. Chapter 18 examines the World Wide Web. WWW is a collection of hyperlinked information about companies, products, technologies, and just about any other topic that you might come up with, that provides highly formatted and readable information on its many subject matters. Thus, it too offers content as well as navigational power.

THE GOALS OF THE EXERCISE

Throughout these chapters our goals are as follows:

- to help you understand how to find and use the tools that are covered
- to expose you to further resources and information on the tools, should you wish to learn more
- to teach you the fundamentals of how to use these tools, and to provide information to help you teach yourself as much detail as you need

We strongly recommend that you make exploration of these tools, and the information they can lead you to on the Internet, a part of your learning experience. That way, you'll understand the tools in the concrete sense of usage, rather than the abstract sense of concept. In other words: Don't just sit there—go out and try something!

INTERNET E-MAIL

9

WHAT IS E-MAIL?

Since electronic mail, or e-mail, is one of the most ubiquitous computing services, you are probably already familiar with it. Perhaps you use it in your workplace or school, or maybe you have access to a bulletin board service such as CompuServe, Prodigy, or America Online, all of which offer e-mail among their other services. E-mail is software that allows you to send messages—a few lines of text or large data files—between networked computers. If you have a LAN in your office, the local e-mail system works between users on that LAN, and if you are attached to a larger network, like the Internet, e-mail works between all the computers attached to that network.

In your Internet tour in Chapter 6 we showed a sample e-mail session, where we read some incoming e-mail messages. This demonstration hinted at some of the uses of e-mail but really only scratched the surface. In this chapter you'll get a better idea what e-mail can do, along with some tips on using it effectively and solving problems that might come up.

Advantages of Communicating via E-mail

In case you're not already sold on e-mail, we'd like to point out some of its main advantages. This should help give you a clearer idea about the uses for which e-mail is best suited, because like any tool, e-mail is better for some things than others.

Speed

E-mail is fast, much faster than sending a letter through the post office or even express mail. In many cases, e-mail delivery is nearly instantaneous. For the message to maintain this advantage, though, the recipient must read it in a timely manner!

Asynchronous

Telephone communication occurs synchronously, which means that both parties must be available and on the same telephone connection at the same time. E-mail, on the other hand, occurs asynchronously, meaning that you can send a message to someone who is not currently available. To the recipients, this means that they can deal with e-mail matters on their own schedule, rather than being slaves to the interruptions of the telephone. It also means that communication can occur across time zones—nobody has to get up at 3 AM to make a phone call.

Inexpensive

If you are sending e-mail via the company network, e-mail messages are effectively free, since the network and connections are already there and paid for. If you access e-mail via an account on which you must pay for connection time, e-mail is still likely to be less expensive than other means of communication, such as sending a fax or placing a phone call.

HOW INTERNET E-MAIL WORKS

To use Internet e-mail effectively, you need to understand a little bit about how it works, so this section gives you a very general introduction to the necessary concepts.

The Post Office Parallel

The easiest way to think about e-mail is by comparing it to the post office. The message you send out is analogous to a letter, and the envelope corresponds to the e-mail message header. This is where all the information about the sender and receiver goes. Note that when you send a letter you do not need to include any information about how the Post Office should route the letter to its destination; similarly, you do not need to know how your e-mail message gets to the recipient. The computers between you and your recipient should handle all of that.

Consider what happens, too, when you want to send a letter to someone in another country. You must make sure that the address is in the format and language of that country, or your letter may come back to you as undeliverable. In the world of e-mail, this situation is comparable to sending e-mail between different networks. Many networks have different addressing conventions, and in some cases you have to adjust for these conventions when you address the e-mail message. You do this by addressing the message to a *gateway*, which is a computer that translates the incoming address to one that is compatible with the target network. We discuss how to send Internet messages to some of the more popular gateways later in this chapter.

Store and Forward

E-mail is what is known as a *store-and-forward* system, which means that when you send a message, it gets added to a collection of messages that other people have sent. At some point, either a preset time interval or when the storage area starts getting full, the e-mail system sends the group of messages out to their next destination. At that computer the messages get sorted, stored again, then sent on to their next destinations.

The implication to you, the user, is that you can send messages and log out, confident that the system will do its best to send your messages, and you don't have to babysit it. This is distinct from a real-time system, where everything happens as you type it, and you have to be there for anything to happen.

Addresses and Mail Headers

Recall from Chapter 3 the structure of Internet addresses. Each address has a name component, usually to the left of the @ symbol, and a domain name to the right. This is exactly the same address you use to send e-mail to someone. The address goes in the mail header, which, as you recall from our post office analogy, contains all the information about the sender and receiver of the message.

By far the most common reason for mail delivery problems is that something is wrong in the destination e-mail address. If an e-mail message comes back saying that it could not be delivered, double-check that address. If it looks right, you might need to resort to calling the recipient on the telephone (yes!) to confirm the address.

What You Can Do with E-mail

To make this discussion a little more concrete and to bring you up to speed if you are not already familiar with e-mail, let's look at some common and some not-so-common features of e-mail systems.

- View a list of all incoming messages
- Respond to a selected message
- Create and send a new message
- Create mailing lists, so that you can send messages to groups of people
- Create folders in which you can store messages, organized by topic
- Save messages in files or on diskettes
- Delete messages (very important!)
- Attach files to messages, including word processing documents, graphical images, audio files, or video clips
- Dial into your account to download your messages to your portable computer while traveling, respond to them off-line, then dial back in to upload your responses
- Send messages between different e-mail systems

Not all e-mail systems offer all of these features, but the good news is that many mail systems are available in the public domain, so you can try out different systems and features at no cost. See Chapters 13 and 15 for information on finding and retrieving software from the Net.

Selecting an E-mail Package

Clearly, without an e-mail package, e-mail would be pretty unmanageable. The next step is to select an e-mail package that serves your needs and works with your system. Do you need to be able to send and receive full multimedia e-mail messages, with sound, video, and drawings, or is a character-based interface sufficient?

If you work in an office on a LAN with an Internet gateway and that is to be your principal interface with Internet e-mail, the choice has been made for you. But if you are selecting your own software, you have many possibilities. Unfortunately we have too little room to discuss the features and differences of all the e-mail software available, so instead we direct you to the best source of information on these programs, the following set of Usenet newsgroups:

comp.mail.elm	Discussion and fixes for the ELM mail system.
comp.mail.mime	Multipurpose Internet Mail Extensions.
comp.mail.sendmail	Configuring and using the BSD sendmail agent.
comp.mail.misc	General discussions about computer mail.
comp.os.msdos.mail-news	Administration of mail and network news under MS-DOS.

For simple e-mail needs, the most commonly available mail readers on UNIX are called *elm* and *sendmail*. While they don't have a lot of fancy features, both are quite serviceable. More capable and less available is the newer pine, and readers compatible with multipurpose Internet mail extensions (MIME) can handle just about any type of attachment you can think of.

How Not to Drown in E-mail

It might seem improbable if you're just starting out with e-mail and get only a few messages per week, but many people who are heavy e-mail users get upwards of 100 messages per day. If you reach this point—or even better, *before* you reach this point—here are some tips to get your e-mail life under control.

Limit Your List Subscriptions

Depending on the topic and activity, some mailing lists can generate 20 or more messages per day. If you subscribe to only one or two of these, the volume can quickly overwhelm you. Sounds great, you say? For information on subscribing (and unsubscribing) to mailing lists, see Chapter 11.

Note that many mailing lists are also available for reading as Usenet newsgroups. If you have Usenet access, consider this alternative to trim the flow of incoming e-mail messages.

Filters and Smart Readers

Some e-mail readers let you set filter parameters, which effectively makes the software act as a secretary, automatically handling certain types of routine messages. It is possible, for example, to instruct your e-mail system to automatically reply to all messages with a preset message—something like an answering machine. This is useful if you are going to be away for an extended time.

Filter features are fairly new, and not yet widespread. As the software continues to improve (and the volume of e-mail continues to grow) look for more improvements along these lines.

Stay on Top of It

Your best defense against getting overwhelmed by a flood of e-mail is to check it often and keep your messages well-organized. Maintenance is the key virtue when dealing with e-mail. If possible, establish a filing system early in your e-mail use and stick to it. The system might be based on the projects about which you correspond with people, your various hobbies and interests, or simply be chronological. Whatever system you choose, adhere to it faithfully and you'll be rewarded with a happy system administrator and lots of easily accessible information.

EXCHANGING E-MAIL WITH OTHER NETWORKS

Suppose you have your Internet e-mail system functioning nicely but you need to send a message to someone who is not on the Internet. If you have that person's address for his or her particular network, you can often send the mail by addressing it to that network's gateway. In this section we describe how to do this with some common e-mail networks.

Before you send the entire text of your latest novel to your sister's CompuServe account, though, be warned. Many of these systems charge their users extra fees for sending or receiving Internet messages or for storage of large volumes of data. Be sure your message is welcome before you send it.

We list only a small number of the many possible networks, but the general pattern should be clear. If you have the user ID and know the name of the network, try some combination of the network name followed by .com or .org.

We assume in these examples that you know something about the person's user ID. If you don't, or want to find addresses on other networks, see Chapter 23.

Service	User ID	Internet Address
CompuServe	12345,4321	12345.4321@compuserve.com *Note:* The comma in the userid is a dot in the Internet address
America Online	janesmith	janesmith@aol.com
Delphi	johndoe	johndoe@delphi.com
MCI Mail	1234-567	1234567@mcimail.com

E-MAIL'S DOWNSIDE

There are a few disadvantages to using e-mail, most of them very easy to handle. The problems range from overefficient autoreply software to hostile network users, but a little bit of awareness and caution can keep any of them from affecting you.

Mail Storms

Earlier in this chapter we described a feature of some e-mail systems whereby you can automatically reply to certain types of messages. Some mailers let you do this in response to all messages, so if you're on vacation, for instance, your system sends mail to all senders until you get back. The problem arises when one of those senders has her e-mail system on autoreply as well. Your mailer gets the response, and politely issues another note explaining that you're out of town. Her mailer does the same, and before too long, the disks on both systems are full of automatic replies.

Unfortunately, the only reliable solution to this one at present is to have a limit on how much disk space your mail is allowed to use. If that space gets full, the system notifies your system administrator. Smarter e-mail software is very likely on the way to solve this. Meantime, consider whether you really need to inform everyone that you're gone.

Harassing E-mail

Every now and then you might run into a particularly vindictive (and bored) individual who has nothing better to do than to send you insulting, rude, or vicious e-mail. You can often run into these characters on political newsgroups, although they roam everywhere. If you become the target of one of these creatures, you have three courses of action.

1. Join in. Not recommended. This person is probably much more experienced at this than you and probably also has more time to devote to the battle. But if escalating makes you feel better, we can't stop you.
2. Ignore it. A good first step. Eventually this person will go in search of someone who responds; your silence gets boring fairly quickly.
3. Report the harassment to the individual's system administrator. In some cases, this has resulted in the person losing Internet access. If the individual's e-mail address is cretin@myorg.com, try sending a note about the behavior to postmaster@myorg.com, or perhaps hosts@myorg.com. Two caveats here—the person might have created an alias for his e-mail address so that attempts to track him down would be futile, or the person might operate his own Internet system, in which case you'd be complaining to a wall. In either case, you're back to option 2.

Mail Bombing

Someone who flagrantly violates the customs of the Usenet community might find herself getting mail bombed. This is when irate users in turn violate all of the principles we established in this book for considerate usage and send hundreds or thousands of e-mail messages to the perpetrator. These messages can flood the recipient's system disk and even cause her computer to crash.

This situation is a bit similar to committing a heinous crime in a country that punishes offenders by stoning them to death. The best defense, in both cases, is to observe the local customs.

Forged Messages

E-mail messages are just collections of characters. No one can do a handwriting analysis to verify their authenticity, and they are rather easy to forge if you have some time on your hands and know what you are doing. In some cases, though, it is possible to trace a message back to its sender, as was swiftly demonstrated in the case of a cocky university student who sent a forged death threat to the president in early 1994. Your defense here is simply to remember that if you get a message that looks odd (from the head of your university, for instance, congratulating you on your honorary Ph.D.), take it with a grain of salt.

Summary

This chapter gave you a whirlwind tour of some of the capabilities, interfaces, and caveats of Internet mail. It is by no means an exhaustive discussion of this vast topic. The best way to learn about e-mail, like so many things on the Internet, is just to jump in and start experimenting with it.

USING USENET

10

THE CENTRAL NERVOUS SYSTEM OF INTERNET LIFE

It is difficult to talk about the Internet without at least a mention of Usenet. While (as many people will hasten to point out) Usenet is not strictly part of the Internet and the Internet is certainly not Usenet, for many people access to Usenet is the main reason to get on the Internet. You might call Usenet the giant convention center and neighborhood bar of the Internet. It's a gathering place for discussions of everything from physics to stamp collecting to politics. Through Usenet you can make friends, discuss topics that interest you, and find out answers to almost every imaginable question.

If you've ever used a forum on CompuServe or some other bulletin board or information service, you have an idea what Usenet is like. The whole thing is organized by topic, with varying degrees of rigidity. In some cases you can turn to Usenet with a question in mind and go straight to the answer, while other queries might take weeks to answer. Persistence, coupled with a knowledge of how Usenet works are the keys to success.

Since Usenet is so vast, we can't begin to give you a comprehensive picture of it—such a description could be a book in itself. Instead, this chapter gives you the tools and information you need to find things on your own. In particular, we devote a section to Usenet etiquette. Usenet is really a community of hundreds of thousands of people and has its own set of guidelines and customs, so you need to understand the guidelines to make use of it and to keep it useful for everyone else.

Usenet Basics

In our short Internet tour in Chapter 6, we browsed through a single newsgroup having to do with cultural issues relating to Northern Africa. We didn't look at any of the messages in the group, though, so let's do that now, to give you a point of reference as we discuss the organization and terminology of Usenet.

Suppose we want to find out when we can buy the next release of our word processor for our Macintosh computer. Figure 10.1 shows a sampling of the newsgroups devoted to various computer systems, and we see that Macintoshes are well-represented. (We describe how to get such a list in Chapters 6 and 26.) It looks like the group called comp.sys.mac.apps is the one most likely to have what we're looking for. Let's take a look. We do this with a piece of software called a *newsreader*, which presents the tremendous volume of Usenet news to you in a logical format.

Figure 10.2 shows a list of the topics that people are currently discussing in the comp.sys.mac.apps newsgroup. These topics are called *threads*, and everyone who has something to say about that particular topic adds it to that thread. In turn, most newsreaders present the

```
comp.sys.amiga.hardware    Amiga computer hardware, Q&A, reviews, etc.
comp.sys.apple2.usergroupsAll about Apple II user groups.
comp.sys.atari.st.tech     Technical discussions of Atari ST hard/software.
comp.sys.ibm.pc.hardware.chips  Processor, cache, memory chips, etc.
comp.sys.ibm.pc.hardware.comm   Modems & communication cards for the PC.
comp.sys.mac.announce      Important notices for Macintosh users.
                           (Moderated)
comp.sys.mac.apps          Discussions of Macintosh applications.
comp.sys.mac.comm          Discussion of Macintosh communications.
comp.sys.mac.databases     Database systems for the Apple Macintosh.
comp.sys.mac.hardware      Macintosh hardware issues & discussions.
comp.sys.mac.misc          General discussions about the Apple Macintosh.
comp.sys.newton.announce   Newton information posts. (Moderated)
```

Figure 10.1 *Newsgroups that cover Macintosh-related topics*

```
comp.sys.mac.apps          537 articles

a 1  >Teach-yourself C/C++
b 2  >Norton and Mac Tools
d 3  [Q] Anyone know when the next version of MS W...be out?
f 1  24 bit X server software ?
g 1  At Easy 2.0
i 1  >Mac password protection program needed!!!
j 1  SUN TIFF file into MacWord doc?
l 1  Word Menu Bar Problem
o 1  System 6 or system 7?
r 2  >Quicken checks

— Select threads (date order)—Top 3% [>Z] —
```

Figure 10.2 *Current topics in the comp.sys.mac.apps newsgroup*

threads to the user in order by topic, so that you can read all the responses to a particular topic, then go on to another thread.

It appears that we're getting closer to what we seek. Let's take a closer look at the "Anyone know . . .?" thread. Our newsreader lets us look at these three postings one at a time, giving us a display that looks something like Figure 10.3.

As you can see in Figure 10.3, the people in this thread are answering exactly the question we came to ask! Of course, this is a very contrived example. But it does give you an idea how Usenet works and introduces you to the key terms. Now let's back up and see how all this started, then explore the organization and workings of the Usenet system.

A Brief History of the Usenet

Usenet started out as a small information exchange system between two universities in the late 1970s. The users at those institutions wanted to exchange notes and observations in a fairly loose format and to organize the information by topic. Further, they wanted the information to be available to a group of people, rather than single recipients as in e-mail. Hence Usenet was born. Within a couple of years it spread to many more universities, then worked its way into corporations and other institutions. During the early 1980s the software underwent a major revision to enable it to handle larger volumes of messages. This

```
comp.sys.mac.apps #12522 (11 + 525 more)                        [1]—[1]
From: "Travis M. Preston" <tmpreston@cs.illinois.edu>
[1] [Q] Anyone know when the next version of MS Word will be out?
Organization: Illinois University
Date: Wed Apr 20 11:29:55 CDT 1994
Lines: 4

I'm thinking of buying MS Word for my Mac at home, but I've heard
that the next version is due out soon. Does anyone know when? I
don't want to invest a bunch of money in something that's about
to become obsolete. :-)

End of article 12522 (of 12641)—what next? [npq]

comp.sys.mac.apps #12534 (10 + 525 more)                        (1)—[1]
Distribution: world
From: "Susan Phillips" sphillips@aol.com
Date: Mon Apr 25 18:43:31 CDT 1994
[1] Re: [Q] Anyone know when the next version of MS Word will be out?
Lines: 5

If I were you I'd just buy it now. I was talking to the MS folks the
other day and they said there would be a free upgrade policy for people
who bought the current version within six weeks of the new release. But
you might want to check and make sure the release is on time! Last I
heard it was due the middle of next month.

End of article 12534 (of 12641)—what next? [npq]
```

Figure 10.3 *Sample postings in a thread*

work resulted in the Usenet of today, which extends to sites all over the world, covers thousands of topics, and has millions of readers.

How Do You Find Anything? The Organization of Usenet

We keep talking about how enormous Usenet is—you must be wondering how anyone ever finds anything. You saw one way in Chapter 6, where we downloaded the list of all active newsgroups and searched through that file for keywords relating to the topic we wanted. You'll be glad to hear, though, that there is some organization among the newsgroups.

The structure of the Usenet newsgroups is hierarchical, similar to a family tree or an organizational chart—or the directory arrangement of many operating systems. (For this reason you often hear people refer to groups of newsgroups as hierarchies.) At the top level are some very general topics, and under each of these the subdivide toward more and

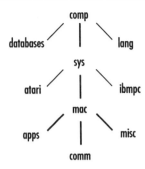

Figure 10.4 *The comp.sys.mac portion of the comp hierarchy*

more specific topics. Figure 10.4 illustrates the hierarchical structure of some newsgroups we already looked at, the comp.sys.mac groups.

Originally the Usenet groups were divided into seven subgroups, which are still called the *Big Seven*. New hierarchies have come into being since then and because every site receives different subsets of the entire Usenet cornucopia, it is impossible to predict which of these you can access. (Many sites get all the groups, which means they have to deal with around 50 MB of data per day!) We describe below some of the hierarchies you are most likely to find, with the Big Seven listed first.

comp   topics related to computers and computer science. From languages to hardware to games.

sci   scientific topics, both research and applications. Physics, biology, psychology, and more.

rec   recreational topics. Everything from sports to music to video making to cooking.

news   not, as you might assume, current events. Rather, this is the hierarchy where Usenet talks about itself. Very important, especially for new users.

talk   loosely formatted discussions on unresolvable questions. Politics and religion are hotly debated in these groups.

soc   discussions about the social issues relating to countries or regions.

misc   things that don't really belong in one of the preceding categories, including jobs postings, for-sale postings, and other miscellany.

alt   a sometimes bizarre mix of topics, from alt.chinese.computing to alt.tv.simpsons. The main distinguishing feature of the alt hierarchy is that it's easier to create a new group than in the other hierarchies, and it shows. Still, some alt groups are quite useful.

k12   groups relating to education from kindergarten through twelfth grade, for both teachers and students.

fj   discussions of hundreds of different topics, in Japanese.

de   a hierarchy rivaling the scope and size of alt, but all in German.

Under each hierarchy heading, the name of the group should become more specific as you read it left to right. So to find a group devoted to the discussion of college basketball, you'd first check the rec hierarchy, then the subtopic sport, then perhaps the subtopic basketball. Sure enough, there you find rec.sport.basketball.college, right between rec.sport.baseball and rec.sport.basketball.misc.

The list describes only a few of the hierarchies—many universities and regions have hierarchies for topics only of local interest. The chi set of groups, for instance, covers announcements and discussion about the Chicago area. Your system administrator can tell you which hierarchies and groups are available at your site.

How It Works

Knowing how the groups are organized, though, is not going to help you deal with the huge amount of information that Usenet offers you. This is where your newsreader software comes in. With a newsreader, you can search for groups and keywords within groups and can respond to articles with articles of your own. If you think your comment is not of general interest, you can send e-mail to the author of the article instead of posting it to the whole world—most newsreaders let you do that too. Best of all, your newsreader keeps track of which articles you have already seen, so that the next time you come in to read news, it shows you only the articles that are new since the last time you read news.

Where Did That Article Go?

A common complaint from new users about their news reading software is "Every time I go back into news, all the articles I was looking at are gone! How do I keep it from deleting articles after I read them?" There are two answers to this question, and which one is correct depends on how your site is configured and how long it has been since you last read news.

In the first case, the articles aren't gone at all. The newsreader has simply marked them as "already read" so that you won't be bothered with them the next time you read news. Most newsreaders have a command, though, that allows you to toggle whether you view read or unread articles—consult the manual on your particular newsreader for information on how to do this.

In the second case, the articles really are gone. Recall that Usenet traffic amounts to something like 50 MB each day, and you can understand that no system in the world can keep it all around indefinitely. Therefore after an article has been around for some length of time, your system removes it from its disk to free up that space for other articles. Just how long this time is depends on a number of factors, most of them having to do with your system's policies and disk space. If you find you often miss articles in certain groups, ask your system administrator to increase the expiration time on that group—he or she might be willing to do this in some cases.

READING NEWS AND POSTING YOUR OWN ARTICLES

Now that you have a good idea what Usenet is, how it is organized, and what you can do with it, you're ready to jump in, start reading news, and posting your own articles. The first thing you need, then, is some software.

Newsreading Software

The best newsreader for you depends on several factors, the most important being what system you are using to read news, since not all newsreaders work with all types of computers. Another consideration is whether you want your display to appear in graphical or text format, but if you have a simple terminal emulation dial-up connection, you have to use the latter. This section describes some of the various news-readers available. Happily, much of this software is available free on the Internet!

UNIX Text-Based Readers

If your access to the Internet is a simple dial-up connection to a computer that runs UNIX, you can probably use rn, trn, nn, or tin as your newsreader. You should be able to invoke them by simply typing their names at the shell prompt (or perhaps by selecting them off a menu, depending on your system). If none of these appears to be available, check with your system administrator.

UNIX Graphics-Based Readers

Perhaps you have a Silicon Graphics workstation on your desk with a direct connection to the Internet. In this case some very powerful and fun software is yours to play with. Again, your system administrator is the best person to advise you on what's available for your particular configuration.

Reading News on a DOS Computer or a Macintosh

If you have a SLIP or PPP connection to the Internet and have a DOS-based computer, your newsreader choices are more limited. Check in the newsgroup news.software.readers for suggestions on software and where to get it.

Off-line Readers

For true electronic environmentalists and those folks who have to pay for their connection time, it is possible to dial in to your Internet provider, download the data that contains the latest Usenet news, and disconnect. Free of the worry of connection charges, you can browse through your chosen newsgroups at leisure, composing responses and digesting the collective wisdom, then reconnect to upload your replies. (Of course by then more articles will have arrived, which you must then download and answer—people have been known to go on like this for days.)

Many people use qwk as their off-line news reading software, but unfortunately it does some unfriendly things with the article headers. Therefore, if you possibly can, use *soup* (simple off-line Usenet packet) as your off-line reader. Reading software is readily available for DOS, Windows, and UNIX environments; you might have to dig a bit more to outfit your Macintosh.

You can find out where to get this software, and answers to all of your questions, in the newsgroup alt.usenet.off-line-reader, and the FAQ for this newsgroup gets posted periodically in news.newusers.questions as well.

Selecting Which Groups to Read

One way or another, you have found a newsreader, fired it up, and . . . wow. You appear to be subscribed to 2000 newsgroups!

Most newsreaders maintain a list of newsgroups for you, and you can add or delete groups from the list using the commands for your newsreader. This process is called subscribing and unsubscribing. When you subscribe to a newsgroup, it thereafter displays for you all the postings in that group. If you don't want to see any more postings on that topic, you can unsubscribe—the newsreader software keeps track of all this for you. Now, the first time you start the newsreader it doesn't know what groups to show you, so it will often just show you all of them! The best way to deal with this is to unsubscribe to all of them (most readers have a command to do this), then resubscribe only to those in which you are interested. Every reader is different, so check the manual on yours to determine which commands to use.

Don't Miss These
Here are a few of the most useful groups, especially for new users. Just by reading these groups for a while, you'll find out about lots of other groups that may be of interest.

    news.newusers.announce

    news.newusers.questions

    news.answers

    alt.answers

    alt.internet.services

Besides these, many of the hierarchies have their own "answers" news-groups. If you are interested in general topics relating to computers, for instance, you might want to subscribe to the comp.answers newsgroup.

USENET ETIQUETTE

Thousands of people use the Usenet to keep up with developments in their fields and gather information. Like you, these people are busy and don't want to be bothered with trivial or oft-answered questions, so they have developed some rules and customs to make the time on-line as productive as possible for everyone.

Selecting Your Audience

If you needed a picture of the molecular structure of benzene, you probably would not go to a meeting of coin collectors to ask for it. They might at best ignore you, or at worst respond with a fair amount of annoyance to your inappropriate query.

So it goes on Usenet. With over 5000 different discussion groups, every group has a rather narrow focus of topics, and the people who read that group do not want to spend their time—or money, if they have to pay for their connect time—on discussions that are not relevant to the topic at hand. (If they did, they'd be reading that newsgroup instead.) So before you post a question or a comment, be very sure that it is relevant to the readers of the group.

In most cases, since newsgroup topics are so finely divided, your comment is likely to be of interest to the readers of only one news-group. In rare circumstances, though, there may be more than one group to which your words are relevant. In these cases, the proper course of action is not to post to the two groups separately, but to cross-post, which means the same message goes to both groups. This way, people who read both groups only have to see your message once.

To crosspost, edit the Newsgroups: line in the article's header to contain the names of all the groups you wish to include, separated by commas (but no spaces!).

Read Before Posting!

Once you find a group that looks like it covers your topic of interest, it is a good idea to subscribe to it and read it for a while, at least a few days. That way you make sure that your question is relevant to the topic of the group, and the answer might even appear during that time. Also, if the group has a list of frequently asked questions (FAQ), read through them for your answer before posting your question. These collections of the wisdom of the group free up the discussion space and save everyone's time (including yours). See Chapter 26 for more information on FAQs.

Test Messages

Before you launch your first real posting to a particular group, you probably will want to make sure you know what you're doing by issuing a test post. The most logical thing to do is to create a message with the subject "Test" and perhaps a message body saying something like "Does this work?" or "Please ignore." Post that to a group that discusses English grammar, though, and you'll annoy a lot of people. They have to pay to read your test, after all, and although by itself it might not amount to much, several of them can take up a significant amount of resources.

Never fear, there is a solution. The groups alt.test and misc.test were created explicitly for that purpose. There you can post as many tests as you like, refining your technique until you are confident enough to go public.

Advertising

As we discussed in Chapter 5, advertising is perfectly legal on the Internet, as long as your access is via a provider that does not run over NSFNET or other networks subject to the Acceptable Use Policy. If in doubt about this, check with your provider.

The other issue to consider regarding test postings is one of audience. As we discussed earlier, one of your responsibilities as a Usenet user is to limit your audience to the people who are likely to be interested in your message. If you have something to sell or a service to advertise, the appropriate groups are in the biz.* hierarchy and the *.forsale groups. There is no surer way to evoke fury and hate mail than to post an advertisement to an inappropriate newsgroup. See Chapter 21 for some examples.

Some General Posting Tips

When you post a response to an article, you usually have the option to either copy the original article in your response or not. If you choose to do so, it is good practice to trim everything but the minimum amount of information needed for context instead of including the entire previous posting. Most people following the discussion already read the previous posting, so they need not read it again.

Additionally, in the continuing spirit of electronic environmentalism, make sure your response offers something to the discussion. A particularly effective way to generate some testy responses is to quote an entire article and add a line at the end that says "I agree!"

You frequently see posts that say something like "Does anyone know where I can find an electronic version of War and Peace? Please respond via e-mail, since I don't usually read this group." While some groups encourage answers to questions to happen via e-mail, most Usenet users consider this rude. Compare it to running into a crowded room, shouting, "If anyone knows what the capital of France is, could you please call me at home and tell me?" and running out again. No one else in the room gets the benefit of hearing the answer.

The usual position on this matter is that if you are going to use the resources of the group to get the answer to a question, you should be reading the group enough to find the answer. The exceptions are those groups whose policy is to reply to questions via e-mail (check the FAQ for the customs in each group) and for people who have only e-mail access and therefore can't read Usenet newsgroups. Every group is different, so again, know your audience.

Some Legal Issues

After posting advertisements in inappropriate places, the second best way to generate lots of hate mail, and perhaps lose your Internet access, is to post a chain letter. Please, resist the temptation. Chain letters and other pyramid schemes not only don't work, they're also illegal in the United States (and many other countries as well).

Another legal matter is new to the Internet and much less clear-cut. This is the matter of libel. While flame wars flare up frequently and the participants usually can count on the conflict being taken in good spirit by all involved, this is less and less often the case. There are those who regard a good flame war as a form of recreation, but with an estimated 2 million new users per month, the character of the community is changing. For one thing, more lawyers are now on-line, and we know of several cases where an exchange of insults turned into a lawsuit. We'll look at some of these in Chapter 21. In the meantime, be careful.

SUMMARY

We hope we have whetted your appetite in this chapter by giving you a broad overview of what it is and what it can do. The resources available through Usenet are so varied and fascinating that some people find themselves spending hours a day staring at the screen, devouring information on every topic imaginable. If this sounds like a bit much for you, turn to Chapter 26, where we offer some tips on how to hone your searches or break free of the Usenet spell if you are already ensnared.

MAILING LISTS

DIRECT MAIL OVER THE INTERNET

Certain topics are so specialized that they do not generate enough interest to sustain an entire newsgroup, though there still may be people who are interested in discussing the topic. Other topics are of a sensitive nature, and people want to discuss them outside of the public nature of the Usenet, where there could be thousands of "lurkers" (people who read the group silently without entering into the discussion). Also, some announcements are not really appropriate to post to a newsgroup, and occasional readers of the group might miss an announcement that was posted there.

For these situations were mailing lists created. Once you get your name (or, more accurately, your e-mail address) on a particular mailing list, you receive all the announcements, discussions, and other items that the list's members or moderator think might be of interest to the group. And you get these messages right there in your own e-mail box!

Mailing Lists and You

To get your name on a mailing list, you must *subscribe* to the list, and removing your name from the list is called *unsubscribing*. Both are usually accomplished by sending an e-mail message to someone, as we describe later.

Once you have subscribed to a list, you will get messages relating to the topic of the list via e-mail. Depending on the list, this could amount to a few messages per month or dozens per day. The messages might arrive separately, mixed in with your other e-mail messages, or they might arrive in digest form, so you get a single e-mail message containing all of the latest announcements for the list.

LISTS AND NEWSGROUPS

Some mailing lists have gateways into Usenet. This means that interested people can access the list either by subscribing to it or by reading the messages with their newsreader programs. If you've browsed the list of newsgroups, you've probably seen some groups whose names start with bit.listserv, for instance. This means that these groups are BITNET mailing lists available to Usenet via gateways. In other cases it's not so easy to tell whether a group is also a mailing list. The moderated newsgroup comp.risks, for instance, is actually a mailing list.

If It's a Newsgroup, Why Subscribe?

If you can access the mailing list messages via Usenet, by all means do so. Not only does it help keep your mail flow to a manageable level, it also helps save resources, requiring your local system to store only one copy of the message.

There is one case when you would want to subscribe to the list instead of reading the newsgroup. If you don't plan to read the group very often, but want to miss no messages that might expire before the next time you read it, you should probably subscribe. By subscribing, you assure yourself that you will see every message that comes through the list. This situation is more likely to apply in the cases of announcement-oriented groups than discussion groups.

FINDING THE MAILING LISTS

The number of mailing lists is huge—over 3000 by one estimate. You just can't find out about them all, for a couple of reasons. First, some are private and restrict their readership. Others are small or relate to topics of limited interest—you may hear about these if you start frequenting places where other interested people can clue you in. Finally, there are just too many lists, and no comprehensive index of all of them. You can find out about a lot of them, though, as we describe in this section.

The List of Lists

Your first stop in looking for mailing lists should be what is fondly known as the *List of Lists*. The person who maintains this list of mailing lists posts it to the news.answers newsgroup periodically, so keep an eye on that newsgroup and you'll see the list within a couple of weeks. Or if you're in a hurry, you can get it via ftp at the ftp site where all the FAQs and other news.answers files are archived: rtfm.mit.edu.

> **Note:**
> This list is quite long, so be sure you have room for it before you retrieve it.

The List of Newsgroups

As we already noted, many mailing lists are available via Usenet through gateways. Those that come to Usenet from BITNET, for instance, have newsgroup names that start with bit.listserv. Also, some of the moderated newsgroups are available as mailing lists, though there is no way to be sure of this from their names.

Informal Sources

The least predictable way to find out about a mailing list can also be the most useful. Suppose you read a Usenet article in which the person posting mentions four-leaf clover. Now, it just so happens that four-leaf clover is your particular passion, and you have a huge collection of specimens. You strike up an e-mail conversation with this person, and she tells you about a mailing list for four-leaf clover collectors.

Word of mouth is a great way to get information, so don't be afraid to contact people if you think you might share some interests.

THE MECHANICS OF MAILING LISTS

Once you find the mailing list of your dreams, the next step is to get your e-mail address added to the list so that you can start receiving its messages. How you do this depends on the type of list you're dealing with. The List of Lists has instructions on how to subscribe to most of the lists that it indexes, so check there for information about your particular list. If yours is not among those, here are some suggestions.

BITNET Mailing Lists

The maintenance of BITNET mailing lists is handled by a software program called a *list server* (listserv for short). This means that you have to subscribe to such lists with a precise format, so that the computer knows what you want to do. You subscribe by sending an e-mail message, usually to the machine that maintains the list, using the user name listserv. So if you know that the list is maintained on a machine with the address comp.edu, you would send mail to "listserv@comp.edu". The body of the message should contain a single line instructing the computer to add you to the list, for example:

```
subscribe clover-1 Dorothy Anson
```

It's not always obvious whether your list is a BITNET list. If it appears in the list of newsgroups as a group that starts with bit.listserv, you can be sure it is. Or if the group name ends with a "-l," that often indicates a BITNET mailing list as well. Otherwise, try this method, and if it doesn't work, try one of the methods that follows.

Getting your name off the list, or unsubscribing, works the same way. You send the same e-mail message as the preceding, using the word *unsubscribe* instead of *subscribe*.

Other Types of Lists

Many of the other types of mailing lists are maintained by humans, so they do not require as rigid a format as list servers. However, in the interest of making that person's job easier, it's a good idea to keep your request short and to the point.

Again, you subscribe by sending an e-mail message. If you send the message to the list address, though, your request to be added to the list will appear in the mailbox of everyone who is already subscribed! Therefore, a computer that handles a mailing list has two mailboxes for the list, one for messages intended for the list at large, and the other for administrative requests, such as subscriptions and cancellations. This second mailbox is the one you want, and usually has the name list-name-request.

So to subscribe to our clover list, we would send e-mail to "clover-request@comp.edu". We can use any subject we like; it's generally ignored. The body of the message should be something like "Please add me to the list—Thanks!"

Once You're On the List

Some lists will send you an acknowledgment, indicating that the administrator has added you to the list. If your list is one with rather low traffic, this can be reassuring, since it might be weeks before any messages come through it.

Be sure to save that notice or a copy of your subscription message or both. Someday you will probably want get your name off the list or inform them of your new e-mail address, and at that point you'll be glad to have the information at hand.

MAILING LIST CAUTIONS

Like everything on the Internet, mailing lists have some quirks. Knowing about a couple of common mailing list problems might help you minimize them.

Replying to a Person or the Whole List?

Suppose someone on the list sends a message that describes a problem in a particularly elegant way. You want to compliment the writer on his use of language, so you issue a Reply command and send your message. To your embarrassment, your note goes not only to the original writer but to everyone on the list!

On the other hand, you might want to send a response to the list, continuing the discussion of the current topic at hand. If you use the wrong type of reply, your clever prose might go only to one person on the list instead of the entire list.

These are benign examples of an unfortunately rather common problem. It happens just as easily in e-mail messages that are addressed to a group of people and in Usenet newsgroups. Unfortunately, we can only warn you about it, because—ready?—the reply command is different for different lists, depending on how the list gets distributed.

Your best defense against these types of problems is to carefully check that To: field in the message. Your e-mail program fills this out for you when you reply to messages; you may have to change it by hand to make sure your message goes where you intend.

Overload

Since the volume of messages on some lists can be very high, you can get completely overwhelmed with messages. Imagine logging into your account one day and getting a notice saying "You have mail (348 unread)." It would take you the entire day to read them all! Deleting them all takes some effort, too.

Because of this, most mailing lists limit their traffic, and those with high traffic generally warn you. If you really must subscribe to a high traffic list but lack the time to read everything that comes through it, consider getting yourself acquainted with the filtering and automatic sorting features of your mail reading program.

SUMMARY

Mailing lists are a convenient way of getting certain types of information and participating in discussions, and in this chapter we discussed how to make the most of them. With thousands of mailing lists available on the Net, there is bound to be one that relates to your particular area of interest.

chapter

GOING
INTERACTIVE
TALK AND CHAT

12

THE ART OF ON-LINE CONVERSATION

Today, with a few experimental exceptions, the closest you can get to real conversation on the Internet is through your keyboard. In this chapter we cover two utility programs that let you interactively communicate with other individuals over the network. The first is a program called *talk* that lets you use the Internet to perform the equivalent of a telephone call—that is, to request an interactive link to at least one other party, and then to type messages back and forth. The second is a conferencing program called *Internet relay chat* (IRC) that lets you join into ongoing conversations that can involve anyone anywhere on the Internet or create new conversations that you can control. If *talk* is like a telephone call, then IRC is like using a CB radio, where you pick a channel and participate in whatever conversation is taking place (unlike a real CB, though, the number of channels is unlimited and you can create one if you like).

Before we launch into the details on these two utilities, a few remarks on interactive on-line conversation might be useful. The first thing to remember is that the other parties to a conversation can easily create a permanent record of whatever gets said. While on-line conversations may feel private and intimate, that is not necessarily the case. It is equally advisable to avoid profanity, slander, or other questionable conversational ploys, especially in the more public IRC venues.

The second thing to remember is that because it's slower to type words than to speak them, there's a profound tendency to employ lots of abbreviations and shorthand when using these utilities. For this reason, we include a table of common abbreviations and symbols in Table 12.1. (*Note:* At least two books we know of are devoted entirely to smileys, so our two samples of the genre doesn't come close to capturing the phenomenon).

The final thing to remember is that interactive conversation can be a tremendous boon, but also a tremendous time waster. Make sure you fit this activity into the rest of your life in a balanced way and that you don't presume too much on the other parties to your on-line conversations. That way, you won't regret the time you spent on-line (when you should have been doing something else), and your friends and colleagues will remain willing to converse with you on-line.

Abbr./Symbol	Explanation
ASAP	As soon as possible
BCNU	Be seeing you
BRB	Be right back (to announce a momentary interruption in conversation)
BTW	By the way
BYE	Good-bye (ready to end or leave conversation)
BYE?	Is this good-bye? (are you ready to end or leave conversation)
CU	See you
CUL	See you later
DWIM	Do what I mean (not what I say)
FWIW	For what it's worth
FYI	For your information
<G>	Symbol for a grin (used to indicate joking or humor)
GA	Go ahead, type away (I'll wait till you're done)
IM(H)O	In my (humble) opinion
JAM	Just a minute (to request a momentary halt in conversation)
OBTW	Oh, by the way
OTOH	On the other hand
ROTFL	Rolling on the floor laughing (sometimes spelled ROFL)
RU THERE?	Are you still online?
ALL CAPS	When in used in text, indicates emphasis
:-)	Smiley symbol, happy face
;-)	Winking smiley, indicates humor, tongue in cheek

Table 12.1 *Common Interactive Abbreviations and Symbols*

USING THE TALK COMMAND

The talk command lets you use your computer to request an on-line conversation with one or more other computers and then to type messages back and forth to your heart's content. To have a successful conversation, all parties—of which the most typical number is two—must be connected to the Internet, all parties must currently be on-line, and all parties must be willing to accept a talk connection. And, as you'll learn a little later on, all parties must be using versions of the program that are the same, or at least similar enough to permit them to communicate with each other.

We're not aware of too many PC-based implementations of talk, so you'll probably end up using one of its several versions while conducting a Telnet session. This means that the talk program has to be installed and usable on your Telnet host machine for you to use it; if it isn't, when you try to run the program, you'll get a message saying something like this:

```
talk: command not found
```

back from the Telnet host. If that happens, don't panic—try one or all of the other versions that might be available. If that fails, call your system administrator or drop him or her an e-mail and ask that the program be installed for you.

Most Internet service providers will already have some version of talk loaded, so don't worry about this until you have tried and failed. Here's how to use the talk command:

```
talk <username> [@<domain-name>]
```

For <username> insert the name of the party you want to talk to. If the party is on the same host you're on, you can skip the @<domain-name> part; but if the party is on another Internet host, insert the domain-name for that host after the @ sign. Here are some examples, first of local usage, then of usage to reach a remote host:

```
talk mrobbins
talk brendan@zen.org
```

When you use the talk program, passing messages between the parties involved is handled by an underlying program on each Internet host that is participating in the conversation. This program is called the *talk daemon*, which is a communications program that always runs as a background task on the host, so as to be ready to pass and field talk-related messages and direct them to the proper parties involved.

What You'll See On-Screen

Once you've initiated a talk request, the program sends a message to the designated recipient's computer and sends an audible beep along with it, to get his or her attention:

```
Message from Talk_Daemon@zen.org at 10:17 ...
talk: connection requested by etittel@zilker.net
talk: respond with: talk etittel@zilker.net
```

To accept the talk request, Brendan would have to type in the command as indicated in the last line of this message:

```
talk etittel@zilker.net
```

If Brendan wants to talk, he can follow the directions; if not, all he has to do is ignore it and keep on doing whatever he's doing. If he does ignore it, the talk daemon will keep bugging him by sending him a message at regular intervals—about every ten seconds, on most systems. If this happens, talk will send the following message to your screen:

```
[Ringing your party again]
```

After a couple of tries, it's a good idea to cancel the attempt. To do this, type **Ctrl-C** (hold down the Ctrl key and hit the C key at the same time) and this will terminate the talk program (by the way, this is what you do to end a successful talk session as well).

Once your talk daemon succeeds in connecting with the other party's talk daemon, you'll be informed that it is time to start talking by this message, and an accompanying beep:

```
[Connection established]
```

At this point, the talk program will take over the screen and draw a line of dashes through the middle. Whatever you type will appear in the upper part, and whatever the other party types will appear below. Talk is a public display of your typing skills, in that whatever you type (including mistakes, backspaces, and corrections) will appear on the other party's screen as well as yours. For that reason, we recommend a little practice if your skills are rusty and checking out some of the keyboard shortcuts in Table 12.2. If you must use talk, you should do it well!

Keystrokes	Explanation
Backspace	Back up and erase one (character) space
Ctrl-H	Same as Backspace
Ctrl-W	Back up and erase one word
Ctrl-U	Back up and erase entire line
Ctrl-X	Use instead of Ctrl-U on some systems
Ctrl-L	Redisplays entire talk screen

Table 12.2 *Talk Keyboard Shortcuts*

When Talk Doesn't Work

Inevitably, you'll encounter some difficulties in using talk, very often for circumstances well beyond your control. Making a connection doesn't always occur, so we'd like to warn you about the circumstances that might prevent things from working:

- *The party you wish to reach may not be on-line.* It's hard to talk to somebody who isn't there. If this happens you'll see this message:

```
[Your party is not logged on]
```

You have two options in this case: You can send an e-mail, asking the person to contact you when on-line, or you can wait a while and try again later (just like trying to reach someone by phone).

Before you give up, though, make sure you typed the name of the party correctly; if you mistype the name, the computer will probably tell you that party's not logged on because the name doesn't match that of any real user, not because he or she isn't logged on!

The other thing to check is that you use your party's real account name and not an alias. While e-mail can handle aliases, the talk program has no knowledge of them and therefore cannot recognize them.

- *The computer you are trying to reach is not on the Internet.* Lots of computers that are reachable by e-mail across the Internet aren't actually attached to the Internet. If this happens, you'll see a message like this:

```
bogus.nohope.com is an unknown host
```

Here again, you'll want to double-check the typing of the domain name for the host; if you made a mistake, chances are what you typed isn't the name of any real Internet host, either.

- *The other party may have turned off talk.* In this case you'd see a message like

  ```
  [Your party is refusing messages]
  ```

  when you try to initiate a talk session. If this happens, use e-mail instead. Before you try talk on someone for the first time, you might want to use Finger on their Internet name. In addition to telling you if the person is logged on or not, Finger can often tell you if that person is accepting or rejecting messages.

- *There's a mismatch between talk versions on the two hosts that are trying to connect.* This problem happens, but it is insidious because it produces a less-than-diagnostic error message:

  ```
  [Checking for invitation on caller's machine]
  ```

  This looks like it's probably just a matter of time before the connection happens, when the "invitation" gets found. Unfortunately, it typically means that the talk on your host and the version on the other party's host cannot communicate with each other. If this happens, try one of the other flavors of talk; some of the newer versions know how to overcome the mismatches that can occur when dissimilar hosts try to talk to each other.

As long as you treat talk somewhat like the telephone and don't expect an answer every time you try to run the program, you shouldn't get too frustrated. Nevertheless, you should be able to work your way through these common gotchas and talk to at least some of your friends and colleagues some of the time!

Several Flavors of Talk

In addition to the original version of the program, called *talk*, there are several other implementations that you might find on your local host machine. These include:

- *ntalk* (short for new talk). One ntalk daemon can talk to another, regardless of what kind of computer either one is running on. Use this version if you get the "invitation" message discussed in the previous section.

- *ytalk* (short for Yenne talk—Britt Yenne is the developer or "Why talk?"). ytalk works with either talk or ntalk on the other side of the connection, plus it will let you conference in multiple parties. In fact, ytalk can probably handle more parties than you can, if you want to push the envelope.

    If you elect a three-or-more-way conversation, ytalk will carve up the screen into as many areas as there are speakers, each with his or her own labeled area for text (ytalk labels each area with the username of the speaker as part of the dividing line between areas).

    To fire up ytalk in multiparty mode, put the names of the callees on the command line after the program name, each one separated by a space like this:

    ```
    ytalk mrobbins@bga.com brendan@zen.org
    ```

    This will initiate a call to both Margaret and Brendan and, with a little luck, start up a fascinating three-way conversation.

We recommend that you use one of these versions, rather than talk, if they are available on your system. Other than the program name (and ytalk's multiparty abilities), they behave pretty much the same as talk.

Controlling Idle Talk

Lest you fear inundation by requests for idle talk sessions, we would like to reassure you that you can control whether or not to receive such requests. If you're working on a deadline or simply don't want to be disturbed, you can use another special command to inform the talk daemon that you will not accept any such requests. If you follow these simple instructions, you can refuse all invitations: Simply type

```
mesg n
```

at the command line on your host system. This tells the daemon not to forward you any messages, which of course turns off all talk requests. To begin receiving requests again, type

```
mesg y
```

at the command line.

That's about all there is to using the talk utility. Try it out on your host sometime and you could discover a whole new way to use the Internet!

INTERNET RELAY CHAT (IRC)

We already compared talk to using the telephone and likened IRC to using a CB radio, except with lots more channels (and the ability to create new ones as desired). IRC falls into a class of programs known sometimes as *conferencing* or, more formally, as a *chat facility*.

The difference between talk and IRC ultimately rests on the way communications are managed within the two programs: When you use talk, you decide when to talk (or if you're even interested in talking) and who to talk to—you initiate the connection, try to reach the party, conduct a conversation, and break the connection when you're done. When you use IRC, you tap into a large set of ongoing conversations, any of which you can decide to join, and you have the option of starting new ones. While you can limit participation in conversations that you started, you can't use IRC to invite anyone not already using IRC to join your conversation.

The etiquette of using IRC makes private conversations largely invisible to most users. IRC's real appeal comes from leaving a conversation, known as a channel, open to anyone and everyone who wants to participate. The only way that IRC users have of selecting a conversation is by deciding whether or not its channel name sounds interesting or by being invited by others to join a private conversation. Given a vast number of browsers, and a small number of private channel operators, the odds clearly favor the browsers.

At any given moment, in fact, it is typical for thousands of participants to be active across hundreds of channels. Because IRC involves people from all over the world, while most conversations are in English, it's not unusual to find them going on in other languages as well. Obviously, it's best to join only those where you have at least one language in common with the other participants!

How IRC Works

Here's how IRC works: You must use a special client program, usually called *irc*, to obtain access to IRC. If the program runs, it will connect you to an IRC server, and you can then enter IRC commands to participate in what's going on at the moment. Because each IRC server is connected to other IRC servers in its immediate vicinity, ultimately all IRC servers are indirectly connected to each other. When you use IRC, you tap into a vast, worldwide web of IRC servers and can talk with all the individuals connected through each of them.

IRC uses channels to organize ongoing conversations, to keep the amount of chaos down to a manageable level. Most channel names begin with a # (pound sign or crosshatch character), which makes them easy to recognize. In addition to public channels, there are also private channels and secret, "invisible" ones.

Every time you enter the command to join a channel, IRC checks its list to determine if that channel name has been defined. If so, you can join in. If not, IRC will create a new channel with the name you have supplied. If you create a new channel, you'll be the only person on it for a while, so you must wait for others to join you or use other IRC commands to specifically invite them from other channels.

When the last person leaves a channel, IRC shuts it down and removes it from the channel list. A channel's creator is called the *channel operator*. The channel operator has special powers: The channel may be made private, so that people can join only by invitation; the topic for discussion can be set and controlled; and operator privileges can be delegated to others (so that the conversation can continue when the original operator leaves, for instance).

Starting up an IRC Client

Firing up a connection to IRC means running IRC client software. Once started, the client will automatically hook you into an IRC server and, hence, to the whole world of IRC servers and ongoing conversations. To start IRC with the nickname "TechTalk," type the following line:

```
irc TechTalk
```

Of course, you can substitute whatever nickname you'd like to use for yourself, as long as it's nine characters or fewer in length.

If your Internet host is a UNIX machine, you can get information on irc by reading its pages from the on-line manual. The command to get this information is

```
man irc
```

This command is a UNIX program too, so remember to enter it at the command line level, not from inside irc. To get help inside the program, simply type /help (all IRC commands start with a slash character), and it will show you a compendium of all the IRC commands at your disposal. In the next section, we talk about how IRC commands work, and how to use them, along with a few other significant details.

IRC Commands

We summarize some of the more important IRC commands in Table 12.3, but a few are absolutely essential to good conduct and survival. We recommend you predefine your nickname when you invoke the irc program, as explained earlier. You can use the **/nick** command to change your nickname at any time, however. For instance, typing

```
/nick Jim-Bob
```

would immediately change your name to Jim-Bob and would result in the following message being displayed to everyone tuned into the channel you're currently on:

```
*** TechTalk is now known as Jim-Bob
```

The most crucial command is **/quit**, which gets you out of IRC altogether. Other crucial commands include **/list**, which lists the channels in operation; **/join**, which lets you attach to a channel of interest; and **/whois**, which will identify a participant from his or her nickname.

The only other thing you really need to know is how to contribute to the activity. Our advice is to wait for a lull in conversation, or a request from a speaker for input, before joining in. The channel operator, and anybody else with delegated operator authority, can throw you out of a channel on a whim, so start out gently and don't be surprised if you get bounced anyway.

What's in a Nickname?

As with CB radio, and most other on-line conferencing systems, every IRC participant has a nickname. When you start an IRC session, you must specify a nickname, which can be up to nine characters in length. You can call yourself anything you want, as long as that nickname isn't already in use by someone else. Should you wish to make your nickname permanent, you can register it with a special IRC database and keep the same name thereafter (assuming, of course, it isn't already taken). Nicknames provide a certain license for expression, by preserv-

Command	Parameter	Explanation
`/flush`		clear current line for a fresh IRC command; halts output from last command
`/help`		Displays one-page list of all IRC commands
	`<command>`	Shows help on command
	`intro`	Shows intro file describing IRC
	`newuser`	Helpful information for new users
	`etiquette`	Rules of behavior for IRC users
		Hit enter at the help prompt to exit help
`/join`	`<channel>`	Join channel (don't forget the # character!)
`/leave`	`<channel>`	Exit channel
`/list`		Displays list of all active channels
	`<channel>`	Shows information about channel
	`-min <n>`	Shows all channels with at least *n* people signed on
	`-max <n>`	Shows all channels with no more than *n* people
`/me`	`<action>`	Types "nickname action" on-screen
`/msg`	`<nick> <text>`	Sends private message to nick consisting of text
	`, <text>`	Sends private message to last sender of same
	`. <text>`	Sends private message to last recipient of same
`/nick`		Displays your current nickname
	`<name>`	Changes nickname to name
`/query`	`<nicknames>`	Sends all your messages privately to names in list Separate names with commas, no spaces by itself, **/query** stops sending to private list
`/quit`		Exit IRC facility
`/who`	`<channel>`	Shows list of users attached to channel
	`<nickname>`	Shows information about user with nickname
	`*`	Shows all users attached to current channel
`/whois`	`nickname`	Shows information about user with nickname

Note: `<text>` means insert appropriate text; all items inside should be replaced with real names, etc.

Table 12.3 *A Minimal Set of IRC Commands*

ing a degree of anonymity, but they also say a lot about their owners. Choose yours with care—it's how other people will come to know you!

Although nine characters leaves lots of room to be naughty, it's probably a good idea to stick with nicknames that other people won't find offensive or off-putting. You'll still be identified by your Internet name whenever you join a channel, and there are ways of finding out who you really are from your nickname, so you won't want to take the anonymity thing too far. It's better to be creative and positive, than creative and risqué or negative, especially if you want to register your nickname for continued use.

Where to Go for IRC Details

There is a lot more to IRC than we can cover in this book. We'd like to help you get more information about this program, which has a deserved reputation as a fabulous way to waste time! We certainly recommend using the **/help** command, especially **/help newuser** and **/help etiquette** to get acquainted with IRC before getting too ambitious. Also, if you scan the list of channels you'll often see one named **#IRC_Prefect** or something like that, where you can hang out to ask questions and see what other questions (and answers) other users have. Finally, be sure to read the man page on irc on your host system (if available).

There is also an on-line document called the *IRC Primer*, and an accompanying tutorial—both of these are worth reading. Here's how to locate them:

1. FTP to cs.bu.edu
2. cd to the directory named /irc/support
3. For the Primer, get one of the files named IRCprimer (.PS stands for PostScript, .txt is a regular text file, and .tar.z indicates a compressed file that requires special techniques to unpack—check Chapter 13 for the details)
4. For the tutorial, download all of the files named tutorial*n* (i.e. tutorial1, tutorial2, etc.) You can use the **mget** command like this:

```
mget tutorial.*
```

You can find the Frequently Asked Questions (FAQ) file for IRC in many of the Usenet newsgroups, including alt.irc and news.answers (see Chapters 10 and 11 for more information on how to use these resources) or you can do the following:

1. FTP to rtfm.mit.edu (remember, RTFM stands for "Read The Fabulous Manual!")
2. cd to the directory named /pub/usenet/news.answers
3. get the file named irc-faq.

Finally, IRC is covered by RFC 1459, so you can follow the RFC download instructions from Chapter 3 and use them to retrieve this document, to get all of the details. This should furnish you with more information about IRC than you ever wanted to know!

In the final analysis, the more you learn, the less strange and stressful your initial exposure to IRC will seem. If you're the adventurous type, go ahead and dive in. Then, if your fingers get burned, go back and do some reading. Otherwise, enjoy!

SUMMARY

In this chapter we looked at the two primary interactive tools for online Internet conversations. The talk function is a useful ability, especially when you need to work directly with someone over the Internet. IRC, on the other hand, is a world unto itself! Be sure to give yourself some time to get oriented and expect to spend some serious time immersed in the many channels of conversation, gibberish, and repartee you're sure to find on-line.

FILE TRANSFER PROTOCOL (FTP)

EVERYTHING IMAGINABLE IS IN A FILE, SOMEWHERE OUT THERE

One of the most underappreciated aspects of the Internet is the sheer volume of *stuff* that's out there on some server, perhaps even languishing in undeserved obscurity. For good or ill, most of this incredible conglomeration of material—which ranges from electronic books, to catalogs, to "free" software (shareware or freeware), to recipes, to computer graphics, to you-name-it—lives in one file or another, somewhere out on the Internet.

You need not look around too hard or too long to be swamped by items that might conceivably be of interest to you, even if you've got pretty esoteric tastes. A world of information is out there on the Internet, just waiting for you to grab hold of it and bring some home to your desktop machine!

WHAT DOES FTP DO?

FTP is the Internet tool you'll want to use when you know that the information you seek is in some kind of file format, and when you know where that information resides. FTP lets you reach across the network, attach to a remote host, root around in its file system—or at least, that portion that you're allowed to see and investigate—and copy what you need (or go the other way, for that matter).

Also, because the type of computer you're copying from may differ from the one you're copying to, FTP is equipped to deal with some basic file format conversions to aid the process along, too. It's not smart enough to convert a 1-2-3 file into a 20/20 equivalent, but it is smart enough to be able to move text formats among PCs, Macs, UNIX machines, and others as well.

Like many other TCP/IP programs, FTP is broken into two parts: a client part (which runs at your PC or as a front-end program on your Internet host, depending on how you use the software), and a server part (which runs as a daemon program on a remote server somewhere). The FTP daemon's job is to listen for FTP connection requests and grant those that survive the login process (meaning that the connection uses a valid account name and password and thus demonstrates its ability to access the files on a system), an FTP session that they can use to send and receive files to or from that host.

FTP's Operations, Step by Step

If we take a look at how FTP works, step by step, in terms of the sequence of actions required to use it, an awful lot about what it can and can't do will emerge. Here is what a typical flow of events might look like, from a sequential perspective (the details will vary from system to system and implementation to implementation, but the basic flow will stay the same):

1. You begin by firing up the FTP program. Most versions of FTP will let you specify the target host on the same line as the program invocation. Thus, you can start up FTP by typing either one of these two lines:

   ```
   ftp
   ftp ftp.zilker.net
   ```

2. The next step is to get permission to use the other system. This means supplying a valid account name and password to be allowed entry onto that system. This dialog will typically look something like this:

   ```
   Connected to ZILKER.NET
   220 oak.zilker.net FTP Server (SunOS 4.1) ready.
   Name (bogus.com:etittel) etittel
   ```

```
331 Password required for etittel
Password:
230 User etittel logged in.
ftp>
```

For security reasons, your password won't show on-screen (to prevent its being read over your shoulder perhaps).

The numbers at the beginning of every other line are FTP status code numbers, which tell programmers that the program is behaving properly. The final line shows the **ftp>** prompt, which indicates that you're inside FTP (at last). You'll see this prompt at the beginning of each line where you're expected to give the program some input, sort of as a reminder for you to do just that.

3. At this point, you want to change to the directory where the file you want to copy (or place) should reside. It will look something like this:

```
ftp> cd /docs/internet
250 CWD command successful.
```

The message indicates that the directory change (from the UNIX command Change Working Directory) has been successful.

4. You can now get a listing of files in the directory by using the **ls** command, like this

```
ftp> ls
200 PORT command successful.
150 Opening ASCII mode data connection for file list.
index
interviews-to-g++.diffs
226 Transfer complete.
remote: *
32 bytes received in 0.071 seconds (0.44 Kbytes/s)
```

This will produce a listing of all the files in the directory (for brevity, we show only the initial response lines and a few files, followed by the command response and information about the data transferred to meet the listing request).

5. Now, you can either use the **put** command to copy a file from your local machine to the remote host (a process known as *uploading*), or use the **get** command to copy a file from the remote host to your machine (a process known as *downloading*). We skip the computer response—try it and see what happens!

6. When you are done, use the **quit** command (**bye** works, too). You have just ended an FTP session. Congratulations!

Put more succinctly, the basic flow of FTP is to start the program, log in to the remote host, get situated in the directory you want, copy or place the files you want, and either continue on or quit the program.

Basic, Unvarnished FTP

As we stepped through the sequence of activities needed to run FTP, you also had a good chance to experience some of its flavor. What we showed is the basic, command-line implementation of FTP, like you would run on any UNIX host or similar machine (say, from a Telnet session or using a terminal directly).

This unvarnished implementation of FTP uses a purely character-oriented interface, with sometimes cryptic commands. But the command syntax (and many of the commands themselves) are similar if not identical to UNIX, and the behavior of the program is simple and straightforward. If the only way you can get access to FTP is through a host-based version, you can still move files around the Internet (or your local network). And, you can do that job with dispatch and precision, if not flair.

Getting Help on FTP

We can't cover every command and every switch for FTP in this book, but we can point you at some excellent sources of help and further information. Standard implementations of the FTP program—and FTP is definitely a required TCP/IP standard, no bones about it—will always include a help facility. To use help within the FTP program, simply type **help** or **?** at the ftp> command prompt. This will show you a list of all the available FTP commands, and you can then investigate further by asking for help on specific commands (or by typing **help <command>** to get help on a specific command).

The governing RFCs for FTP are 959 (and the "host requirements" RFC, 1123). These will be a bit dry, so unless you're a real bit-head, you'll probably want to check out the Frequently Asked Questions for FTP, instead.

1. FTP to rtfm.mit.edu (remember, RTFM stands for "Read The Fabulous Manual!").

2. **cd** to the directory named /pub/usenet/news.answers.
3. **get** the file named ftp-faq.

Don't forget that your host may have man pages on FTP, too. If you look for help and information, you will be sure to find what you need!

Anonymous FTP

A special variety of FTP in fact, really acts as an underpinning to the free exchange of information on the Internet. It's called *Anonymous FTP* because it makes files available on the network to anyone who wants them, as long as the user logs in using the account name Anonymous. The password is usually one of the following possibilities (in decreasing order of popularity):

1. **Guest** (any spelling is usually OK, as is any mixture of upper- and lowercase characters).
2. Your e-mail name (most often used on heavily accessed public servers like rtfm.mit.edu, to help them keep track of who's downloading from them).
3. Any password (type whatever you want; actually, 2 is just a subcase of this possibility, but occurs less frequently, unless you stop to consider that 2 is the same as 3, except that FTP is asking for information which it will review later on).
4. No password (hit the return or enter key when prompted for one) required.

Given that there are multiple password possibilities, how will you know what to do when you try to log onto some particular Anonymous FTP server?

The answer is quite simple: When you start to log in to one of these servers, it will usually tell you exactly what to do to gain access. For example, when logging in to the main usenet FTP server, here's what you see:

```
Name (ftp.uu.net:etittel): anonymous
331 Guest login ok, send your complete e-mail address
as password.
Password:
```

In other words, follow the instructions that show up when you provide the account name Anonymous and you can't go wrong!

Now that you are over the password hurdle, why should you care about Anonymous FTP, anyway? The reason is simple: Anonymous FTP is the primary tool for the distribution of software, documents, and other information on the Internet. Chances are very good that the administrator on your Internet host uses Anonymous FTP all the time, for everything from obtaining the utilities you use to read newsgroups, to all kinds of help files, and perhaps even for the software you're using on your own computer to talk to that host! As you become more familiar with the Internet, you'll find that Anonymous FTP is invaluable for all kinds of things, too.

FTP Commands

We base our discussion of the FTP commands around Table 13.1, which covers a pretty complete set of all the FTP commands available from most implementations. You will find slight differences among versions, but the basic commands must stay the same to meet the RFC requirements.

For your convenience, we indicated the most important and commonly used commands in **bold** in Table 13.1, leaving the rest in plain text. For the same reason, we also categorized the commands and included the one-line help text for each one from our own handy-dandy FTP implementation.

Here's what the categories we used to divide up the commands mean:

- *File System Control.* These are the commands you use to view and navigate around in both local and remote file systems. For example: ls (list remote directory), delete (remove remote file), rmdir (delete remote directory), lcd (change local directory).
- *File Transfer Control.* These are the commands that let you move files to and from the remote host. For example: **put** (transfer file from local to remote), **get** (transfer from remote to local).
- *File Transfer Management.* These are the commands that let you manage file format translations, character modes, and file names when moving between local and remote machines. For example: **ascii** (treat file as ascii text), **binary** (treat file as binary), **mode** (set file transfer mode).
- *Program Management.* These are the commands you use to control the FTP program itself. For example: **open** (connect to a remote host), **close** (disconnect from remote host), **bye** or **quit** (exit FTP and close any open connections).

File System Control Commands

Command	Description
cd	change remote working directory
cdup	change remote working directory to parent directory
delete	delete remote file
dir	list contents of remote directory
lcd	change local working directory
ls	nlist contents of remote directory
mdelete	delete multiple files
mdir	list contents of multiple remote directories
mkdir	make directory on the remote machine
mls	nlist contents of multiple remote directories
pwd	print working directory on remote machine
rename	rename file
rmdir	remove directory on the remote machine

File Transfer Control Commands

Command	Description
append	append to a file
mget	get multiple files
mput	send multiple files
put	send one file
recv	receive file
send	send one file
get	file transfer control; receive file

File Transfer Management Commands

Command	Description
ascii	set ascii transfer type
binary	set binary transfer type
case	toggle mget upper/lower case id mapping
cr	toggle carriage return stripping on ascii gets
form	set file transfer format
glob	toggle metacharacter expansion of local file names
hash	toggle printing `#' for each buffer transferred
mode	set file transfer mode
nmap	set templates for default file name mapping
ntrans	set translation table for default file name mapping
runique	toggle store unique for local files
sendport	toggle use of PORT cmd for each data connection
struct	set file transfer structure
sunique	toggle store unique on remote machine
tenex	set tenex file transfer type
type	set file transfer type

Table 13.1 *A Compendium of FTP Commands (continued)*

Table 13.1—Continued

Program Management Commands

Command	Description
!	escape to the shell
$	execute macro
?	print local help information
account	send account command to remote server
bell	beep when command completed
bye	terminate ftp session and exit
close	terminate ftp session
debug	toggle/set debugging mode
disconnect	terminate ftp session
help	print local help information
macdef	define a macro
open	connect to remote tftp
prompt	force interactive prompting on multiple commands
proxy	issue command on alternate connection
quit	terminate ftp session and exit
quote	send arbitrary ftp command
remotehelp	get help from remote server
reset	clear queued command replies
status	show current status
trace	toggle packet tracing
user	send new user information
verbose	toggle verbose mode

Table 13.1 *A Compendium of FTP Commands*

When using FTP, it is important to remember the distinction between local and remote file systems and to use the corresponding commands within these categories. That is, to list the local directory, you have to use the ! (bang) command to run **ls** locally (i.e., **!ls** at the **ftp>** prompt); if you use FTP's **ls** command, it will list the contents of the remote directory instead of the local one. This will be somewhat confusing at first, so make sure you read the header lines on the FTP screen displays—in most cases, these will tell you if they are responding to a local or a remote command.

In the next subsection, we explain how to use some of the most important commands, as we tell you what you need to know to use FTP to copy files to and from a remote host machine over the Internet.

How to Copy Files Using FTP

Let's take a more detailed look at the example we showed you at the
beginning of the chapter, which provided an overview of the steps
involved in using FTP:

1. Invoke the FTP program. Most versions of FTP will let you specify
   the target host on the same line as the program invocation. Thus,
   you can start up FTP by typing either one of these two lines at the
   host prompt:

   ```
   ftp
   ftp ftp.zilker.net
   ```

2. The next step is to log in to the other system. This means supplying a valid account name and password, or using Anonymous
   FTP. This dialog will typically look something like:

   ```
   Connected to ZILKER.NET
   220 oak.zilker.net FTP Server (SunOS 4.1) ready.
   Name (bogus.com:etittel) etittel
   331 Password required for etittel
   Password:
   230 User etittel logged in.
   ftp>
   ```

   If it was anonymous FTP, it would look more like this:

   ```
   Connected to ZILKER.NET
   220 oak.zilker.net FTP Server (SunOS 4.1) ready.
   Name (bogus.com:etittel) Anonymous
   330 Guest login permitted; normal restrictions apply.
   Please enter e-mail name
       so we can track server usage.
   Password:
   230 User Anonymous logged in.
   ftp>
   ```

3. At this point, you change to the directory where the file you want
   to copy (or place) should reside. If you're using Anonymous FTP,
   you'll be following instructions from a file or other resource and
   should be able to **cd** right to the directory you want:

   ```
   ftp> cd /docs/internet
   250 CWD command successful.
   ```

   The message indicates that the directory change (from the UNIX
   command Change Working Directory.) has been successful.

4. You can now get a listing of files in the directory by using the `ls` command, like this

```
ftp> ls
200 PORT command successful.
150 Opening ASCII mode data connection for file list.
index
interviews-to-g++.diffs
226 Transfer complete.
remote: *
32 bytes received in 0.071 seconds (0.44 Kbytes/s)
```

This will produce a listing of all the files in the directory (for brevity, we show only the initial response lines and a few files, followed by the command response and information about the data transferred to meet the listing request).

5. Now, you can either use the **put** command to copy a file from your local machine to the remote host (a process known as *uploading*), or use the **get** command to copy a file from the remote host to your machine (a process known as *downloading*). If you want to transfer multiple files, use **mput** (to transfer multiples from your local machine to the remote host) or **mget** (to transfer multiples from the remote host to your local machine). Here's some **put** dialog, followed by a **get** example:

```
ftp> hash
Hash mark printing on (8192 bytes/hash mark).
ftp> put internet.text
200 PORT command successful.
150 Opening ASCII mode data connection for internet.text.
############
226 Transfer complete.
local: internet.text remote: internet.text
92854 bytes sent in 14 seconds (6.7 Kbytes/s)
```

Note the **hash** command. We used this so that the computer would tell us each time it transferred a block of text from the remote host to the local one (as the display indicates, each hash mark stands for 8KB of data). Note also that put tells us the names of the files, local and remote, and information about the total amount of data sent and the time it took. Here's the **get** example:

```
ftp> get internet.text
200 PORT command successful.
150 Opening ASCII mode data connection for internet.text
(91155 bytes).
############
226 Transfer complete.
local: internet.text remote: internet.text
92854 bytes received in 29 seconds (3.1 Kbytes/s)
```

Notice that the number of bytes sent is greater than the file size; this is because of the overhead imposed by TCP and IP in the packet and frame headers that get shipped across the network.

6. When you're done, use the **quit** command (**bye** works, too) and you will be through.

The best way to become more familiar with FTP is to spend some time with the program. Start out by practicing: Create a short text file and copy it back and forth from your machine to the local host. Experiment with the various commands, read the **man** pages on FTP, and over time you will start to get comfortable.

Making FTP "User Friendly"

Up to this point, you have been exposed only to the standard UNIX implementation of FTP, which is strictly character mode and command oriented. Many vendors offer client-side implementations that are a great deal easier to use, because they've taken the time and effort to adapt FTP to a graphical user interface (GUI). We're aware of such implementations for the Macintosh, OS/2, MS Windows, and a variety of X-Windows versions for all kinds of platforms, UNIX and otherwise.

Figure 13.1 shows one example of such an interface. The beauty of this approach is that all file system navigation is by point and click operations on files and folders and that the FTP commands are largely hidden underneath buttons and menus that require far less training and understanding to operate.

Given that these tools are so snazzy, why would anybody use anything else? The short answer is cost. The command line FTP implementation can be found on virtually any Internet host and is free for the using. The GUI versions must be acquired for the user's desktop platform and, while some shareware or public domain implementations are to be had, most of these versions cost somewhere between $100 and $400, depending on the platform, the number of TCP/IP utilities included in the package (you can't buy FTP by itself today, at least that we're aware of; you'll invariably have to buy a TCP/IP package that includes FTP, Telnet, utilities, protocol software, and more).

Our recommendation, notwithstanding the budgetary strain that a purchase might cause, is to investigate shareware and freeware implementations first. If those don't meet your needs or expectations, spend the money and buy a commercial version. Because it simplifies things

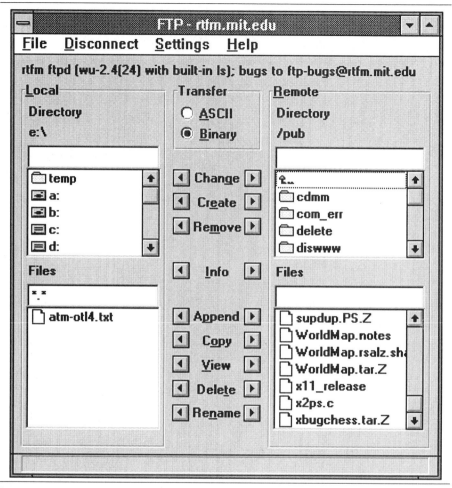

Figure 13.1 *A GUI Interface Makes FTP Easier to Use!*

so much and saves so much time, such an investment will actually pay for itself if you have to do much with the Internet (please consult Chapter 29 for more information on TCP/IP vendors).

MAXIMIZING FTP

Even after you have mastered the program, still other information about FTP usage and convention is worth knowing. Because shipping files across the Internet takes time—especially for large files—you'll quickly learn that many FTP servers (particularly for Anonymous FTP) store files in compressed format. This reduces the amount of data that has to be sent across the network, speeding file transfer and conserving precious bandwidth.

Unpacking compressed files takes special tools, though. It would do you no good to copy a file that you can't read. In the next section we cover the various file compression schemes you are likely to encounter on the Internet and talk about the tools and techniques necessary to deal with them.

After that, we talk about a possible FTP substitute based on e-mail, for those of you who may not have access to FTP, but who do have access to Internet e-mail. We conclude this section with a brief discussion of some typical compatibility issues that may surface when you get files from systems different from your own and try to use them on your machine.

File Compression Schemes

While there are many ways to compress files and lots of different programs can do the job nicely, all approaches depend on the same basic technique: of performing statistical analysis on the bit patterns that make up a file and applying mathematical encoding techniques to represent longer bit patterns with shorter ones. Some techniques eliminate repetition, others perform pattern matching and build so-called compression dictionaries, while yet others use specialized encoding techniques.

No compression scheme is worthwhile unless it is a two-way street: that is, a compressed file that can't be decompressed is no good to anyone. Although we only scratch the tip of the iceberg here, in this subsection we cover the most widely used compression and decompression techniques on the Internet and explain how to apply them to your best advantage.

One important thing to remember about compressed files is that they typically contain multiple files when unpacked. This means that it's always a good idea to set up a separate workspace whenever you unpack such a file, especially if you don't know what it contains. The easiest way to do this is to create a new directory with nothing in it, and then to copy or move the compressed file into that directory before you unpack it.

Tape Archive (.tar) Format

The term **tar** is short for tape archive, a very popular tape backup format used on many UNIX systems. You'll still find many files stored in tar format, or a compressed variant, on FTP servers, Anonymous and otherwise. These kind of files, known as *tarfiles* (or compressed tarfiles), must typically be unpacked on a UNIX host for further use. Whereas most uncompressed tarfiles end with the extension .tar (for example internet.tar), a compressed tarfile ends with the extension .tar.z (again internet.tar.z)

For more information on the tar program, check the man pages, or consult a UNIX reference (if you don't know of any good ones, please consult the Publications List at the end of this book). Our discussion is very tightly focused and doesn't begin to cover all of the program's many capabilities.

Unarchiving tarfiles

The **tar** command is used on UNIX systems to archive and unarchive files. Fortunately, this means that most UNIX systems will be able to handle such files for you. To unarchive a tarfile named internet.tar, enter the following command at the UNIX command line:

```
tar -xvf internet.tar
```

The *x* stands for extract, which is what you want to do. The *v* stands for verbose, which means that tar will tell you exactly what it is doing; that is, it will list each file as it gets extracted. The *f* indicates that the name of the tarfile follows.

To create your own tarfile named nonet.tar that contains the files first.txt, second.txt, and third.txt, enter the following **tar** command:

```
tar -cvf nonet.tar first.txt second.txt third.txt
```

The *v* and *f* mean the same as before, and *c* stands for create.

Uncompressing Compressed Tarfiles

By convention, a **.z** (uppercase is important) at the end of a UNIX file name means that it has been compressed with a special utility named *compress*. There is a matching utility called *uncompress* that you must use to unpack such files. Therefore, unpacking a compressed tarfile is a two-stage process. Using internet.tar.Z as our example, here is what you have to do to get at its contents after using FTP to transfer it to your home system:

```
uncompress internet.tar.Z
tar -xvf internet.tar
```

If you want to see what **uncompress** is doing, you can also add the -v switch to the command like this:

```
uncompress -v internet.tar.Z
tar -xvf internet.tar
```

To compress a file, you can use the **compress** program. Just be aware that this program automatically deletes the original file and creates a compressed replacement with the **.z** extension on the filename. Here again, you can use the **-v** option if you want the program to tell you what it's doing:

```
compress -v internet.text
```

For more information on compress and uncompress, check the man pages on a UNIX system somewhere.

Finding Compression/Decompression Tools on the Internet

There are also PC-based versions of these programs, including tar, compress, uncompress, and all of the other programs we mention in the next two subsections. These are available from a number of sources if you want to obtain the software for use on your own machine. One good reference is a file that refers to itself as "The Ultimate Guide to MSDOS Archive Files," compiled by Samuel Ko; it contains references to many other programs of interest and can be obtained by Anonymous FTP from rtfm.mit.edu in the /msdos-archives directory in two files, named part1 and part2.

Compressed PC Formats

Lots of file compression formats are used on PCs and still more on Macintoshes. Table 13.2 summarizes the more common file extensions, supplies the name of the software programs you need to deal with them, and includes Anonymous FTP servers where you can get them, with directories and file names.

Of course, each of these compression methods has its own software and its own way of doing things. We boldfaced the most popular and recurring formats in Table 13.2, and recommend that you obtain the software to at least deal with them. Over time, though, the more work you do with FTP, the more of these packages you'll find accumulating on your hard disk (at least you know where to get them now, anyway!)

Extension	Program	Srvr: Directory	Filename
`*.zip`	PKZip software	oak: /pub/msdos/archiver garbo: /pc/arcers	pkz204g.exe pkz204g.exe
	Info-Zip's Zip	oak: /pub/msdos/zip garbo:/pc/arcers	zip20x.zip zip20x.zip
	Info-Zip's Unzip	oak: /pub/msdos/zip garbo: /pc/arcers	unz50p1.exe unz50p1.exe
`*.arj`	ARJ file archiver	oak: /pub/msdos/archiver garbo: /pc/arcers	arj241a.exe arj241a.exe
`*.lzh`	LZH Archive pgm	oak: /pub/msdos/archiver garbo: /pc/arcers	lha213.exe lha213.exe lha255b.exe (Japanese only)
`*.arc`	ARC packer/unpacker	oak: /pub/msdos/archiver garbo: /pc/arcers	pk361.exe or arc521e.tar-z pk361.exe
`*.zoo`	Dhesi's ZOO archiver	oak: /oub/msdos/zoo garbo: /pc/arcers	zoo210.exe zoo210.exe booz20.zip is extract-only
`*.hpk`	Hpack cross-platform archiver	oak: /pub/msdos/archiver garbo: /pc/arcers	hpack78.zip hpack78.zip
`*.sqz`	Squeeze compressor	oak: /pub/msdos/archiver garbo: /pc/arcers	sqz1083e.exe sqz1083e.exe
`*.sit`	Aladdin Systems StuffIT (Mac) compression	check file mirror-list.txt sumex: /infomac/hlp	stuffit-expander-35.hqx (expand only, no compress)

Note: this product is also available as a commercial package called StuffIT Deluxe, from Aladdin Systems, Inc. at (408) 761-6200 E-mail: aladdin@well.sf.ca.us

`*.tar`	UNIX tape archiver	oak: /pub/msdos/fileutil garbo: /pc/unix	tar4dos.zip tar4dos.zoo
`*.z`	UNIX compress & decompress formats	oak: /pub/msdos/compress garbo: /pc/unix	comp430d.zip comp430d.zip
`*.gz`	GNU compression tools	oak: /pub/msdos/compress garbo: /pc/arcers	gzip124.zip gzip111.exe

Note: these GNU tools also handle another compression format that uses a `.z` (lower case) extension, and the UNIX compress `.z` (upper case) as well.

Notes

	Server abbreviation	Full name	Location/Explanation
1.	oak:	oak.oakland.edu	United States site
2.	garbo:	garbo.uwasa.fi	European site (Finland)
3.	sumex:	sumex-aim.stanford.edu	Master Macintosh reference

Please don't use sumex: except in dire need; this system is already *WAY* too busy!

Table 13.2 *Common PC/Mac File Compression Formats*

An Important Caveat (for FTP, and for Life in General)

While writing this book, we checked all of the server names, directories, and file names to make sure they were still accurate. But the Internet is like the desert: Its boundaries keep shifting, and the sands eventually cover everything. We apologize in advance, because we know that by the time you read this, some of this information will be out of date and incorrect. If that is the case, don't give up: Start asking for help via e-mail to these sites (admin@domain-name will get you to the system administrator, who might have some good ideas on where to go to look for the stuff that used to be there, or he or she might be able to point you at a replacement). Join Usenet groups on the topic that you're interested in. Use Archie (covered in Chapter 16 to help you locate other sites where files might be located).

The moral of the story is this: If you keep looking, you may not find what you started out after, but you'll definitely find a way to solve your problem or meet your needs!

Getting Files via E-mail

Much of the software and information that you will find on the Internet is the result of people working at projects on their own and in their spare time. However, it is also true that organizations around the world have donated the time and effort of their employees and their equipment and network links to make the Internet more accessible and its information more available.

Thanks to a program called *ftpmail* written by Paul Vixie and publicly available on a server located at (but not supported by) the Digital Equipment Corporation (DEC), you can use Anonymous FTP to request files—both ASCII and binary—to be delivered to you by Internet e-mail.

FTP by Mail

The request procedure is quite simple: All you have to do is to send a properly formatted e-mail message to ftpmail@decwrl.dec.com and, in a day or so, the file you requested will appear in your e-mail's inbox. While your request is being processed, but before the actual file arrives, you'll probably receive several automated status reports on your request.

The essential element in the preceding information is the idea that your request has to be "properly formatted." What this really means is that your request will be handled entirely by a computer—no human beings who might be able to interpret any mistakes will be involved—thus, the formatting must be perfect, or the request will fail.

One part of the message that is not sensitive is the subject field. You can put anything you like here, but we recommend that you supply information that will remind you of what you're requesting, should you ever need to review the message again. The FTP-by-mail program simply doesn't care what's in the subject field, so you might as well have it do yourself some good.

An ftpmail Test Drive

We include two sample messages, with comments, that we used to request the IRC FAQ. The first message is addressed to the FTP server at MIT (rtfm.mit.edu) where we told you to go to get the Frequently Asked Questions file (irc-faq) for Internet Relay Chat in Chapter 12. The second message goes to the main Usenet server (ftp.uu.net) to obtain a Windows version of the Eudora e-mail mail reader program.

These messages reference comments that are keyed to bracketed numbers at the end of each line. This information only appears for your benefit: Please do not include either the bracketed numbers, or the comments they reference, in your message to ftpmail@decwrl. dec.comand or it won't work.

Script Line	Comment
`reply etittel@zilker.net`	[1]
`connect rtfm.mit.edu`	[2]
`ascii`	[3]
`chdir /pub/usenet/news.answers`	[4]
`get irc-faq`	[5]
`quit`	[6]

1. This entry tells the server where to send its status reports and the file you requested. The default is to use your e-mail address as the reply address, but it is best to be safe and explicit.
2. Identifies the Anonymous FTP server where the file to be obtained is located.
3. Specifies that the file is in ASCII format; the other legal value is binary. While the default is ascii, being explicit is a good idea here

too. Use ascii for all text files, binary for everything else (including when you're not sure).

4. Identifies the directory specification for where the file is located. Please note that this program uses UNIX directory notation, which requires the use of forward (i.e., **/pub**) not backward (i.e., **\pub**) slashes, as is normal for DOS.

5. Identifies the file to get. UNIX file names are case sensitive, so make sure you type the name exactly as it appears on the FTP server's directory (copy it carefully from your information source).

6. Tells the FTP server to terminate and break the service connection.

By now, knowing what you already do about FTP, ftpmail's design should be obvious: It's an e-mail-based remote control program for FTP. You using an e-mail message to drive an FTP client on the DEC machine, and it gets you what you request, acting entirely on your behalf.

Here is the second example, which downloads a larger file. Because these files have to be moved in fixed-size chunks, to successfully be transferred as e-mail messages, this introduces a little more complexity into the message we have to send:

Script Line	Comment

```
reply etittel@zilker.net                            [1]
connect ftp.uu.net                                  [2]
binary                                              [3]
chdir /systems/ibmpc/msdos/eudora/windows           [4]
uuencode                                            [5]
chunksize 100000                                    [6]
get                                                 [7]
quit                                                [8]
```

1. Set destination for requested file.
2. Specify FTP server to download from.
3. File type is binary; transfer as such.
4. Specifies directory where file to be transferred is located.
5. Tells the server to "encode" this binary file in ASCII format, using the standard UNIX uuencode system. (See the next subsection on uuencode and uudecode.) This encoding increases the file size by a bit more than one third.
6. The server will split large files into sections for mailing. This entry tells the server the maximum size for each chunk. The default is 64KB but the maximum that the FTPMAIL program will

accept is 100,000. That is what we use, to reduce the number of chunks (you might want to check with your system administrator if this causes problems, to find out if there's a ceiling on the maximum allowable size for an e-mail message on your system; if so, adjust accordingly).

7. Tells the server to get the file named.
8. Terminates FTP and breaks the remote connection.

These two examples should tell you most of what you need to know to use ftpmail. One additional note is worth making: If you need to get more than one file from the same server, simply insert the appropriate FTP commands into the script that makes up the message body, and the program will be happy to oblige. Except for the need to use uuencode to split up large files, you can script it out just as if you were using FTP interactively.

More on uuencode and uudecode

Although lots of the files available using Anonymous FTP are in binary format, Internet e-mail can transport only ASCII text in the body of a message. The proper workaround for this problem is to use an encoding/decoding routine to change binary files into ASCII form and later to restore the ASCII to binary. The programs that do this are called *uuencode* (short for "unix-to-unix encode") and *uudecode* ("unix-to-unix decode"), respectively.

These programs are available on most Internet hosts. Thus, the decwrl.dec.com host will uuencode binary files before sending them to you via e-mail, providing you include the proper command in the e-mail message body.

When encoding, every 3 bytes of a binary file gets turned into four ASCII characters. This means a uuencoded file will be about a third again as large as the binary file from whence it originated (because of file overhead, the file winds up 35% larger).

When you receive a binary file using ftpmail, it will arrive in uuencoded ASCII format. You can restore it to binary form using uudecode, either on a UNIX machine or by installing one of the DOS versions available on your PC. The restoration process is straightforward:

1. If the uuencoded file is contained in a single message, simply save the message as a file.

2. Next, issue the following command:

```
uudecode <filename>
```

3. The uudecode program automatically detects the beginning and end of the uuencoded file contained in the message, converts it to binary, and writes it to disk using the name FTPMAIL. You can then rename FTPMAIL to its "real" name to restore it to its original condition.

4. If the uuencoded file you receive is larger than 100,000 characters, it will be broken up into several messages. From your e-mail program, save these individual messages as separate files (you could name them SEG1.UUE, SEG2.UUE, etc.). Then, if you issue the command

```
uudecode SEG
```

uudecode will automatically process all of them, removing their headers and other extraneous material, and write the resulting binary file to disk as FTPMAIL, just as in the preceding example.

FTPMAIL offers nearly the full capability of FTP to anybody with access to Internet e-mail. If you have e-mail access to the Internet but no FTP, this could be an invaluable tool! Before taking undue advantage, though, make sure that the FTP server you're trying to reach doesn't have its own mail server already—many of the larger, more popular sites already offer their own tools to send files via e-mail.

Compatibility Issues

Inevitably, there will come a time in your use of FTP when, having copied a file from a remote host to your local system, you will try to examine or use it and find that it's just not readable. Don't feel too bad when this happens, because it happens to everyone.

The most common cause of such problems is file format incompatibilities between the remote host and your own system, whatever they may be. When moving files from UNIX to PCs, be aware that even text files are incompatible, because on a UNIX system, lines of text end with only a linefeed, whereas on DOS (and most other microcomputer systems) they end with a carriage return and a linefeed character as well. Part of what FTP does when transferring files is to detect the conventions in use and try to convert from one set to another when necessary.

Nevertheless, things will go wrong from time to time. When they do, the first thing to try is to copy the file again with explicit format settings included (i.e., make sure you specify binary or ascii mode transfer in your FTP commands and make sure that you're using the right mode for the file you want to transfer). If that doesn't work, try converting the file on the remote host (or asking for help from the system administrator if you can't Telnet to that machine) and then ship it over. Sometimes, it is just as simple as running uuencode before file transfer and then reversing the procedure with uudecode after you have brought it local.

If you still have problems, it's time to ask for help. See if you can identify the creator of the file; if you can, describe your symptoms and ask for advice. In many cases, the creator will be able to help. Here again, you can contact the system administrator (admin@<domain-name>) by e-mail, describe your difficulties, and ask for help. Or, you can find a newsgroup that specializes in FTP and post a general question to the readership. Very often, this will produce lots of useful suggestions, maybe even including advice from someone who's had the same problem.

The main thing is don't give up. If the file couldn't be transferred, it wouldn't be in an FTP archive. If you persevere and ask enough people the right questions, you'll eventually be able to get what you need.

SOME INTERESTING ANONYMOUS FTP RESOURCES

Table 13.3 lists all the Anonymous FTP references from the entire book, in alphabetical order, by the server's domain name. We invite you to go exploring and see what's interesting out there. Look in the root-level directories of these servers for files named things like ReadMe or Index or TOC (table of contents). Downloading these will often let you know exactly where to look for the items of real interest!

Domain name	Directories	Mail Server Explanation
ftp.uu.net	/usenet/news.answers	unknown usenet information, documents, mail tools
garbo.uwasa.fi	/pc/...	unknown UNIX, Mac, PC Internet documents and tools
oak.oakland.edu	/msdos/...	unknown UNIX, Mac, PC Internet documents and tools
rtfm.mit.edu	/pub/...	mail-server@rtfm.mit.edu ("help" in message body) all kinds of Mac and PC stuff
sumex-aim.stanford.edu	/infomac/...	info-mac-request@sumex- aim.stanford.edu check .../hlp/mirror-list.txt for alternative sites

Table 13.3 _Interesting Anonymous FTP Servers_

SUMMARY

We started this chapter by pointing at the sheer volume of _stuff_ out there on the Internet. Then we proceeded to point you at one of the major tools to help you go out and get some for yourself. Along the way, we covered FTP from a number of angles and dealt with some interesting alternatives. As long as you know what you're after, nothing beats FTP for getting it. In upcoming chapters we cover tools to help you figure out what you're after. But when you do, chances are extremely good that you'll be back to FTP so that you can get your hands on what we sincerely hope is the right stuff!

TELNET

WHY WOULD YOU WANT TO?

Like FTP, Telnet is an important window into the resources of the Internet. Rather than providing a method to obtain files, it provides a method to obtain computing services from hosts that can be reached over the Internet. Like so many TCP/IP applications (including FTP), Telnet is a client-server program. This means that you must run a client program on your workstation or your local host to talk to a Telnet daemon that can start a Telnet session up for you on a remote host and then manage communications thereafter. Again like FTP, Telnet normally requires an account (with accompanying password) on the remote host to permit access, but it comes in a variety of anonymous flavors.

The answer to the question "Why would you want to use Telnet?" therefore has to be: "To be able to use programs and resources on other hosts around the Internet." This can range from simple activities like reading and writing Internet e-mail to obtaining a home base to store files and materials. But Telnet also allows access to a broad variety of specialized applications and databases around the world in places like the Library of Congress or your local public library for research and catalog information, to the National Weather service for global and local weather maps and reports.

Originally, Telnet was developed as a way of stretching the length of the connections that could exist between a computer and its users, in an era when a terminal was the Cadillac of user access and punch cards were the norm. Today, Telnet makes it possible for a user sitting in his or her office at a PC to be able to access a computer anywhere in the world—as long as it's on the Internet!

OBTAINING A TELNET CONNECTION

Anonymous Telnet is somewhat less common than Anonymous FTP. In most cases, it's necessary to have an account on a host to Telnet to it. The **telnet** command can be issued with the domain name or IP address of the host as an argument like this:

```
telnet zilker.net
telnet 198.252.182.200
```

But, to log in (except for Anonymous Telnet, or a special service-based connection for Archie, Gopher, etc.) you must have a valid account name and the right password to go with it. Even Anonymous Telnet requires a valid account name—which, unlike Anonymous FTP, may not always actually be the word *anonymous*—though it may not require an accompanying password.

If you sign up with an Internet access provider or obtain an account through your school or employer, you'll be issued the information you need to get on the system. Then, as Telnet responds to your connection attempt, you must survive the dialog that ensues immediately after you attempt to attach to the host to truly gain access to that system:

```
oak.zilker.net> telnet bga.com
Trying 198.3.118.20 ...
Connected to bga.com.
Escape character is '^]'.

Real/Time Communications (zoom.bga.com) (ttyp2)

login: etittel
Password:
```

Let's assume that you do have a valid login and a valid password to go with it, so that you will survive the ordeal of making a Telnet connection. Then what happens?

Basically, running Telnet to access a system makes you a user of that system. Other than some items related to interacting with the Telnet program itself—on the client side, on "your side" of the network connection—all the activity you engage in is determined by the capabilities of the remote host. What does this mean?

It means that you have to know how to get around the remote host's operating system, for one thing. It also means that you have to have some goal in mind, or a task at hand, on that system, or you will be all connected up with nothing much to do!

What's on the Other Side of a Telnet Connection?

Since so many Telnet hosts are UNIX machines, using Telnet means learning how to work inside a UNIX environment. Here again, we recommend consulting some of the UNIX materials referenced in the Publications List in Chapter 27 to make yourself familiar with the most likely commands and activities that you'll find on the remote side of most Telnet sessions. We also recommend that you plan out what you're going to try to investigate or accomplish during the course of a Telnet session before you log in, at least while you're still making yourself familiar with a new computing environment. That way, you'll have a clear set of objectives against which to measure your learning and progress.

Communicating with Telnet, Not the Remote Host

Let's take another look at the login dialog from the preceding screen shot. Notice the line that says

```
Escape character is '^]'.
```

The notation '^]' means "strike the Ctrl key and the right square bracket key (]) at the same time" (usually expressed as Ctrl-] in the PC world). This is the special character that our example local Telnet client looks for to grab your keystrokes and examine them for itself; otherwise, everything you type at your keyboard gets forwarded across the network to the remote host. Be sure to pay attention to the login dialog when you fire up Telnet for the first time on a new system: If the escape sequence is different from '^]' take note and use that sequence instead, should you need to switch from terminal mode to command mode.

If you do type in the escape sequence, you'll see a different prompt appear on your screen:

```
telnet>
```

This lets you know you're talking to Telnet, rather than the remote host. What you can do at list point will be the subject of the subsection entitled "Telnet commands." Suffice it to say at this point that this is how you control Telnet's behavior, including running multiple sessions or switching from one remote host to another at will.

Using Telnet

One of the beauties of Telnet is its transparency. In most cases, you won't even know it's there. Thus using Telnet is really using the remote host, with only an occasional need to interact with the program directly. Unless you have special requirements or need to run multiple Telnet sessions simultaneously, your only encounters with Telnet will be when you invoke the program and then when you exit from it.

How Telnet works

Once you start up the program, the Telnet client on your computer (or your local host) captures each keystroke as you enter it. It packages each one into a separate TCP packet, emplaces it into an IP datagram with the remote host's address and socket ID, and ships it across the network. The Telnet daemon on the other side will have created a special Telnet session process on the remote host, which receives the incoming packets and forwards them to the host operating system.

The remote host then ships an acknowledgment packet back to the client, which includes the same character it just received. This character will be echoed to your screen, to show you that the remote host received exactly what you sent. This approach is known as *remote echo* since the characters you type come from across the network rather than from your local keyboard, otherwise known as *local echo*.

You can change Telnet's mode of operation from a character at a time to a line at a time, but this will interfere with its ability to respond immediately to the escape sequence (it won't see it until you hit the Enter key). But for most uses, the single character method works just fine, primarily because humans are so slow compared to computers (to them, it is an eternity between keystrokes; to us, the blink of an eye).

Telnet Configuration

For some versions of Telnet, especially those that run as clients on your local desktop machine, it will be necessary for you to tell the software what kind of terminal you want it to emulate. In most cases, choosing the DEC VT100 as your terminal type is a very safe choice, because it is as close to a standard emulation as it's possible to get. Also, if you're going to connect to an IBM host of some kind, you may elect to emulate a 3270 terminal (for older 370-class mainframes) or a 5250 terminal (for AS/400s and System 3x machines). If that's the case, you'll probably run a specially adapted version of Telnet called *tn3270* or *tn5250*, respectively. Please consult your software manual for the details.

Most PC- and Macintosh-based Telnet implementations give you all kinds of bells and whistles you can't get from host-based versions. The local power of the desktop machine and access to a GUI (for Windows and Macintosh users) makes all kinds of things possible that a character-mode terminal can't do. These bells and whistles include things like keyboard reassignments, virtual keyboard (windows with little keys on them that you can select with the mouse or define alternate keystrokes for), task switching, file paste and copy, and much, much more. Again, consult your software manual and be prepared to learn about some pretty amazing things!

Telnet Commands

Another way to get to the command mode in Telnet is to start the program without including a domain name or IP address on the invoking line. This will produce the `telnet>` prompt, where you'll stay in command mode until you open a Telnet session on a remote host.

Once you are connected to a remote host, most Telnet commands will execute and then return you to terminal mode. Otherwise, if you simply hit the enter or return key at a `telnet>` prompt, you should immediately drop into terminal mode.

Table 14.1 includes a list of the most common Telnet commands, with brief one-line explanations taken from the help file. There are only ten such commands in our implementation, which is about on a par with most others we have seen. For your convenience, we include the most important and commonly used commands in boldface, with the others in plain text. Telnet commands can be abbreviated, as long as they're unique—in other words, `c` is good enough for close, because it's

Command	Explanation
close	Close current connection
display	Display operating parameters
mode	Try to enter line-by-line or character-at-a-time mode
open	Connect to a site
quit	Exit telnet
send	Transmit special characters ("send ?" for more)
set	Set operating parameters ("set ?" for more)
status	Print status information
toggle	Toggle operating parameters ("toggle ?" for more)
z	Suspend telnet
help, ?	Print help information

Table 14.1 *The Telnet Commands*

the only command that starts with a *c*, but **sen** is necessary to distinguish it from set.

If you use the **z** command, Telnet will suspend its operations and return you to the command shell automatically. To restore it to action, enter the **fg** (foreground) command, which takes the process most recently moved into the background and puts it back into the foreground. It's sort of equivalent to the **!** (bang) command in FTP, but requires more action on your part to get back into the program.

Getting Help

To learn more about Telnet, you can consult a variety of sources. We recommend that you start with the program's help facility. Entering **help** or **?** inside the Telnet program will only produce one-line help information. The Telnet program will also tell you more about itself if you go into command mode and then enter a command followed by a **?** (question mark).

Your next stop should be the program's man pages. The **man** file for Telnet is worth printing, so you can use it as a reference. After that, you could consult the governing RFCs for Telnet (RFCs 854 and 855), but we recommend obtaining a detailed TCP/IP reference like one of those documented in the TCP/IP section of the Publications List at the end of chapter 27. Also, if you purchased a TCP/IP implementation for your desktop computer, chances are its documentation will include pretty detailed coverage of the version of Telnet that it includes.

Multistage and Multisession Telnet

Sometimes you'll have to piggyback Telnet sessions, where you Telnet from one host to another and then from that host to yet another, to make connections that otherwise would be impossible. In some cases, this will be because you can't get directly from your local host to the remote host; but by Telnetting to an intermediate host, you can get to the desired host. In other cases, you'll Telnet into one host to get access to high-speed modems or network links that might not be available if you went direct.

Multistage Telnet takes a little getting used to and requires you to pay attention to your links and the time and resources you consume in the intermediate stages. A computer, after all, resembles a pie to the extent that it can be cut into only so many pieces. By using a host machine as a Telnet intermediate, you consume CPU cycles, a pair of Telnet ports, and a login session. This may not sound like much, but it does cost the other users some diminishment of that machine's capacity and capabilities. And, you're not really using it as anything but a step-ping-stone to get to where you really want to go. The rule here is to be considerate and not use this technique during prime working hours if at all possible, and to get it over with as soon as you can.

Multisession Telnet happens when you fire off multiple copies of the Telnet program to allow yourself to access more than one remote host simultaneously. Here again, the same consumption phenomena (multi-ple Telnet ports, extra CPU consumption, etc.) happens as with multi-stage Telnet, except it is all on the same machine. If that machine is your own desktop, who cares—you're the only one that will suffer. If it isn't a desktop machine, observe the same rules we suggested in the preceding paragraph. Taking away CPU cycles from yourself is one thing, taking them away from other users is entirely another.

USING ANONYMOUS OR
SERVICE-BASED TELNET

Some Internet hosts will let you log in to them to use Telnet without requiring an individual account and password. This can happen through an advertised "Guest" or Anonymous Telnet facility, or it might be happening when you access an advertised service for Gopher, Archie, or some other Internet utility (under the hood, Telnet is in use as a part of the program that makes the connection to the remote host and handles communication between you and that machine).

Here again, the watchword is consideration. The resource you are accessing belongs to somebody else, and that user must bear its associated equipment, software, and maintenance costs. Chances are, the number of ports is limited and your use of one may deprive somebody else of the opportunity. Therefore, be quick to get in and get out—do as much investigation ahead of time as you can, so that you need not spend too much time wandering around to figure out where things are or what you want to do—and limit your consumption of CPU cycles, disk space, and other shared resources.

If you do have to mess with large files, or run compute-intensive software, try to arrange your schedule to work around periods of peak use. If in doubt, send an e-mail to admin@domain-name and describe what you want to do, requesting advice about how to do it in the least disruptive manner. You might be surprised how helpful others can be when you approach them respectfully and try to work within their guidelines!

Summary

In this chapter we examined the innards of Telnet, the other major workhorse Internet application. The most important thing to remember is that Telnet opens a window across the network for you onto another machine. To make the best use of this window, you have to learn how things work on the other side. Most of your interactions using Telnet will be with the operating system and software on the remote host. The more you can learn about these things, the better-equipped to handle them you'll be. For most of us, this means learning more about UNIX. For all of us, it means being respectful of the rest of the computing community that's sharing the resources of whatever remote hosts we are using Telnet to get to!

GOING FOR IT
YOUR INTERNET
RUNNER

THE FAMOUS RODENT

You learned in previous chapters about ftp, the program that lets you transfer files to and from other computers all over the world. You also read about telnet, a program that enables you to log in to other computers and look around, retrieve articles, search catalogs, or whatever else those machines do. The problem with these tools, though, is that every machine you go to has a different directory structure or method for navigating screens. Still, if you know pretty much what you want and more or less where it is, you can't beat ftp and telnet for effectiveness.

This is all fine, but it would be a lot easier to find information if we had some way of accessing these resources that behaved the same way on every machine. Well, that is where Gopher comes in. As you might have guessed, the name is a pun, because you tell the program what you want and Gopher goes for it. This chapter describes a bit about Gopher and what you can do with it.

A LAYER OF FRIENDLINESS

One of the main advantages of Gopher is that it uses the same set of commands no matter where you are. Whether you launch a Gopher client on a computer in Texas, Switzerland, or Canada, you always get a set of menus that lead you through your search, and you always use the same commands to get around in those menus.

Even better than the consistent user interface across Gopher clients is that every Gopher client has links to other Gopher clients. So no matter what client you start working with, you can still get to all other Gopher clients in the world by following the links.

Best of all, Gopher conceals all the details from you. That is, it knows whether it needs to get to the next computer in the chain via telnet, or whether it needs to access a certain document by issuing an ftp command, or whether it should perform a search using Veronica or WAIS. You need not know any of it. If Gopher uses telnet to get to another computer, all you see is a new Gopher menu. If Gopher retrieves a document for you using ftp, you simply see that document arrive on your client computer. And if Gopher performs a search for you using an indexed database, all you need to do is enter the keywords for which you want to search. Well, indexed searches are actually slightly more involved than that, as we discuss later in this chapter, but you can see that Gopher does a lot for you, by hiding all the tedious work of connecting to sites, navigating the directories, and retrieving files.

It is easier to show you how it works than to describe it, so let's go find some Gopher clients.

GETTING TO GOPHER

Gopher operates on the client-server model, which means that the computer you are using needs to run client software before it can access one of the computers where the Gopher server software (and all the data) is. The next step, then, is finding a computer that is running Gopher client software.

Finding a Gopher Client

The first place to look is on your very own Internet access computer. If you have a command line interface, try typing **gopher** at the command line prompt. If you have a menu interface, look through the menus for something called gopher. Of course, it can't hurt to check with your system administrator to see whether your system even has a Gopher client.

If you have no luck locally, head for the Usenet newsgroup called comp.infosystems.gopher, where you will find the FAQ about Gopher, which gets posted every few weeks or so. That should give you some tips on where to look for public Gopher clients from which you can start exploring. This newsgroup is also the place to go if you want to download the Gopher client software and set up a Gopher client on your own machine—you need a SLIP, PPP, or direct Internet connection to do so!

Assume you don't want to do that right now, you just want to try your luck gophering. If you still have found no public clients, telnet to one of the following machines and log in as "gopher." These machines are all in North America.

```
consultant.micro.umn.edu
gopher.msu.edu
sunsite.unc.edu
ux1.cso.uiuc.edu
ecosys.drdr.virginia.edu
gopher.ORA.com
```

Note that these machines are very busy, so you're better off trying them in the evenings (their time). Otherwise, they might be very slow, or might even refuse your connection if too many people are already using them.

One nice thing about Gopher clients is that they are already configured to take you to the nearest Gopher server, so you don't have to worry about finding a server. Also, as we discussed, every Gopher server is connected to every other Gopher server, so you don't have to worry about which server is the best one on which to start your search.

Nevertheless, if you must use a public Gopher client, try to find one that is not too outrageously far from you. If, for instance, you live in Idaho and know about two public Gopher clients, one in Arkansas and the other in Australia, head for the one closer to home. Not only does this minimize your impact on the Net, it can greatly improve your transmission speeds!

SOME FEATURES OF USING GOPHER

The first menu on any Gopher server is likely to have information of interest to the people who usually use that computer. If the server is maintained by a university, for instance, the first menu might have information about classes, campus events, and so on. See the example screen in Figure 15.1.

```
                    Gopher Courtesy Account Client v1.12S
                    Root gopher server: gopher.uiuc.edu

-> 1.  Welcome to the University of Illinois at Urbana-Champaign Gopher.
   2.  Campus Announcements (last updated 04/15/94)/
   3.  What's New?  (last update: 3/15/94)/
   4.  Information about Gopher/
   5.  Keyword Search of Gopher Menus <?>
   6.  Univ. of Illinois at Urbana-Champaign Campus Information/
   7.  Champaign-Urbana & Regional Information/
   8.  Computer Documentation, Software, and Information/
   9.  Libraries and Reference Information/
  10.  Newspapers, Newsletters, and Weather/
  11.  Other Gopher and Information Servers/
  12.  Phone Books (ph)/
  13.  Internet File Server (ftp) Sites/
```

Figure 15.1 *Main menu for the Gopher client at University of Illinois*

Gopher to Gopher

Every Gopher client is a bit different, but you can count on one thing: every Gopher server has an item that lets you access other Gopher servers. This item might be called *Other Gopher and Information Servers*, as it is in this example, or perhaps *Gopher Tunnels (To Other Gopher and WAIS Sites)* or some other similar title. It might also be on another menu; it's important to be flexible when dealing with Gopher. But no matter what they call it, they all have a menu item that you can use to get to other Gophers, which is one of the most powerful features of Gopher.

Types of Resources

You might notice that each menu item in the example has a symbol at the end of it. No, these are not typographical errors, rather they indicate what type of resource you get if you select that item. A dot at the end of the line, for instance, indicates that the item is a text file. If we select item #1 in the preceding example, we see a file that tells us a bit about this Gopher server and perhaps the restrictions governing its use. Other menus might direct us to files that contain more useful types of documents.

The slash symbol at the end of the menu item indicates that it is a directory item, and you can probably expect that when you select such an item, you would get—what else?—another Gopher menu. This is how you get around between servers.

Notice that item #5 ends in a question mark. This indicates that this type of resource is an indexed searching tool. When you select such a resource, Gopher prompts you for keywords on which to base the search, then passes those on to a searching program. The problem here is that every search program works slightly differently, so you might want to tailor your keywords to a particular program if you know which one Gopher is using. We address these programs, and some search techniques, in Chapters 16, 17, and 18.

You might encounter several other types of resources in your Gopher tunneling, but these are enough to get you started. We discuss some of the others in upcoming chapters.

Getting Around the Menus

Gopher usually displays some helpful instructions on the screen to help you get around, but in case you can't see them, remember that *u* always takes you up to the previous menu, and that the arrow keys move you around within menus. Typing a question mark (**?**) usually brings up a help screen in case you have more questions.

SUMMARY

This chapter gave you a brief overview to using Gopher. As you learn more about indexed searching services in the next few chapters, you'll find that Gopher is even more powerful and useful than we indicated here. So find yourself a Gopher client and start looking around—it's even easier to use than it sounds!

ARCHIE AND VERONICA

16

LOST IN RIVERDALE?

In this chapter we continue our examination of the preferred Internet search tools that we began in the last chapter with Gopher. Here, you'll learn about two additional tools named Archie and Veronica. While it might sound like we wandered off the Internet and onto the pages of a comic book set in the mythical middle American community of Riverdale, that is not the case. Like the names of many of the second generation Internet programs, these two have their humorous side. Who knows, maybe this is a reaction to the somewhat somber and sterile names for first-generation Internet programs like *ftp* or *telnet*.

While their names don't appear to be any more self-documenting that those for the first-generation tools, both Archie and Veronica offer considerable functionality to their users. We discuss both of these programs in detail shortly, but for now it's wise to think of Archie as a tool that can search the directories of Anonymous FTP servers all over the place, and Veronica as the equivalent search tool for the vast collection of Gopher information on the Internet that has come to be known as *Gopherspace*.

In fact, it is safe to think of both of these programs as intelligent indexing tools, developed primarily to help users locate and wade through the vast amount of information stored in FTP and Gopher servers around the world. Think of them as your navigational assistants, able to help you find where to go and what to ask for when looking for particular items. Once you've spent much time navigating directories on FTP servers or plowing through menus on Gopher servers, you'll really appreciate the "cut to the chase" directions that these two tools can give!

Because the root servers for much of the information we cover in this book are often hard to log in to, you could use Archie to help you find a closer, less heavily used FTP server that could provide a file that you otherwise might not be able to get to. Likewise Veronica might help you to find a Gopher server off the beaten track that nevertheless contains just the material you're looking for.

Archie = Archive – V

Like we said, there is some humor in the name of this program. Its inventors claim—with their tongues stuck firmly in their cheeks—that Archie really stands for "archive minus the letter v (for volume)," as the strange heading of this section is meant to indicate. This is pretty consistent with Archie's job of handling searches of Anonymous FTP server directories to locate files by name, in that it will comb through a large collection of such servers on your behalf and let you simply decide if it has found what you want, rather than having to go look for it all by yourself.

The way Archie really works is to plow through a collection of comprehensive directory listings for a large number of Anonymous FTP servers (over 2,000 of them worldwide, as this book is being written, with more being added daily). When using Archie, it is important to remember that it doesn't actually examine the contents of any files; it examines merely a set of comprehensive directory listings for a large number of FTP servers on the Internet.

Archie: The Early Years . . .

Like many Internet tools and technologies, Archie is a program that started life as the result of a "throwaway" task, but that succeeded beyond its inventors' wildest dreams. The whole thing stems from a project assigned to a McGill School of Computer Science graduate student, named Alan Emtage, who was assigned to monitor what public-domain software could be found for free on Anonymous FTP sites.

Because McGill had little budget for software, this meant they had to stretch what dollars they had.

At first, Emtage would connect to each of the FTP sites he knew about, one at a time, and obtain a comprehensive directory listing. He could then compare this listing to a previous one to see what had been added since his last visit. Emtage quickly realized that the degree of monotony in this task made it unusually well-suited for computerization, so he started off by writing UNIX shell scripts to automate the Anonymous FTP sessions that generated the file listings. He then added the ability to compare a prior listing to a new one, to identify what was new (and potentially interesting).

The results of all this work was a list of files for each FTP server, with all the necessary directory information needed to uniquely identify and locate any file. Since this list was itself a file, by using the UNIX pattern-recognition program, **grep**, Emtage could quickly locate any file by name on demand. This practice attracted notice from his colleagues, and his boss Peter Deutsch, and became a popular local activity.

At some point later, Deutsch noticed a Usenet newsgroup request for a particular file with definite location restrictions (it had to come from outside the United States). With Emtag's tool in hand, by now polished to a high gloss, Deutsch had no trouble coming up with lots of possibilities and was rapidly able to reply to the request. This quick response led to more requests, which in turn led Deutsch to commission his group to build some tools to query the file listing files so that any user could do (and leave him and his staff alone).

Thus, Archie was born. From these impromptu beginnings, it has gotten big—today, most Archies cover over 2,000 file collections—and popular—it is widely recognized as one of the most popular Internet tools currently in use!

Archie Architecture

Archie consists of multiple components, all of which work together to handle end-user queries, examine the relevant databases, and report the results. We examine these elements in the subsections that follow.

Data Collection and Database Construction

Archie's ultimate value still derives from its access to comprehensive listings of FTP and other servers out on the Internet. Just as in the

McGill days, special programs still regularly visit a targeted (and growing) list of archives out on the Internet. Today, the resulting files are processed and added to a comprehensive database that includes file names, directory locations, and related server names. This data collection and database generation software has been made widely available, so that sites can build their own Archie databases at will, and they contribute to the overall availability of information to the whole Internet community. This also lets new sites provide Archie access almost immediately, as soon as one brings an Anonymous FTP server on-line.

Once installed, an Archie server regularly polls other Archie servers to update its own databases. The polling and update intervals can be established by the system administrator, so that local archives could be polled frequently but remote ones only occasionally. This lets administrators trade off the freshness of the Archie information against the time and resources required to access remote servers across the Internet.

The Archie DBMS Servers

Once the data has been collected and the underlying databases constructed, Archie uses special programs to maintain these databases, to support information queries and provide the server end of the Archie program (which, like so many other TCP/IP applications, adheres to the client-server model). This software handles the queries that you direct to Archie across the network, looks things up in the related databases, and sends back a reply.

In addition, the Archie programs have been explicitly designed to coordinate and cooperate with their peers around the network. This makes it possible for multiple copies of the entire Archie database to exist and for them to remain relatively well-synchronized. Because the database can be accessed at multiple locations, no one location gets swamped with requests, and everybody's query load can be balanced. This makes Archie an inherently distributed information service, which is something of a rarity, even on the Internet.

Archie Client Software

Following the client-server model, Archie requires a local front-end program to permit users to access the Archie database. Today Archie front ends are available for PCs, Macintoshes, OS/2, and a variety of UNIX machines. If you can't find a version for your desktop machine, you can still probably get access via your local Internet host. To find out, simply Telnet to that host, and type

```
Archie ?
```

at the command prompt. If you get a response from the program, rather than a "Command not found" message, you're ready to go!

Archie's Other Database "Hits"

Today, Archie has been put to work to manage multiple collections of data, not just the holdings in FTP archives around the Internet. Though this still remains its best known and most popular use, Archie offers at least one other interesting alternative applications. Likewise, there is no inherent limitation to its abilities that says that other distributed databases of information built around Archie won't be showing up from an Internet service provider near you soon!

The "Whatis" DBMS

Starting in 1992, Archie's interactive users gained the ability to access the so-called whatis database, which includes a collection of descriptions of over 5,000 public-domain or freeware programs, data collections, and on-line documents located all around the Internet. For each entry, the database contains a brief text description of its contents. This makes it less far-reaching, but more informative, than the FTP database because it references much less material, but provides the ability to search by subject or keyword as well as by file name.

Archie: Commands and Search Methods

Archie comes in two flavors: interactive and noninteractive. The interactive version requires you to obtain a copy of the Archie client software for your computer. The noninteractive version is one you would use on most Telnet hosts (except for those listed in Table 16.1; these offer Telnet-based interactive Archie, too). We briefly discuss each kind in the subsections that follow.

Noninteractive Archie

The following screen shot is typical of the response you get if you enter "archie" at the command prompt on an average Internet host running UNIX—that is, from one of the legion of hosts not in the list in Table

Server name	IP Address	Location
archie.au	139.130.4.6	Australia
archie.edvz.uni-linz.ac.at	140.78.3.8	Austria
archie.univie.ac.at	131.130.1.23	Austria
archie.uqam.ca	132.208.250.10	Canada
archie.funet.fi	128.214.6.102	Finland
archie.univ-rennes1.fr	129.20.128.38	France
archie.th-darmstadt.de	130.83.128.118	Germany
archie.ac.il	132.65.16.18	Israel
archie.unipi.it	131.114.21.10	Italy
archie.wide.ad.jp	133.4.3.6	Japan
archie.hana.nm.kr	128.134.1.1	Korea
archie.sogang.ac.kr	163.239.1.11	Korea
archie.uninett.no	128.39.2.20	Norway
archie.rediris.es	130.206.1.2	Spain
archie.luth.se	130.240.12.30	Sweden
archie.switch.ch	130.59.1.40	Switzerland
archie.nctuccca.edu.tw	N/A	Taiwan
archie.ncu.edu.tw	192.83.166.12	Taiwan
archie.doc.ic.ac.uk	146.169.11.3	United Kingdom
archie.hensa.ac.uk	129.12.21.25	United Kingdom
archie.unl.edu	129.93.1.14	USA (NE)
archie.internic.net	198.49.45.10	USA (NJ)
archie.rutgers.edu	128.6.18.15	USA (NJ)
archie.ans.net	147.225.1.10	USA (NY)
archie.sura.net	128.167.254.179	USA (MD)

Table 16.1 *Master Archie Servers, Worldwide (as of 7/94)*

16.1. We use this screen to explain how to use noninteractive Archie, including the options and its workings.

```
oak.zilker.net> archie
Usage: archie [-[cers][l][t][m#][h host][L][N#]] string
        -c : case sensitive substring search
        -e : exact string match (default)
        -r : regular expression search
        -s : case insensitive substring search
        -l : list one match per line
        -t : sort inverted by date
       -m# : specifies maximum number of hits to return
             (default 95)
    -h host : specifies server host
        -L : list known servers and current default
       -N# : specifies query niceness level (0-35765)
```

The first thing to note is that this version of Archie expects to get command switches and arguments on the same line where the program is invoked. Using Archie without any such additional information results in the help message you see above.

After the command name (archie) comes a range of possible switches, as follows:

-c *case-sensitive substring search.* This means pay attention to upper and lower case when searching for substrings (parts of) file names, or other database fields.

-e *exact string match* (default). This means that Archie should search for the string exactly as you specified it; (default) means that this is the option that's set if you specify none of **c**, **e**, **r**, or **s**.

-r *regular expression search.* Lets you specify different kinds of substitution mechanisms for pattern matching on strings (check **man** pages for "regular expressions" for more information).

-s *case insensitive substring search.* This means match all case variants for a supplied string (i.e., the string **ABC** would therefore match ABC, abc, Abc, ABc, aBC, abC, aBc).

-1 *list one match per line.* This shows one file specification per line (default is two lines per match, which makes listings more compact).

-t *sort inverted by date.* This lists newest files first, instead of last.

-m *specifies maximum number of hits to return* (default 95). This indicates the maximum number of matches to report (normally it stops at 95).

-h *specifies server host.* To search only a single host follow *h* with a host name; to search a domain, follow *h* with *.edu*, or whatever.

-L *list known servers and current default.* This shows a list of the Archie servers that the client knows about (Table 16.1 comes from one of the master servers and is a comprehensive list of its peers).

-N# *specifies query niceness level (0–35765).* This is a good-neighbor switch; the bigger the number you supply, the less resources you will consume on the remote host (but the longer your replies will take).

Please note that you can select only one of **c**, **e**, **r**, or **s** (that is what their grouping inside a single set of square brackets means). If you do specify the **h** switch, it should come last, since you have to leave a space between it and the host name you're supplying. If you use either **m** or **N**, follow it immediately with the number of your choice (e.g., **m20** or **N16535**).

The string you specify is the most important part, because it's what Archie will look for. Unless you're absolutely sure you know the file name (perhaps you could try Archie to look for one of the files we mentioned in this book), use the **-c** switch to make the search case insensitive. This improves the odds of finding what you're looking for, even if it does result in larger replies to your queries.

Here are some sample noninteractive Archie commands, with explanations (following the exclamation point, don't type these or what follows if you try them out!):

```
archie -cth *.edu whatis.archie      !get file named
                                     whatis.archie from any
                                     education server; sort
                                     newest first


archie -s archie                     !get all files that include
                                     archie, in !upper or lower
                                     case, in their names
```

Interactive Archie

If you've got an Archie client for your desktop machine or log in to one of the interactive Archie hosts (like those named in Table 16.1), you'll interact with Archie in much the same way as ftp or command mode for telnet. That is, you'll see a prompt that looks like **archie>** at the beginning of each line, at which point you can start entering commands from the list in Table 16.2.

We strongly recommend that you start your first encounter with this version of Archie with the following commands

```
set pager
help manpage
```

The first command tells Archie to use the UNIX **less** command to show you only a screenful of information at a time before moving on (hit the spacebar for the next screen, the **q** key to quit when you get to the end). The second command tells Archie to show you the system's man pages on itself. These are chock full of useful information, so you'll probably want to turn on your screen or file capture capabilities, if you've got them, as well.

If you need to do complicated pattern matching on file names, you'll want to read the man pages on "regular expressions" as well as what's in the Archie man pages. This is a pretty complicated, but powerful, notation that will really let you manage the hits that Archie can generate when searching its database.

Program Control Commands

Command	Explanation
quit	end Archie session and exit program

Help/Information Commands

Command	Explanation
help ?	show list of commands
help *command*	show help information for *command*
manpage	show Archie manual page
servers	show list of Archie servers

Search Commands

Command	Explanation
find *string*	search FTP database for *string*
whatis *string*	search whatis database for *string*
mail	ship results of last search to **mailto** address

Variable Settings

Command	Explanation
show	shows values for all definable variables
show *variable*	show setting for *variable*

Settable Variables	usage: set *variable* from list below
Command	**Explanation**
autologout	idle time before autologout in minutes
mailto	Internet e-mail address to ship search results to
maxhits	maximum matches, total, returned; default = 99, you may want to set this lower)
maxmatch	maximimum filename repetitions allowed
output_format	can be **terse**, **verbose**, or **machine**-readable
pager	use UNIX **less** command to control screen enter **unset pager** to turn off
search	establish search behavior for pattern matching similar to noninteractive, with values of **exact**: match pattern exactly **sub**: search for any string containing pattern **subcase**: any string but distinguish upper/lower case **regex**: search for regular expression **exact_sub=e**, then **sub**; **exact_subcase=e**, then **subcase** **exact_regex=e**, then **regex**
sortby	**none, filename, hostname, size, time** **r** in front (e.g. **rsize**) reverses sort order
status	display status line during search (completion time info) enter **unset status** to turn off

Table 16.2 *Interactive Archie Commands*

After that, you should be able to get by with the bold commands in Table 16.2. Note that find searches the FTP database, and that whatis searches the whatis database. Remember to quit to exit the program, and you should be able to get right to it!

The Archie E-mail Alternative

So far, you've learned that, in addition to using an Archie client on your own machine or local Telnet host, you can Telnet to one of the Archie servers that supports interactive Archie and drive the program for yourself. For those in no rush for results, those who have trouble logging in to an interactive Archie server (these are really busy—we had to try many, many times to get logged in), or who have no client access to Archie, yet another method is available: You can also send Archie commands by e-mail and receive the results the same way.

To use Archie via e-mail send a message at the userid archie at the address of one of the servers listed in Table 16.1 (e.g., archie@archie.sura.net). When composing the body of the message, remember that the subject field is treated as the first Archie command (or you can leave it blank, if your e-mail software will permit it), and that each line in the message is treated as an Archie command.

With only a few exceptions, e-mail Archie commands are identical to the interactive ones. The only ones you shouldn't use are the display controls (like **set pager** and **unset pager**) that mean nothing for a batch-oriented, e-mail-based use of Archie. For equally obvious reasons, your first command should always be the **set mailto <username>@<host-name>**. Even though Archie will use the sender's address from your message by default, you can never be too explicit when doing things by e-mail! Finally, make sure the last command in your message is always **quit**—that way, you'll be sure to consume only the minimum necessary amount of machine resources on the Archie server, rather than force an autologout on an e-mail inquiry (which is kind of rude, we think).

VERONICA

As Archie is an FTP-based tool—at least in its original implementation, anyway—so Veronica is a tool for searching Gopherspace. Actually, what Veronica does is to search menu entries in Gopher menus on Gopher servers everywhere (or everywhere that it can get to) to look for the search strings you specified. That means it's quite like Archie, in a lot of ways.

A Tool Within a Tool . . .

Unlike Archie, though, you'll find Veronica within the Gopher menus on your client software, rather than having to run it as a separate program (in fact, many Gopher implementations will let you run Archie from inside them as well as WWW, WAIS, and other Internet tools).

To find where Veronica hangs out, look for a menu entry that reads something like

```
4.   Search titles in Gopherspace using veronica/
```

Many times, Veronica shows up under the same heading as the list of Gopher servers, so it might show up under a menu item like:

```
5.   Other Gopher and Information Servers
```

In fact, this is the kind of entry where you would find Archie, WWW, WAIS, and other tools, too!

Using Veronica

Once you locate and select the right menu entry, you'll be ready to use Veronica. If you place this entry into your personal bookmark list by using the **add** (**a**) command, you'll be able to get back to it at any time by using the **view** (**v**) command, which displays a menu of those bookmarks.

The top-level menu for Veronica typically looks something like this:

```
           Search titles in Gopherspace using veronica
  ->1. Search Gopherspace using veronica at NYSERNet <?>
     2. Search Gopherspace using veronica at AT&T InterNIC <?>
     3. Search Gopherspace for GOPHER DIRECTORIES (NYSERNet)<?>
     4. Search Gopherspace for GOPHER DIRECTORIES (AT&T
        InterNIC) <?>
     5. How to compose veronica queries.
     6. FAQ: Frequently-Asked-Questions about veronica.
```

To make a general query, select items 1 or 2 (the principle of locality holds here: always choose the server closest to you; for us that would be the InterNIC). Once you select the server, Veronica will prompt you for a search string:

```
+----Search Gopherspace using veronica at AT&T InterNIC----+
|                                                          |
|Words to search for _____ |
|                                                          |
|                         [Cancel ^G] [Accept - Enter]     |
|                                                          |
+----------------------------------------------------------+
```

We're going to ask Veronica about Archie, so we type **archie** and press the enter key. As soon as this happens Veronica will search Gopherspace for menu items that contain the word *archie*. The results will be displayed in a menu that you can then make further selections from. Unfortunately, since most Gopher implementations include a way to invoke Archie, the results are pretty useless, but it does show that wherever Veronica is, Archie is not far away.

The best thing about using Veronica is that it behaves like Gopher and uses the same menus and display conventions you are already used to. Moreover, Veronica is capable of doing some interesting search operations. For instance, by specifying the string **faq** along with **archie** on the search request, we would find all menus that relate to Frequently-Asked-Questions documents and Archie on the same line. This might be more of what we had in mind.

Furthermore, Veronica supports Boolean operations on the strings you specify, including **and, or,** and **not**. This means you can ask Veronica to find menu entries where both words are present (**and**), or only one and not the other (word1 **and not** word2) **or** (word2 **and not** word1), or either one or the other (word1 **or** word2).

To round out its capabilities, Veronica also supports the wild card character * (asterisk), so that you can match substrings within words. For example, you could tell Veronica to look for *fondness, fondue,* and *fonts* by telling it to look for **fon***. Actually, you could find any menu entry with the consecutive letters *fon* by telling Veronica to look for ***fon***.

Take another look at the screen output for the top-level Veronica menu and take note of the distinction between Gopherspace and GOPHER DIRECTORIES. If you are sure that what you're looking for is a menu, not a document or program, select a directory-focused search. This will speed the search time, get you your answer quicker, and save more CPU cycles for other users. What more could you possibly want?

Getting to Know Veronica Better . . .

If you want to learn more about how to use this tool, a good place to start is with menu entry number 5, "How to compose veronica queries." This document covers all of the gory details of the Boolean operators, using wild cards, and a great deal more on how to tell Veronica exactly what you want. The next stop on the way to getting to know Veronica better is on item number 6, which will help you retrieve the Frequently-Asked-Questions file on Veronica. This, too, will provide lots of useful information on how to use the program.

Beyond that, you could try asking Veronica to tell you about herself. Over the years, we've learned that a question like that can provoke all kinds of interesting answers. Make sure you do some creative query phrasing, or you'll learn only that Veronica is a common menu entry on Gopher servers everywhere.

And Now . . . It's Jughead!

In keeping with the Riverdale tradition, there's even a special edition of Veronica available in some locations. It's called *Jughead*, and represents a kind of Gopher menu search tool that limits itself to purely local Gopher servers. It's used in campus or organizational settings, where it's useful to be able to search information about nearby resources, documents, and more.

SUMMARY

In this chapter we investigated two powerful search tools, Archie and Veronica, that should help you get a handle on the tremendous amount of information stored in FTP archives and Gopher servers all around the Internet. We suggest that you try these programs to locate some of the other files and resources we mentioned in the book thus far, as a way of proving to yourselves just how useful these tools really are. It's no wonder that some people think that, without them, neither Gopher nor FTP would be as useful as they currently appear to be.

WIDE-AREA INFORMATION SERVICE

17

"WE HAVE WAIS OF MAKING YOU TALK!"

At this point, you've learned about Internet tools that can help you search Anonymous FTP archives and software collections (Archie), and to browse through Gopher menus (Veronica and Jughead). You've also learned that these tools attach to servers that offer database engines that browse through text information that has been collected from archive directory listings and from Gopher menu items by specialized software that knows how to go out and obtain this information on a regular basis.

This is really great, because it means that as long as you know the name of a file or some text from a menu entry, one of these programs can go out and find it for you. But what happens when all you know is the topic you need information about or you're not sure that the keywords you know correspond to the ones that have already been indexed. Over time, as you get familiar with Archie and Veronica you'll notice that some searches will come back empty, simply because there's no match between what you've requested and what is in the respective databases. You may also encounter collections of data that are so big, or have so many potential sources of information, that neither Archie nor Veronica can handle them.

This is where WAIS comes in: The program is designed to spread itself across the network, to work on multiple archives and data formats, and to search tirelessly for the information you request throughout the Internet. WAIS is pronounced "ways" (as in the *Ways* and Means Committee in the United States Senate) or "wase" (as in *waist* without the final *t*). WAIS can help you find things, especially when you're not sure of exact file names, menu entries, or other indexing characteristics.

LOOKING FOR CONTENT? USE WAIS . . .

In fact, WAIS differs from the tools we covered so far in that it looks inside the items that are stored, rather than just looking at file names and locations (Archie's FTP database), program names and descriptions (Archie's "whatis" database), or Gopher menus and document names (Veronica and Jughead). This means that WAIS examines an even more stupefying amount of information that any of these other programs and can find things that no index-only search could ever turn up.

WAIS differs from the other programs in another significant way: It was developed as a commercial application of database technology by the now-bankrupt supercomputer vendor Thinking Machines Corporation, working together with Apple Computer, Dow Jones' News Retrieval Division, and featured KMPG Peat Marwick as a sort of corporate guinea pig that would use, and help to refine, the resulting software.

Why this combination of organizations, you ask? Well, here comes an explanation based on enlightened self-interest. Each organization had a lot to gain from a successful implementation of such an experiment, as follows:

1. Thinking Machines saw supercomputers as necessary tools to deal with the volume of data involved and sought to develop a new market for its products. WAIS could conceivably create more demand for supercomputers capable of dealing with huge volumes of information quickly and efficiently.

2. Apple saw a need for broad-based information access for end-users and sought to find a new application to make its desktop machines more attractive to purchasers. A powerful WAIS client could make its machines much more useful in the workplace; Apple could also trade on its user-friendly image to induce more people to try the software than otherwise might.

3. Dow Jones is in the content business and is always looking for new ways to deliver that content to its customers. Growth in the popularity of WAIS could easily lead to more information sales for

the News Retrieval group and could help it exploit some internal developments in information retrieval technology.

4. KPMG Peat Marwick, as a consulting and business development company, is in the information analysis business; the more high-quality information it can get to its analysts, the more money it can make. WAIS stood to make the company much more capable at finding and analyzing the information it needed, and letting it handle more customers better than ever before.

Given that everybody had a lot to win, it's no wonder that they all pitched in with a vengeance to help build this environment.

WAIS Design Principles

Given that WAIS was a commercial venture, its designers had to justify the program first and then build it. This, too, is a big difference from many of the other Internet tools available, many of which emerged from toolsets that system administrators put together for themselves or from the "Wouldn't it be neat if . . ." school of computer programming. Here is what the WAIS designers set out to accomplish: They wanted the program to be

- Inherently networked, and they aimed it at distributed collections of data from the very first.
- Super easy to use, and they used a "natural language" approach in building the query interface.
- Fast and efficient, and they used a friendly, simple front-end hook-up to a superpowerful, superfast back end.
- Smart, so it would look for partial matches on search terms and could even use synonyms to help find unexpected material (this was based on a search technique developed at Dow Jones called *relevance feedback,* which lets a user select an example of what he or she wants and use "find some more like this" as a search instruction).
- Automatic, so that users could save searches and have them automatically repeat at certain intervals (to provide notification when new information shows up).

Judging from its enthusiastic reception on the Internet, WAIS has met its designers' expectations and really wowed its users. The initial test at

Peat Marwick, even at $300 per hour per user, was a howling success. It was so successful, in fact, that by mid-1992, developers at Thinking Machines (and other Internet sites) had built WAIS client software for a variety of UNIX hosts, VAXen running VMS, and for PCs or workstations running DOS, MS Windows, Macintosh, and NextStep.

Working with WAIS

Even though the initial use of WAIS was in a pay-as-you-go commercial environment, the program has still attracted a great deal of attention and use on the Internet. Because the program's developers used the Internet to communicate with one another and because the Internet has been an ongoing testbed where users around the world can test-drive the application (it remains that way to this day), the connection between WAIS and the Internet has always been a strong one. At present, many information collections for resources and services on the Internet can be searched by WAIS, and WAIS is becoming a tool of choice for individuals seeking either free or fee-based access to information via the Internet.

By the time WAIS started showing up on all kinds of computers around the Internet in 1992, it also began to assert itself as an important search tool for information. In addition to a great variety of databases, both free and commercial, WAIS can also access things like Internet mailing lists, Usenet newsgroups, and newsfeeds, among others. This means that it can cover a huge amount of territory to find what you're looking for, including much of the news traffic from the Internet itself.

Firing up the Program

The only way to use WAIS is first to gain access to a WAIS client (like most other TCP/IP-based applications, WAIS follows the client-server approach). If WAIS is available on your system, run that version. Most experts agree that a GUI-based implementation such as those for MS Windows, Macintosh, or X-Windows is superior to a text-based version, so use one of these if you can. Otherwise, use what you can get!

If you have to Telnet to a public WAIS server, like the one operated by Thinking Machines at quake.think.com, simply login as "wais" and provide your real Internet name as a password (this helps them keep track of who's using the equipment). In this case, you'll be presented with a character-mode interface. Be sure to use the "?" to get help on the syntax for WAIS commands.

Selecting Data Sources

The WAIS application typically begins with a "directory-of-servers" screen, where you'll pick the information sources you want to browse or use keywords to help you find such sources. Once you've narrowed down the information sources you want to search, select them by highlighting, using the arrow keys, and pressing the spacebar (or doing whatever a GUI implementation wants; typically, pointing, and double-clicking).

You can select as many, or as few, but at least one data source for your queries. When you're done, striking *S* will return you to the sources window to show you what you've selected. Now, you're ready to start querying these sources for the information you're really after.

Searching with WAIS

The command mode for searches is to strike the *W* key, which will then prompt you for a list of keywords. Enter each one, separating individual key words by spaces, to specify your query. For instance, if you wanted to find information on a WAIS client for your computer (let's assume it's a Macintosh PowerBook) you'd enter:

```
Enter keywords (separated by spaces): WAIS client PowerBook Macintosh
```

and then strike the Enter key. At that point, WAIS will go off to the data sources you specified and perform its searches, which will then appear as yet another list that you can examine.

When presented with that list, you can select individual elements and strike the *V* key to view them on-screen, or the *M* key to have them e-mailed to you. Each time you strike this key, you'll be prompted for the appropriate e-mail address (if your front-end program supports a paste buffer, load it with your e-mail address and save yourself some keystrokes).

As before, GUI implementations of WAIS will have equivalent functionality, but vastly different commands and keystrokes. Since we can't cover them all, we simply suggest that you look for menu and program selection equivalents to the actions we describe. Because the number of commands and options, in total, is probably under 30 or 40, even an exhaustive search of everything shouldn't take you that long!

Unlike any of the other tools we looked at before, WAIS also differs in that it will retrieve items for you. For text or other viewable information, this will allow you to learn information you might very well need. For binary files of all kinds, it will allow you to pilot subsequent Anonymous FTP sessions with all the precision you'll need to get exactly what you need later on.

Some Cultural Notes

WAIS servers are in very high demand on the Internet, especially those that are free for public use. As you'll quickly learn when you try to use them, these resources are either extremely slow, because of the load they're carrying, or unavailable, because all their "wais" Telnet connections are already in use.

Whenever it comes to free resources on the Internet, the rules of the road should be very clear:

1. Learn as much as you can about the program or facility before you use it. Read the FAQ, look for tutorials or other training files, talk to others who may have more expertise than you.
2. Try to plan out what you're going to be doing, or at least what you're after, before you try to log into the resource.
3. Try to find the peak usage times, and plan on accessing the resource during off hours.
4. Use only what you need to, for exactly as long as you need to (you'll find very narrow windows—3 minutes on some systems we used—before "inactivity disconnects" log you out in any case.

WAIS Commands

These are the commands you see for *swais*, the "simple WAIS" implementation available by FTPing to accounts named "wais" on servers that support this service. Again, while the commands and their syntax will differ considerably from GUI implementation to GUI implementation, the capabilities should remain pretty consistent (although the convenience factor goes way up—as we said earlier, if you can use a GUI version, please do).

Table 17.1 covers a list of basic WAIS commands, from the swais version. As usual, we boldfaced the ones you'll probably find most important. We now take you through a scenario of how to use them. As you get more experienced with the program, you'll be motivated to learn more about the others. (Remember, the notation ^P means strike the Ctrl key at the same time as the *P* key! Also two keys separated by commas means that one or the other combination works—don't key in *j* Ctrl-N, key in either *j* or Ctrl-N.)

Command Key(s)	Explanation
j, ^N	Move Down one item (arrow keys work, too)
k, ^P	Move Up one item (arrow keys work, too)
J	Move Down one screen
K	Move Up one screen
R	Show relevant documents
s	Save current item to a file
m	Mail current item to an address
##	Position to item number ##
/sss	Position to item beginning sss
<space>	Display current item (when selecting items)
<return>	Display current item (when selecting items)
<space>, <period>	Select current source (when selecting sources)
=	Deselect all sources (when selecting sources)
d	Deselect current source (when selecting sources)
|	Pipe current item into a UNIX command
u	Use this item, add it to the list of sources
v	View current item information
r	Make current item a relevant document
s	Specify new sources to search
w	Make another search with new keywords
o	Set and show swais options
h	Show this help display
H	Display program history
q	Leave this program

Table 17.1 *WAIS Command List*

Once you log in to WAIS, you'll either be presented with a list of sources or simply be presented the opportunity to browse the master directory list (the source of all sources, as it were). When searching this list, strike the v key to examine a description of any item's contents; then strike the u key to select it for future searches. Once you've narrowed down your list, strike w to create a query based on a list of the keywords that you'll supply. Examine the resulting list for items of interest, using v to view, S to save to a file, or m to mail to you.

Then, like the recipes say, repeat as often as necessary! It's really not too complex. The only part you'll see in commercial or GUI clients is the "find something like this" capability, which, unfortunately, is missing from publicly available implementations. As long as you're careful about remembering when you manipulate sources (collections of data) versus items (individual objects stored in collections) you should have no problem figuring out how to get useful information out of WAIS.

SUMMARY

In this chapter we looked at what is possibly the most powerful Internet search or navigation tool available. Because it covers such a wide collection of data and can handle more sophisticated searches than its companion utilities, you'll undoubtedly want to give it a try. Just be prepared to wait a while if you're going to use a publicly available implementation, because the demand for WAIS seriously exceeds the current supply. Although it may hurt your pocketbook, you may want to consider trying a for-a-fee version if you ever need to get any serious work done with WAIS.

You should also look into finding a WAIS client for your desktop, if you're not running with a terminal or only have terminal-emulation capabilities. Use Archie to look for "wais" as a substring search, and you should be able to find exactly what you need!

RESOURCE GUIDE

III

*B*y now, you should be familiar with the protocols and technologies that help to make up the Internet and that make it possible for so many people to access. We sincerely hope that you've acquired an appreciation for the ordinary activities involved in running applications and have a feeling for the extraordinary variety and quantity of information available "out there" on the Internet.

In this part of the book we take a look at some of what is indeed out there, as we examine some rules of the road for traversing the Internet and move on to explore a small fraction of the interesting material that the Internet can deliver.

At this point in the book—assuming you've read Parts I and II—you should be familiar with the history of and protocols on the Internet and with a number of Internet applications that you'll need to know to partake of its bounty. In fact, you should feel comfortable with the difference between TCP and UDP and understand the difference between a fully qualified Internet name and a numeric IP address. You should also know when it's appropriate to use Telnet versus FTP, and what's special (if anything) about Anonymous FTP. Likewise, the term *Gopherspace* should conjure up a particular approach to Internet information, and the names Archie, Veronica, and Jughead should suggest more than a comic book!

If any of this material sounds unfamiliar or strange, dig back into the chapters in Parts I and II and refresh your memory. At this point in the book, we have covered all of the material needed for a general book on understanding and using the basic building blocks and technologies that make up the Internet. This section of the book covers a collection of rules of netiquette and also includes guided tours and explorations of a number of important topics and data collections. Use it as a reference tool before you go out to tackle the Internet or as a guide back into Parts I and II. However you approach it, we hope you find it both informative and useful!

We have to leave you with one important caveat here at the beginning of Part III. The information in this book is in print and was probably collected a while ago. Some of it will be incorrect because it's out of date, and some of it will be irrelevant because of new developments between the time it was written and the time it's being read. Remember, always go out and check what's available on the subject on the Internet (and check the dates on the stuff you look at). The newer the information, when it comes to as fluid and mutable a world as the Internet, the more likely it is to be correct!

THE WORLD WIDE WEB

18

WONDER OF THE INTERNET

The Internet information browsers that we've seen so far clearly give you much more capability than you would get by using ftp and telnet alone. Nonetheless, Gopher, WAIS, and similar utilities are limited, either in their search capabilities or in the types of data they can present. Also, while these browsers were quite powerful and useful when they were first released, the growth of information available on the Internet, in both type and quantity, has rendered them less useful, and users need more powerful search tools than ever before.

Recognizing this, a team of researchers at the European Particle Physics Laboratory (CERN) in Switzerland saw the need for an information-finding system that could handle the expanding data needs of the Internet and came up with the World Wide Web (WWW). It is only a couple of years old, so there are not as many WWW servers as there are Gopher servers, but more Web servers come on-line all the time.

Like its cousins Gopher and WAIS, the World Wide Web helps you sift through the thousands of offerings on the Internet and find documents and data all over the world. Also like Gopher and WAIS, it lets you access many different types of data from a common user interface. The Web differs from these two, however, in several important ways.

Where Gopher can offer you either menus, documents, or indexes and can search only the names of the files it knows about, the Web can search documents as well as indexes. If you need to find a discussion on the effects of climate on traditional cuisine, for instance, you could search for it with Gopher, but your search would cover only the names of the files that Gopher has in its index. Web servers can search the entire contents of documents.

But the major difference that distinguishes the Web from the others is that it is based not on menus but on hypertext-style links. Not only can the Web perform more sophisticated searches than its predecessors, but the hypertext model of presenting information greatly increases the power and flexibility of the searches it can perform.

FROM HYPERTEXT TO HYPERMEDIA

You may be wondering at this point what exactly hypertext is. If you have ever used the "help" system in Microsoft Windows, you have probably used hypertext. It's an information presentation technique, where you can select certain keywords for more information about them. These words are usually indicated by a different color, a box around them, or a different text font. When you select one of those highlighted words, by clicking on it with a mouse, for instance, a new screen appears that gives you expanded information about that particular word.

For example, take a look at the text in Figure 18.1. If this were a hypertext document, selecting the words printed in bold type would bring up information explaining each of those terms. We might, for instance, select the term *basting stitch*, and the program would present us with another screen full of information describing a basting stitch. That text could also have hypertext links, which we could in turn select for more information about those new terms. We could continue in this manner until we ran out of screens, following a meandering path according to our interests rather than the rigid, hierarchical path that a menu-driven presentation requires.

In order to ensure that the sleeve fits smoothly, be sure to **ease** the entire **sleeve cap** before attempting to stitch the seam. Use a **basting stitch** just inside the seam **allowance**, then pull the stitches as necessary until the sleeve fits without puckers or gathers. After stitching, **press** lightly.

Figure 18.1 *Example hypertext screen*

As you can see, hypertext gives us a very flexible way of accessing information. Now imagine the addition of other types of media than just text, such as sound, pictures, and video. For example, you might be reading a document in which you find the sentence, "They heard the familiar strains of the **William Tell Overture**." When you select these last three words for expansion, the system does not give you a text description of the piece, but instead plays a few bars of the music over your speakers.

Now that hypertext and hypermedia have been around for several years and are becoming increasingly common in information and educational systems. The exciting power of the Web comes from its ability to link related media documents all over the Internet. You might, for instance, be sitting at your computer in Wisconsin reading the text in the preceding example. The text might be on a server in Hawaii, and the music might come from a server in Brazil. The Web handles all the linking, and you simply follow the links as your interest guides you.

GETTING THE MOST THE WEB HAS TO OFFER

To take advantage of all this power, you need to find a multimedia browser, and you also need the appropriate hardware. If you want to play video clips on your computer, for instance, you need video decoding hardware and speakers. To display high-resolution graphics you must have a high-resolution monitor and an interface card to go with it. To use WWW, a direct network connection to a web server works best, but you can also use a dial-up link, provided you're running SLIP or PPP (we'd recommend using a 14.4 kbps modem, though).

Like Gopher and WAIS, WWW is based on the client-server model. You need client software running on your own computer (or that of your service provider), and that client software in turn communicates with one or more servers. If you have a SLIP, PPP, or direct Internet link, you can run the client software (called a *browser*) from your own computer. Currently these browsers are available for X Windows systems, VMS systems, Microsoft Windows systems, and Macintoshes, among others. Mosaic is probably the most popular and easiest to find.

We would like to be able to tell you exactly where to get the software, but since availability changes so much and so often, we will suggest where to look for it instead. The newsgroup comp.infosystems.www is devoted to discussions about the Web. While many of the discussions in the newsgroup relate to advanced matters about setting up one's own

Web server, the FAQ answers questions that you are more likely to have as a beginning Web user, including where to get browser software. The FAQ gets posted both to this newsgroup and to news.answers at least once a month.

THE STATION WAGONS OF WEB BROWSERS

If you do not have a flashy graphics workstation with video capability, don't despair. The power of the Web is still available to you through a text interface. If you start using the Web and find that you use it constantly and really need more advanced capability, you can always upgrade your software (and hardware) later.

The text-based browsers are not particularly fancy, but they are quite serviceable. The Web interface is so easy to use that you should have no problems using it either way.

We show a sample screen of a text-based session with a Web browser in Figure 18.2, using a VT100-terminal compatible browser.

```
          The World-Wide Web Virtual Library: Literature and Art[1]
                          LITERATURE AND ART


Information categorized by subject. See also other subjects[2]. Please
mail www-request@info.cern.ch if you know of on-line information not in
these lists.


Art in the age of digital dissemination[3]
                        Class essays from a Fine Arts Course

Irish Literature       CURIA archive of Irish Literature is no longer
                       available due to construction work.

English language Literature
                     . Project Gutenberg[4] : two classic books a month.
                       See their explanations[5] , the index and
                       newsletter[6], books published in 1991[7], 1992[8] ,
                       and reserved for the USA[9] .  See also a new
                       provisional easy-to-use index[10] ., newsgroup[11]
                       for discussion of the project.

1-32, Back, Up, <RETURN> for more, Quit, or Help:
```

Figure 18.2 *Sample Web screen with a text-based interface*

In this example, you select the items with numbers next to them by typing the number. For instance, to find out more about a newsgroup devoted to Project Gutenberg, you would type 11.

With a VT100 browser such as Lynx, you get full-screen capability with highlighting and can move around on the screen using your arrow keys. VT100 terminal interfaces were considered quite luxurious a decade or so ago! The WWW FAQ also gives you information on where to go to get one of these browsers for your own system.

Trying out the Web

Remember in Chapter 15, when we set about trying to find a Gopher client? Well, to try out the World Wide Web, we again have to find a client. We can run a client program locally or we can telnet to a public client computer.

Try Local Access First

Local clients have several advantages. When you run a local client you avoid the overhead of your telnet connection slowing down your session. Additionally, a local connection to the Web means that you can retrieve documents to your own computer. If you run a remote connection via telnet, many documents will simply be unavailable to you, because the system has to retrieve them to somewhere local before it can display them for you. If you are logged in to a public client, you won't write access to the client's hard disk and so can't retrieve these types of documents.

The other advantage of running locally is more a matter of consideration for other users. The more you do on your local computer, the less burden you place on the other computers. So not only from the standpoint of consideration, but also of your own convenience, it is a good idea to try to run your Web client locally if you use it more than occasionally.

Your Internet provider might already have a Web client installed on your access computer. To find out, try typing **web** or **worldwideweb** at the command line prompt if you have one or search through the menus for something along those lines if you don't. If you get a screen welcoming you to the Web, you're off! Otherwise, talk to your system administrator. The client software might be available via some other command, or perhaps your administrator just needs a little nudging to tackle get it installed.

Finding a Public Web Browser—A Short List

If no client is available locally, you can telnet to a couple of public Web client computers. The most famous, and therefore, popular, public client is at info.cern.ch and for these reasons you should try not to make it your first choice. The following list suggests some others; many more may be available by the time you read this.

> `info.cern.ch`—in Switzerland. No log in necessary.
>
> `ukanaix.cc.ukans.edu`—Uses Lynx. Log in as **www**.
>
> `www.njit.edu`—in New Jersey. Log in as **www**.
>
> `vms.huji.ac.il`—in Israel. Log in as **www**.

WHAT IS THE WEB GOOD FOR?

Thousands of documents and other data files are available through the World Wide Web. Not only does the Web give you access to anything that you can get via Gopher, ftp, telnet, and WAIS, you can also read Usenet news with it (though we know of no browsers at this writing that allow you to post to Usenet newsgroups). The Web also has links to many other smaller information organization systems and knows how to handle documents in the format of UNIX manual files.

More exciting is that the Web's flexibility allows anyone with sufficient interest to create hyperlinks to their own data sets. You can access scientific databases through the Web that let you search all known DNA sequences in seconds, for instance. Or you can view a discography of a musical group complete with images of their album covers, with samplings of their hit songs playing in the background. Or you can view pictures of a city you'd like to visit, and see one person's view of the highlights of their town. The limit to what is available on the Web is only in the imaginations of the people creating the links, which could include you. (For information on how to create your own Web server, see the FAQ or the comp.infoservers.www newsgroup.)

SUMMARY

In the continuing story of the Internet, it seems that every time someone develops more powerful software to access the resources, it leads to more resources becoming available. This in turn seems to spur the development of more powerful software to access these new resources. Certainly this held true in the jump between Gopher and the Web, and it will be interesting to see what types of new information systems the World Wide Web will engender.

FINDING OUT
WHAT'S OUT
THERE

19

THE INDEXING PROBLEM

The last few chapters gave you introductions to some of the increasingly powerful tools available to help you explore the Internet. With tools such as Gopher, WAIS, and the World Wide Web, you can follow a train of thought down a series of menus to the document that contains a complete answer to your question. Or if you know the general category of the information you seek and where to get it, you can use one of these tools to retrieve it without explicitly logging in to the necessary computers and searching through the files there—these programs handle all such details for you. But they are far from perfect, and finding data might sometimes be frustrating. In this chapter we discuss the issues around finding things, exploring the reasons it can be difficult and some strategies to help ensure successful searching.

Keeping Track of the Archives

Tools such as Gopher, Archie, Veronica, WAIS, and the Web are all much more powerful than their predecessors, and they are continually improving. They have some limitations, though. They are especially useful and convenient if you know that a particular document exists or if you know where the information is or the name of its file. They are not quite so helpful, though, if you are not sure that the data you seek actually exists, or if you know the data is out there somewhere but don't know where the file might be or what it might be called.

Additionally, all of these systems rely on registration techniques to make data available. That is, someone who creates a set of electron microscope photographs of a molecule and is willing to let other people look at them must register the files with a Gopher, WAIS, or WWW server so that the server knows to point to them. Otherwise users of the search programs never hear about the new data set.

The need for owners to register their files is one aspect of the problem; timely updates are another. Gopher servers, for instance, must periodically query each other to find out what new data are available on other servers, so the information you can get from a particular server might be significantly different from what is actually out there, depending on how often your nearby server performs this update.

Thousands of Libraries

These record-keeping issues, although thorny, are not the only difficulty in finding data on the Internet. The other is one of indexing. Imagine thousands of libraries, each with sophisticated and specialized collections, before the invention of the Dewey Decimal System. Most of the libraries have their own local methods for cataloging and finding data within them, but some have no catalogs at all. Those catalogs or indices that do exist were created by different librarians, each of whom has a different system of organizing information. Moreover, there is no central repository from which someone can find information in all libraries.

This is a pretty accurate picture of the current situation on the Internet. While there is an incredible amount of data out there, it is not organized or indexed in any consistent way. The Internet databases have grown extremely quickly, especially in the past few years, and the searching and indexing tasks have simply not kept up. Library science is just starting to meet the Internet databases.

Working with the System

While the indexing problem does create some challenges in finding data, it's not an insurmountable obstacle. Your best bet is to educate yourself thoroughly on the tools currently available and understand the search mechanisms each tool uses. As you get more comfortable with the tools, you'll learn to be more flexible and creative in generating search strings, and your searches will in turn become more productive. At the same time, lots of very bright and creative people are aware of the problems and working on solutions, so new software comes out all the time to help you. In the meantime, the next section describes search techniques, some simple and direct and some rather oblique.

SEARCH TECHNIQUES

The key to learning to find information on the Internet is cultivating a certain patience. Much of the information you comb through is not indexed professionally, and some of it is not indexed at all, so searching can require attacking the problem from several different angles, with various tools.

With so many resources out there and so many different tools to access them, you can't expect to be proficient with the software as quickly as you might, for instance, with a new word processor on your Macintosh. Give yourself time to develop the necessary skills, and eventually you'll learn to find information more and more efficiently.

In some cases, you have a question in mind, formulate a search query, and locate the information immediately. If this doesn't happen, though, here are some suggestions that might help.

Know Your Search Tool

Every one of the most common Internet search tools formulates queries in a different way, so it's important to know how searching works for the tool you are using. Suppose, for instance, you need to find documents containing the words *salt* and *pepper*. If you use the search string **salt and pepper**, some utilities treat the word *and* as a logical symbol, so they show you all the documents that contain both the words *salt* and *pepper*. Other utilities will treat the entire string as one entity, and so show you only documents that have the phrase *salt and pepper* in them. Which did you want? Which does your current utility do?

Every utility, from Gopher to Archie to WAIS and all the others, has a different way of handling search strings. Familiarize yourself with the search commands for the software you are using by reading the manual for that software. Here are some features of searching software that can affect the success of your queries.

- Does the software allow multiple word searches or only one word at a time?
- If the software allows multiple word searches, does it allow logical keywords such as *or*, *and*, and *except*, or does it treat these words as literally part of the search string?
- Does the software allow wild card matching? In some utilities, for instance, the expression *wi?* matches any string with three characters, where the first two characters are *w* and *i* and the third character could be anything. Other utilities only match this string with a *w* and an *i* followed by a question mark.
- Will the software match only strings in which the upper- and lower-case letters match exactly, or is it case insensitive?

By paying attention to the rules of your software, based on these guidelines, you can greatly increase your chances of finding what you're looking for.

The Overlap Problem

When you are using a tool such as Gopher that gives you a nice uniform user interface no matter whether you're talking to a Gopher, WAIS, or Web server, your gains in ease of use are sometimes offset in the simplification necessary to make all of these programs so easy to use. That is, by giving you one single way to talk to all these types of servers, Gopher must also reduce the way you talk to them down to the simplest of them all. This often means you can formulate only simple, one word search commands, rather than complex logical commands with wild cards.

If this appears to be posing a problem, see if you can get the address of the current resource so that you can telnet to it directly and use the fully featured search capability there.

Other Sources of Information

Now for the less direct strategies. One of the richest resources of the Internet is the people, the thousands of experts on tens of thousands of topics. In this section we offer some suggestions on how to tap into this wealth without taking advantage of it.

FAQs

Many newsgroups have lists of frequently asked questions, or FAQs. These files are full of the collected wisdom of the group and often have pointers to other references across the Internet. Find the FAQ for your topic of interest by looking in one of the answers newsgroups, such as news.answers, alt.answers, or comp.answers. If you don't find it there, look at the FAQ archives via ftp at rtfm.mit.edu, or check in any related newsgroups you can find.

Usenet Conversations

Outside of the FAQs, an enormous amount of information flows through the Usenet newsgroups. Subscribe to a couple of groups that deal with topics related to the information you need, and you are very likely to see references to data that interests you over the course of a few days. Lots of nonuseful discourse tends to flow through the groups, too, though, so this method takes a fair bit of patience.

Books

A number of books now on the market purport to catalog the Internet, and more are coming out every couple of months. These books necessarily become obsolete quickly, so we will not attempt to recommend any, but you might find the paper format convenient to honing in on data sets that interest you.

Mailing Lists

If there is a mailing list that relates to your area of interest, by all means subscribe to it. Some mailing lists appear to be more social than informational, while others offer a much higher ratio of information to conversation, and some can be rich veins of resources, references, and advice.

Keep an Open Mind

Since the index methods are so varied, and so many different views of data are represented in the way information is stored on the Internet, the most important skill is to learn to think creatively and flexibly about how to find the data you need. Information on tracking time, for instance, might be indexed under the word *calendars* on one system, but the word *scheduling* on another. Try to think of as many different ways as possible to describe your target data.

SUMMARY

The state of data availability on the Internet is far ahead of the state of tools to search that data. In this chapter we described the causes of some of the indexing problems and discussed some ways to get around the problems. By remaining flexible and exploring many different avenues, you can maximize your chances of finding the data you need.

APPLIED FOLKLORE

20

SOME THINGS TO AVOID

Every community has a set of legends that define it, and finding out about them is one of the pleasures of joining the group. There are a couple of Internet legends, though, that you need to know about before you get too far into the Net or suffer various unpleasant consequences.

We're stretching it a bit to give the title of legend to all of the incidents in this chapter. Some are events that rippled strongly through the community, others are perennial annoyances. Perhaps it would be better to call these tales *fables,* because they all illustrate behaviors that you should make every effort to avoid!

If you do try any of these, you might get no negative feedback at all. But in many of these cases, the people involved lost their Internet access, and in one case the perpetrator landed in jail.

THE BRAIN TUMOR BOY

In the book *Everybody's Guide to the Internet* (1992, MIT Press, Cambridge, MA), author Shari Steele writes about someone called the Brain Tumor Boy, a.k.a. Craig Shergold. Craig, who lived outside London, was a seven-year-old with terminal brain cancer, whose last wish was for postcards. Some newspapers took up the cause, Craig got lots of cards, and then he decided he wanted to be in the Guinness Book of World Records for having the largest collection of get-well cards. He made it, and not only that, he even recovered from the cancer. In fact, Craig is now a teenager without cancer, and the post office of his hometown is still getting cards. Despite pleas from Craig, his parents, the post office, and even Dear Abby for people to stop, Craig still gets cards, something on the order of thousands per year. The story just refuses to go away, and every now and then, a letter asking people to send cards to Craig makes its way around the Net again.

When we first read this account we scoffed—we had heard about this several years ago and were sure the furor had died down by now. But sure enough, just last week we received a request from a friend, asking us to please send cards to Craig. So it might never really stop, but you can do your part to reduce the flood a little bit!

MY NAME IS DAVE RHODES

Nobody seems to know whether Dave Rhodes ever existed, but the name can provoke your listeners to roll their eyes, throw things, or moan quietly in a corner. This phrase is the beginning of a letter that gets posted to various Usenet groups periodically. The letter goes on to describe how Mr. Rhodes was destitute a while back, but received a copy of this same letter, sent it on (with some money) to the people it named, and became incredibly wealthy and successful as a result.

We probably don't have to tell you that this is a chain letter. Chain letters not only do not work, they are illegal in the United States and in many other countries as well.

The people who post this letter to Usenet groups are probably well-intentioned, and certainly it would be nice to suddenly become rich, but instead they often lose their Internet access. Most providers prohibit illegal activities from their site; they must to protect themselves from liability. If they find that a user is doing something illegal they have no choice but to cancel that user's account, even in some cases where the user was not aware that the action was illegal.

THE WORLD WILL END ANY DAY NOW

Every now and then someone finds that he has a message to share with the world that is so important that it simply can't be restricted to the relevant newsgroups. This person instead posts the message to every possible newsgroup, just to make sure that everyone gets a chance to see it. Not only that, but he posts individually to every newsgroup, rather than crossposting, so that smart newsreaders can't detect that they have already seen the article, and the hapless readers are forced to read the message once for every newsgroup to which they subscribe.

We know of two such incidents in the past year, and in both cases the people involved lost their accounts. The perpetrators in one case are still involved in the legal repercussions of their stunt.

New newsreading software is on the way that can deal with these annoyances by filtering out such posts, so by the time you read this it might be a nonissue from your point of view as a user.

WORMS AND VIRUSES, OR CAN I GET USENET IN JAIL?

With this we move from the ignorant or crude to the malicious. These are software programs designed to remain invisible, replicate themselves in other software, and often destroy data or cause computers to behave erratically. Your best defense against these is to scan frequently for viruses using a reliable virus checking program, especially if you are in the habit of downloading software from public sites. Also, back up your computer frequently, so that if it does get infected, you can fall back to a previous, clean, version of your files.

In a highly publicized case, the Cornell University student responsible for a particularly nasty worm program that incapacitated hundreds of Internet computers received a lengthy jail sentence. Unleashing worms and virus programs is considered a very serious crime and can cost you much more than just your Internet access!

SUMMARY

In this chapter we warned you against some of the pranks and myths that tend to circulate on the Internet. We gave you tips to protect yourself from the negative consequences or to keep from adding to the waste that some of these situations might engender.

GOVERNMENT DOCUMENTS

21

COMPILED BY UNCLE SAM

Since the United States government had such a big hand in the origins of the Internet, you might expect that they would have a large presence in terms of databases and available documents. You'd be only partially correct. A lot of government-created documents are available on the Internet, but it is not always the government that made them available. While old Uncle Sam was willing to invest in the infrastructure of the network, he did not always have the cash available to make all of his data accessible through it.

As it turns out, this is no obstacle at all. Since information gathered with government money is in the public domain, and therefore not subject to copyright protection, any interested party can make government documents available. And lucky for us, many have.

In this chapter we discuss some of the major repositories of government documents and data and give some examples of the types of things these banks contain. We restrict ourselves to United States government documents; every country has its own policies and copyright law variations.

Note that many of these resources are available via telnet, or are on Gopher servers. The commands we list are the ones you would use if your Internet-connected system offers the commands `telnet` and `gopher` from the command line, since this is the most general way of presenting the commands. If you access these services through some other method, adjust according to your system's requirements.

Resources

Weather Reports

If you're headed to the Caribbean tomorrow for vacation and you need to know whether a hurricane might mar your trip, or if your grandfather lives alone in the Great Plains and you want to see the latest tornado warnings, or you want to know what the high temperature was in Rome yesterday, or you just want to know what weather tomorrow is expected to bring to your home town, you're in luck. A couple of Gopher sites are set up to provide you with all this information and more.

Here are a couple of gopher sites that offer weather information. If these commands do not work for your site, talk to your system administrator for help.

```
gopher wx.atmos.uiuc.edu
gopher ashpool.micro.umn.edu (once connected,
   select the Weather menu item)
```

As you remember from our discussion of Gopher in Chapter 15, the arrow keys move you around in the menus, the letter **u** moves you back up to the previous menu, the letter **q** gets you out of Gopher, and every Gopher site has a link to all other Gophers. So you can start by looking up the weather, then move on to the travel advisories that the State Department issues.

State Department Travel Advisories

The United States State Department issues advice on travel to every part of the world. These bulletins include information about political conditions, health issues and medical care, crime, locations of embassies and consulates, and much more.

To access these advisories, enter the following command:

```
gopher gopher.stolaf.edu
```

Once you are connected to this gopher site, select the menu item Internet Resources. This presents another menu; select the Travel

Advisories item. Now you can search for the country or region in which you are interested. When we searched for Bali, for instance, the system presented the advisory on travel to Indonesia. It gave us information on visa requirements (for United States citizens only, of course), areas of political unrest, and economic conditions in the area. Some summaries also contain clippings from news articles about topics of interest to travelers (such as crime against tourists or United States citizens).

Environment

Whether you are interested in the progress of the SuperFund project, or helping your child with a report for school, or just curious about what the United States government is up to with respect to the environment, the Environmental Protection Agency Online Library System offers some interesting browsing. It indexes thousands of articles relating to all aspects of the Environmental Protection Agency's jurisdiction, from keeping the air clear to cleaning up sites of toxic waste. It even lets you search through the documents by keywords. The interface is not particularly friendly, though, so work through the menus slowly, reading all the instructions as you go.

To access this library, telnet to the epaibm.rtpnc.epa.gov by using the command

```
telnet epaibm.rtpnc.epa.gov
```

Once you get connected, select the menu item labeled **PUBLIC**. In the next menu, select the item labeled **OLS**. From there you get into the search screen, where you can search by author, title, or keyword for topics that interest you.

Freedom of Information Act (FOIA)

The Freedom of Information Act states, briefly, that United States citizens have the right to view all nonclassified government documents on request. This act opened up a number of avenues of research that had previously been unavailable because the searcher had to prove a need for the information. Now the government cannot refuse you the information unless it can prove that releasing it would compromise national security.

You must follow certain guidelines to obtain information under this act, though, and this guide shows you how. It's on a Gopher server, so enter the following command:

```
gopher wiretap.spies.com
```

When you connect to the server, select the menu item Government Docs. At the next menu you can retrieve the guide by selecting the item **Citizens Guide to Using the FOIA**.

This server also has some other interesting government documents, including the text of the Maastricht Treaty and the North American Free Trade Agreement. Interesting browsing.

Legislation

If you want to trace any legislation that has been introduced into the United States Congress since 1973, the Library of Congress can help you. Just Telnet to locis.loc.gov by entering the command

```
telnet locis.loc.gov
```

and selecting the menu item Federal Legislation. As you might imagine, this archive is enormous, but it does provide searching facilities.

News Services and Current Events

For the United States government's view of what's going on in Russia, Eastern Europe, and Central Asia, enter the following command:

```
gopher gopher.lib.umich.edu
```

From the menu, select the item News Services. This presents you with a report on the latest events in those areas, updated every day.

For information closer to the United States, take a look at the daily White House press briefings, speeches, policy statements, and other timely documents. This is also a Gopher site, so enter

```
gopher tamuts.tamu.edu
```

From the first menu, select Browse Information by Subject. This brings you a long list of subjects; go down several screens to the item Political Science. Here you see an item labeled Information from the White House. Now you can either search by keywords for the topic that interests you, or browse through what is available. You can even view the president's daily schedule.

The Rest of the World, from the United States' Point of View

The Central Intelligence Agency produces a set of documents called *The World Factbook*, which details the economic and political conditions of countries around the world, as well as their languages, industries, communications networks, and more. Great for those social studies papers and also fascinating browsing. It's a Gopher site, so use this command:

```
gopher wiretap.spies.com
```

Select the item Electronic Books, then the CIA World Factbook. Be patient; it is not a small document! You can browse through it from here, but you might be better off downloading it to your local account; type ? in Gopher to see the command to do that.

If you'd also like to view the text of the constitutions of some those countries, you might be in luck. On the same Gopher server, instead of selecting the Electronic Books item, select instead the Government Documents item (a couple of screens down the list). Only a few countries are represented here, though.

SEND E-MAIL TO AN ELECTED OFFICIAL

The United States House of Representatives is experimenting with e-mail. If you want to tell a representative what you think about the project, or anything else, send an e-mail message to congress@hr.house.gov with a request for information. They will send you back a document describing the project and how to access your representatives.

If you'd prefer to go straight to the top, try the following e-mail addresses:

```
president@whitehouse.gov
vice.president@whitehouse.gov
```

From what we have heard, the president does not answer his e-mail personally.

Summary

Thousands of documents and databases generated by various government agencies are available via the Internet. While much of this might also be available at a library, it is likely to be more up to date and easier to search through when you can access the data with your computer.

FINDING AND MANAGING E-MAIL ADDRESSES

c h a p t e r 22

FINDING PEOPLE

One of the most common questions asked by new Internet users is: I know this person has an e-mail address. How do I find out what it is?

For some reason, many of these seekers are resistant to the obvious answer: Call the person on the phone and ask! It is more interesting and fun to surprise the person with an e-mail note, of course. Sometimes, too, you want to contact someone whom you do not know personally, so calling might be inappropriate. In some cases, you simply might not know how to contact the person—someone you met at a conference, for instance.

Whatever the reason, you want to find the e-mail address of someone. You would expect that this would be an easy thing to do—what a perfect task for a computer, right? They are good at storing large amounts of data and searching through it much more quickly and accurately than a human. Surely some tool exists on the Internet for finding e-mail addresses!

Well, it does. Actually, there are several. This is probably no surprise to you based on what we know about the Internet so far. It's a loosely constructed web of networks, each with its own protocols, usage guidelines, and other quirks. If you are becoming concerned that maybe not all of the Internet e-mail addresses are available or not in one convenient place, you're right. Since every network has its own operating procedures and policies, every network has a different approach to making its e-mail addresses available, and some simply don't, citing security and privacy reasons. Others register their addresses with large, multinetwork databases; these banks are conveniently called *White Pages*.

Clearly there is no single place to go to find the e-mail address of anyone on the Internet—it will take some digging. In a way, this is similar to finding a phone number. If you only know the person's first name and the state in which he lives, you will have a hard time finding his phone number, but if you also know his middle and last names, address, and place of employment, the problem gets much easier. It's the same with e-mail addresses—the more you know about the person, the easier your search.

Why It's Difficult

Before we launch our search for e-mail addresses, it would be helpful to understand some of the obstacles to searching and the limitations to the search information.

As we've seen, the Internet has no centralized authority that organizes it or, in particular, hands out e-mail addresses, so there is no central place where all addresses might be stored. Every network attached to the Internet has its own set of e-mail addresses, and some refuse to give out e-mail addresses at all.

In addition, people change jobs and locations often, but no one necessarily purges obsolete e-mail addresses from the records of a particular institution. You might find an address for someone, but it might be one she hasn't used in years.

Not only that, but the person might have several addresses, one at work and one for personal use from home, for example. Knowing which one to use can be difficult.

One of the largest obstacles is that e-mail addresses do not have any particular standard format, so one system cannot necessarily read the addresses from another system, much less index them. This is why we have gateway software—it performs the translation between different e-mail addressing schemes.

Nonetheless, it is not impossible to find someone. It just means that you need to keep in mind that the address you find might not be the one you want, and you should try many avenues before giving up. In the next section we describe some of these avenues.

WAYS TO FIND PEOPLE

The key to successfully finding a person's e-mail address is to gather up as much information as possible, because the best way to find him or her depends on what you know about the individual. Do you have business cards, letters, postcards from the person? Perhaps a scrap of paper on which he wrote his e-mail address? An e-mail note from him? If you met him at a conference, was he listed in the program or the proceedings? Be creative in thinking of things you might know about the person, and once you have collected as much information as you possibly can, you are ready to begin your search.

If You Know the Phone Number

First and foremost, just ask the person. Many people are resistant to this simple solution, and true, it removes the element of surprise. But is surprising your friend really worth the work? You could dig around and find an e-mail address for an account that she never uses. Asking is the only really reliable method of finding e-mail addresses.

If you have no phone number for the person, try sending her a letter or a fax. You might also try asking someone else in her office, school, or professional field. If you know any other people who know her, try asking them as well.

If you exhaust all these easy methods of finding the address, it's time to take your search out to the Net.

If You Know the Host Name

The Finger command is available on many UNIX systems to let you get information about people who have accounts on the particular computer. The amount of information available through Finger varies, depending both on the way it's implemented on a given system and the amount of information each user chooses to make available.

You can invoke the finger command in several different ways, as we will illustrate. The general form of the command is **finger <address>**, where the address is in the usual name@hostname format.

But the name is exactly what we're trying to find! Luckily, the Finger command will search for people on that machine whose names contain the string you use. So if you know your friend's first name is Michael, and you know the host name, try

```
$ finger michael@cc.nwu.edu
```

This could give you a really long list, so it's a better bet to use the last name if you know it.

```
$ finger walker@cc.nwu.edu
[cc.nwu.edu]
Login name: mwalker              In real life: Michael Walker
Directory: /home/u2/mwalker      Shell: /bin/csh
Last login Sun May  1 12:41 on ttyq0
Mail last read Sat Apr 30 20:43:55 1994
```

Note that Finger searches the name field (labeled **In real life** in the example) for the name you gave. If you lack the correct spelling, or you're using a nickname and the person is listed only by his full name, you're not going to find him.

If You Know the Organization Name

Suppose you know the person has an account with a certain organization, but you don't know the name of the machine. You can try using the Whois command to find the host name, then use Finger to find the person on that computer. For instance, suppose we know that Gina has an account at Rice University, but have no idea which machine.

```
whois "Rice University"
```

which gives you the following list:

```
Rice University (LUCERNE-HST) LUCERNE.RICE.EDU 128.42.4.155
Rice University (NISC-SEQUI)  NS.SESQUI.NET    128.241.0.84
Rice University (RICE)        MOE.RICE.EDU     128.42.5.4
```

It might not be very efficient, but now you can try running Finger commands on all of these machines in turn until you find the person you're looking for.

Whois Servers

The interesting thing about that last example is the use of the Whois command. This is a command that accesses a large database of not only organizations that are attached to the Internet, but also people who have had something to do with it. This is one of the first directories of Internet people ever, and many of the others are at least loosely based on it. It holds close to 100,000 addresses, so if you know that the person has worked on the Internet or has done research on it, you might try looking for them with a whois query.

If you have a command line prompt on your Internet computer, try the following examples:

```
whois margaret
whois marga.
```

Note that if you don't know the whole name, you can just enter the first few letters and terminate the name with a period (.), and **whois** will find anyone whose name begins with those letters.

If You Know That the Person Has Posted to Usenet

Well, unfortunately, your would-be correspondent is not listed in the Whois database, or if she is, you can't figure out how. You do know, however, that she posts to Usenet newsgroups—maybe that was how you got the idea to write to her.

It's not commonly known, but a database of all people who have posted to any of the Usenet newsgroups that passes into the MIT site (nearly all of them). This database is maintained by MIT, so to query it, you have to send a message to MIT.

Note that the success of this search depends on how much information the MIT software can extract from the Usenet posting. If the person's name does not appear in her postings, for instance, you are not likely to have much luck with this approach. Still, it is worth a try. Send e-mail to mail-server@pit-manager.mit.edu with no subject, and the body of the message containing a single line:

```
send usenet-addresses/name
```

For instance, when we sent the query

```
send usenet-addresses/robbins
```

we received the following response (many other entries deleted for space, and because it's not considered polite to publish people's e-mail addresses without their knowledge):

```
Message 1/8  From mail-server@BLOOM-PICAYUNE.MIT.EDU May 1,
94 03:33:25 pm -0400


Date: Sun, 1 May 1994 15:33:25 -0400
To: Margaret Robbins <mrobbins@bga.com>
Subject: mail-server: "send usenet-addresses/robbins"
Reply-To: mail-server@BLOOM-PICAYUNE.MIT.EDU
Precedence: junk
X-Problems-To: owner-mail-server@rtfm.mit.edu

---cut here---
            .
            .
            .
mrobbins@bga.com (Margaret Robbins)     (Apr 18 94)
            .
            .
---cut here---
```

Note that these queries don't work with partial strings. We could have successfully searched for the string "margaret" in this example, but not "marg" or "bbins."

Fred, Whois++, and the Future

Clearly, it's time for someone to bring all these search methods under one roof, and many researchers and developers are trying to do just that. Fred, for instance, is an experimental system that uses X.500 addressing (recall our discussion of these in Chapter 3). When everyone has an X.500 style address, this system could be quite powerful, because it is designed to search very large databases quickly.

Another project on the horizon of e-mail directory management is the Whois++ project. As the name suggests, it's more than just Whois. Whois++ follows the Gopher idea of trying to create a single, consistent interface for all of the many ways there are to search for people on the Internet. You would enter the information you know about the person, be it his or her name, place of employment, phone number, or whatever; and Whois++ would form the appropriate queries and return to you any matches. It's still a fledgling system, but promises to make the whole process of finding people much easier.

Summary

If you need to send e-mail to someone on the Internet and are not sure what the person's e-mail address is, finding it can be quite a challenge. There are a few tools to help you, but their usefulness is limited to narrow ranges. Nonetheless, some persistence and flexibility can pay off, and this chapter gave you some tips to make your searches successful.

GOPHERING FOR GOLD

23

GETTING STARTED

The best way to look for something in particular is to know what you're looking for. If that's your mètier, we strongly recommend that you find the Gopher menu item for Veronica, and use that program to search for the thing you're after. Remember that you can limit your searches to directories and get a much faster response (and shorter menus) or you can go whole hog and have Veronica get you everything it can find. Our best advice, though, is to start small and build from there.

On the other hand, Gopher is a tool that lends itself to hour upon hour of leisurely Internet cruising, too. We spent quite a bit of time with the program, meandering around the menus, pausing occasionally to investigate topics or entries that looked particularly interesting.

Because it's so easy to get lost in Gopherspace and request information from the most unlikely places, we encourage you to explore, but apply a few important principles:

1. *The Principle of Locality*. F. Buckminster Fuller put it best: "Think globally, but act locally." In Gopher terms, this means use the closest servers (local is best) to start your search and try to stay close to home when you can. There is no point in copying files from Finland when you can find the same ones at your local college campus or library.

2. *The Principle of Polite Usage.* Don't noodle around during prime working hours. Exploring is great, meandering is marvelous, but don't do it when other people are trying to work. If you try to use a Gopher server for a query and get a "No more connections available; try again soon!" message, that probably means that you shouldn't be fooling around on that server right now. Our advice is to try again later, rather than sooner!

3. *The Principle of Similarity.* It's not always true that identical Gopher menu entries cover duplicate copies of the same stuff, but it almost always is. Unless you're noodling on purpose, don't open every menu entry that says the same thing! Our advice is that if you try it twice and get a duplicate, skip the other members of the list that say the same thing (this will occur most often when you use Veronica, because it grabs similar or identical menu entries and organizes them alphabetically).

4. *The Law of Net Conservation.* If you want to grab a *big* document using Gopher, consider having Gopher mail it to you, instead of downloading it there and then. Mail delivery lets the server schedule the download at a more convenient time, helping preserve Principle 2 while saving you time to explore even more.

By following these few simple rules, you'll be able to get the best use out of the Internet without impinging too much on your fellow netizens!

VERONICA SEARCH TECHNIQUES

There are two secrets to using Veronica effectively. First and foremost, carefully define the scope your search; and second, choose keywords or search terms correctly. This raises an interesting question—how do you know what to tell the program to look for when you're not exactly sure what you're looking for yourself?

Because Veronica searches menus, not documents, it's easy to be too specific. If you're looking for a Macintosh TCP/IP package why not simply enter "Macintosh TCP/IP package" in the search field when prompted? After all, that's exactly what you're looking for. Unfortunately, unless a menu entry reads exactly like the words you've entered (or in some other order), the search will turn up nothing.

This is where defining the scope of the search comes in. If you looked for *either* Macintosh *and* TCP/IP, or TCP/IP *and* client *or* software *or* package, chances are much better that you'd turn up some interesting items than if you entered all three terms together. By broadening the scope of your search a little, you can include more possibilities and leave room for near-misses to be picked up, as well as exact matches.

Your choice of search terms is important, too, because words that have multiple meanings or uses can lead to unexpected results. For instance, if you were interested in Indian food—let's say curry—it would seem perfectly natural to use curry as the search term when navigating Gopherspace. If you did, though, you'd quickly remember that Curry is also a very common proper name. In addition to numerous recipes for curry dishes, you'd find yourself looking at Curry Awards, papers and mail messages by people named Curry, information on a Curry School of This or That, and all kinds of other extraneous stuff.

How do you avoid this kind of problem? Easy—include another word with your search. Curries usually come in particular kinds or flavors, so you could try chicken curry, beef curry, lamb curry, vegetable curry, or even curry recipes. This might take more time and searches, or perhaps a little exercise of Boolean operators for Veronica, as in "curry *and* (chicken *or* beef *or* lamb *or* vegetable *or* recipes)".

The important thing is to strike the proverbial happy medium between casting your net too wide and having to wade through the mismatches, and casting it too narrow and coming up empty. Practice and experience will help a great deal, but thinking things through will help even more!

GOPHERING IS A VISUAL EXPERIENCE

If you remember to apply the four principles and use Veronica when looking for specific items or topics, you'll be able to research and investigate those kinds of things fairly effectively. To really get the most out of Gopher, we strongly recommend getting away from a character-mode interface like that shown in Figure 23.1, and using a graphical interface like that shown in Figure 23.2 instead.

```
                  Internet Gopher Information Client v1.12S

          Search GopherSpace by Title word(s) (via U. of Manitoba)d IBM PC

->    1. Connection Machine  IBM PC (Mon, 10 Dec 90..s": Conversion Rates).
      2. Connection Machine  IBM PC (Mon, 10 Dec 90..s": Conversion Rates).
      3. Connection Machine  IBM PC (Mon, 10 Dec 90..s": Conversion Rates).
      4. Connection Machine  IBM PC (Mon, 10 Dec 90..s": Conversion Rates).
      5. Generic IBM PC Soundcard FAQ periodic posting                    .
      6. Comp.sys.ibm.pc.soundcard FAQ                                    .
      7. Comp.sys.ibm.pc.rt: AIX V2 FAQ - Index                          .
      8. Comp.sys.ibm.pc.rt: AIX V2 FAQ - Question/Answer, Pt 1 of 2     .
      9. Comp.sys.ibm.pc.rt: AIX V2 FAQ - Question/Answer, Pt 2 of 2     .
     10. Comp.sys.ibm.pc.rt: AIX V2 FAQ - OS Specific Hardware, Pt 1 of 1 .
     11. Comp.sys.ibm.pc.rt: - AIX V2 - Part 1 of 4 - FAQ                 .
     12. Comp.sys.ibm.pc.rt: - AIX V2 - Part 2 of 4 - FAQ                 .
     13. Comp.sys.ibm.pc.rt: - AIX V2 - Part 3 of 4 - FAQ                 .
     14. Comp.sys.ibm.pc.rt: - AIX V2 - Part 4 of 4 - FAQ                 .
     15. Comp.sys.ibm.pc.rt: AIX V2 FAQ - Porting software, Pt 1 of 1    .
     16. Comp.sys.ibm.pc.rt: AIX V2 FAQ - Software questions, Pt 1 of 3  .
     17. Comp.sys.ibm.pc.rt: AIX V2 FAQ - Software questions, Pt 2 of 3  .
     18. Comp.sys.ibm.pc.rt: AIX V2 FAQ - Software questions, Pt 3 of 3  .
```

Figure 23.1 *Character-Mode Gopher*

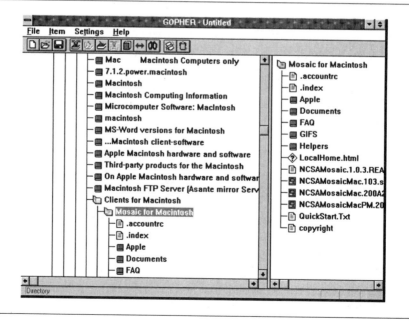

Figure 23.2 *Graphical Gopher*

The benefits of a graphical Gopher interface include the following:

- Menu elements can be tagged with icons rather than characters; a directory or catalog image is easier to interpret than a slash or an asterisk at the end of a line.
- Picking items from menus lends itself naturally to using a pointing device, like a trackball or a mouse. This cries out for a GUI approach, rather than terminal emulation (and will make you much faster and more effective).
- Running Gopher on your desktop, rather than through a host, means that the documents and files you download will be delivered in a single step (rather than requiring a second download from your Internet host to your desktop machine after you're done with the host Gopher).
- GUI Gophers can also let you get immediate access to graphics files and image data, and can let you exploit the capabilities of other graphically oriented Internet tools, like WWW or WAIS clients.

The beauty of Gopher is that it can even help you to find information out about itself. By using Veronica to look for "PC Gopher" or "Macintosh Gopher" or "UNIX Gopher" you can probably find a number of public-domain or shareware Gopher implementations that will let you add a graphical Gopher to your desktop for little or no cost!

Using a graphical Gopher lends itself much more readily to exploration and experimentation. We've tried it both ways and are convinced that the graphical approach works best; at the very least, we encourage you to find someone who has access to a graphical Gopher and watch that person use it. We think you'll agree: seeing is believing.

A-Hunting You Should Go!

In Table 23.1, we recommend a short list of "Gopherspace Attractions" that you should find appealing. These are presented in alphabetical order, which by no means corresponds to any item's interest or importance. Just remember to look around, and to follow the menus that interest you the most. At the very least, you could use these items as jumping-off points; at the most, they could lead you on the search of a lifetime!

Menu Entry	Explanation
Computer Information	A place to find all kinds of hardware and software information, plus the RFC database, plus news and discussion digests
ftp	Yet another way to use Archie, this lets you run the program from inside Gopher
Fun & Games	Games, humor, movies, music and recipes—need we say more?
Gopher Jewels	A collection of menus on a variety of Internet topics ranging from environmental issues to personal development. Cool! See especially "Internet Resources by Type"
News	On-line versions of newspapers, wire services, and all kinds of other publications
The Internet Hunt	A monthly competition, administered by Rick Gates; 10 questions must be answered with Intenet-based information
The top level Gopher hole	May also appear as The University of Minnesota Gopher; this is the granddaddy of all Gophers, the original server!
Weather	Access to weather maps and forecast information from all over the country, and the world.

Table 23.1 *A Sampling of Gopher Attractions*

We conclude this section with one final word of advice: don't delude yourself into thinking that you can do any real exploring in five or ten minutes; once you dive into the Gopher hole, it will take a lot longer than that to get back out!

Summary

The Internet Gopher program can be your entry into a huge amount of information, especially when used in concert with Veronica and Jughead. If you're unsure of where to begin, try our guided tour. If our experience with the program is any indication, though, the real problem is not in knowing where to start, but rather in knowing when to stop! Happy gophering. . . .

TCP/IP
SOFTWARE FOR
YOUR PC

24

WHAT TO EXPECT

Whether you're an individual trying to get a connection to the Internet from home or a systems administrator trying to hook up a number of users, it's wise to consider the benefits of running a TCP/IP protocol stack and related applications right on the desktop machines that you (or they) use. If you're looking for direct TCP/IP connectivity to a network, there's really very little choice; if you're trying to make the best of a dial-up connection, this is an option worth considering as well.

Three fundamental components are involved in setting up this kind of software:

1. A software driver to let the computer communicate with some kind of physical device to attach to the network, be it a network interface card driver if the machine is to be directly attached to a LAN or a communications driver if the machine will be attached via modem.
2. A TCP/IP protocol stack to confer the basic IP protocols needed for communication over whatever physical link gets established; on PCs running DOS and/or Windows the stack usually takes one of three forms: a terminate-and-stay-resident program (TSR); a dynamic link library (DLL; Windows only); or a virtual device driver (VxD; Windows only). On other types of desktop machines,

the protocol stack will be loaded as a part of the network manager (Macintosh) or as a separate background task (OS/2 and UNIX).

3. TCP/IP applications, which provide the capability for a user to take advantage of the physical network connection supplied by the interface or modem and the driver, and the raw communications ability supplied by the protocol stack, to actually perform useful tasks like remote terminal emulation (Telnet), file transfer (FTP), or electronic mail.

Whenever you acquire a TCP/IP package, you'll typically acquire all three of these components, although for telecommunications using TCP/IP, the software will often interface with standard system drivers as well. For instance, most Windows-based TCP/IP software expects to communicate with the Windows-supplied telecom driver called COMM.DRV, or some replacement. A key part of the installation process consists of making sure the hardware, the drivers, and the protocol stack are all properly integrated with the computer's operating system and applications.

SHAREWARE/FREEWARE VS. COMMERCIAL PACKAGES

When it comes to selecting TCP/IP software for a system, the Internet culture virtually guarantees that you'll have more options than you might for some other kinds of programs. Because so much freeware and shareware is available on the Internet, it's possible to find TCP/IP software for most kinds of computers and operating systems for little or no cost.

To begin with, it's important to understand the distinction between freeware and shareware. Freeware (sometimes known as public-domain software) may or may not be copyrighted and may or may not have distribution restrictions, but the reason for its name is that its creators make the software freely available at no charge to users (though they may offer manuals or other materials not available on-line to users for a fee).

Shareware, on the other hand, is always copyrighted and includes a software license that requires its users to pay for the privilege of using the software beyond a certain trial period. Even so, shareware is also freely distributed through BBSs and on-line archives, and its creators depend on the honor system to get paid for their work. Note, however, that if the Software Publisher's Association audits a site and finds shareware in use beyond the trial period, it can assess the same kinds of penalties and charges that would normally be assessed for illegal copies of commercial software.

Commercial software is normally not available on-line, except from for-a-fee access providers, and specifically requires payment before use is permitted. Like shareware, commercial software may not be copied except as the license terms allow, which normally consists of a single backup to protect damage to the original media on which the software is delivered. Some vendors are enlightened enough to make their licenses based on "single use"—that is, multiple copies of the same package are permitted on different machines, as long as only one of them is in use at any one time (this is a real boon to people who own laptops and desktop machines and are able to use only one or the other at any given time).

Given that TCP/IP packages are available on-line at little or no cost, why would anyone use commercial software? The short answer to that question is this: You get what you pay for. The long answer to that question is more than we can go into here, but it includes some important elements that are worth mentioning:

- *Warranty/guarantee*. Most commercial packages come with a 30-day money-back guarantee so that if you try the software and it doesn't meet your needs, you can get your money back. Freeware makes this element moot, but shareware guarantees are a matter of individual choice and are seldom available.
- *Technical support*. Most commercial vendors will mount a presence on-line, and provide either toll-free or toll-call support hotlines; for both freeware and shareware, it's unusual to get telephone support at all, and "whenever they get around to it" e-mail support is the most typical.
- *Features, functions, bells and whistles*. Commercial vendors try to supply value for what they charge; for this reason, it's common to find such packages more robust and reliable and also offering a greater range of functionality than freeware or shareware equivalents.
- *Regular updates*. Even though these usually cost money, commercial vendors are more conscientious about tracking new operating system releases (and new operating systems) than freeware or shareware providers. For organizations that need certain software to conduct business, regular updates and bug fixes are critical.

These elements help to explain why so many organizations and individuals opt to spend $100 or more per desktop to purchase commercial TCP/IP software.

Nevertheless, those businesses or individuals that are willing to spend the time and effort it takes to locate shareware or freeware and to become proficient, if not expert, in the underlying technologies can realize substantial savings and reasonable performance and reliability from such packages. That's why traditionally money-strapped organizations and individuals—especially academic and hobbyist users—continue to act as a source for such software and why this practice is likely to continue for the foreseeable future.

If money is a hurdle to getting connected to the Internet, the shareware and freeware alternatives will be well worth investigating. If you take this road, though, you must understand that what you don't pay for in money, you'll end up paying for in time and effort instead! There's no free ride on the Internet, either.

ABSOLUTE BASICS

No matter what kind of TCP/IP package you decide to use, there are some basic capabilities to look for that you simply can't do without. These are absolute requirements to meet government RFCs, so it's safe to assume that any commercial package will meet these needs; when looking at shareware or freeware, you have to check this out for yourself. (Note: Even though some shareware or freeware packages may not meet this basic requirements list by themselves, you can very often find shareware or freeware add-ons that will round out the list.)

- Support for basic LAN and dial-up interfaces (typically, this means Ethernet and Token-Ring for LANs, and SLIP and PPP for dial-up)
- Support for standard network interface drivers (typically this means at least two of the following: Novell's ODI, Microsoft's NDIS, and the Clarkson/UofU packet driver)
- A fully functional TCP/IP protocol stack, as per RFC 1123 and related requirements; it's also customary to have RARP, BootP, DNS and NetBIOS (RFC 1001, 1002 compliant) support as well
- Telnet
- ftp (client at least, but server as well if possible)
- Basic SMTP mail support

- PING
- Finger
- Whois
- lpr (remote print capability)
- Basic terminal emulation (VT52, VT100)

You'll find all of these to be necessary at some time or another while using the Internet. These are good requirements to look for, and not as arbitrary as they may appear.

BELLS, WHISTLES, AND ADD-ONS

The number of additional features and capabilities available in some implementations is truly staggering. Rather than trying to cover every conceivable item you might find advertised or touted, we stick to the ones that are generally agreed to be useful, and we also indicate if they're recommended (meaning that if you have them, you'll probably use them) or optional (meaning that you may use them seldom, if ever). This information is covered in Table 24.1.

There are lots of other features and capabilities that we omitted here. However, we tried to address only those that would appeal to the greatest audience. For more information on what else is (or might be) available, a quick trip through RFC1600 will fill in any gaps we created; as would a survey of product literature from the commercial TCP/IP providers.

PROVIDER PROFILES

In this section we cover the organizations and individuals offering free-ware and shareware TCP/IP implementations. We try to cover this area as completely as we can, understanding that there are probably nooks and crannies of the Internet we didn't get to and apologizing for our oversights in advance! Table 24.2 covers what we were able to learn, however.

It's very clear from reading this list that there's a gold mine of client TCP/IP software at ftp.cica.indiana.edu (and at its many mirrors). Using Archie on some of these file names, you can probably find the files much closer to home than that.

Feature	Status	Explanation
Gopher client	Recommended	Best if it provides a graphical Gopher interface
IBM emulation	Recommended•	tn3270, tn5250, etc. let you use Telnet to attach to an IBM minicomputer or mainframe via TCP/IP
IRC	Optional[†]	A potentially addictive, but fascinating time waster
NFS client	Recommended•	If your environment offers NFS, you can read and write files across the network as if they were local
NNTP client	Recommended•	If you read network news, this is a better tool than to be forced to read news inside Telnet on the host
POP2, POP3	Recommended	POP mail lets a remote client automatically transfer mail to and from a host account (this lets you use a local text editor and interface for mail)
r-utils	Recommended	A quick way to perform activities on remote machines (across the net)
SNMP agent	Recommended•	If you're in an environment that's being managed with SNMP, a local agent brings your machine into the fold
statistics	Recommended	A great way to check how your IP connection is working (provides throughput and error rate info)
talk	Optional	An invaluable tool for on-line, interactive conversation, but usable through emulation
		The software's capabilities
WAIS client	Optional[†]	Best if it provides a graphical WAIS interface
WWW client	Optional[†]	Must provide a graphical interface to do it justice

Notes: • If you need it, you'll know (or be told you do)
        [†] Optional, usually available as an add-on

Table 24.1 *Potentially Useful TCP/IP Extras*

VENDOR PROFILES

In this section we cover the organizations and individuals offering commercial TCP/IP client implementations. Again, we try to cover this area fairly comprehensively, understanding that there are some we probably missed, and apologizing for our omissions in advance! Table 24.3 includes all that we could find, however.

Given the relatively large number of vendors (there are 15 covered in the table) mentioned here, it might seem a bit daunting to make a selection. Perhaps this will help: Based on recent (since 1992) trade press reviews, the following companies have won awards of one kind or another for their products: FTP Software, Frontier Technologies,

Provider	Product Name	Additional Information
BSDI	BSDI UNIX	Shareware PC UNIX implementation, includes full TCP/IP client/server support anon FTP: freebsd.cdrom.com
Clarkson University	CUTCP	DOS only TCP/IP package Freeware; anon FTP: sun.soe.clarkson.edu
Core Systems	Internet Connect	DOS & Windows PC-based package Shareware; anon FTP: ftp.cica.indiana.edu+ win3/winsock/inetcon1.zip
Ham radio users group	Ka9q	DOS only TCP/IP package Shareware; anon FTP: ucsd.edu /hamradio/packet/tcpip/ka9q
NCSA	NCSA Telnet	DOS, Mac, Windows TCP/IP pkgs Shareware; anon FTP.ncsa.uiuc.edu Mosaic client also available
QPC Software	QVT/Net	Windows-only TCP/IP package Shareware; anon FTP ftp.cica.indiana.edu
Trumpet SW International	Trumpet Winsock	Windows-only TCP/IP package Freeware; anon FTP ftp.cica.indiana.edu win3/winsock/winsock.zip & winapps.zip

Table 24.2 *Some Freeware/Shareware TCP/IP Providers*

NetManage, Novell, and Spry. This may make a better short list to start with, but be sure to check the next section before making any rash decisions.

ADDITIONAL SOURCES OF INFORMATION

Having worked for Excelan (later to become a part of Novell) and been a marketer for PC and Macintosh TCP/IP software, Ed has a confession to make: "I probably know more about this stuff than is good for me." That's why we've tried to stay neutral and objective and point you at the vendors without making too many judgments ourselves. In this section we point you at some sources of information on these (and other) products, so you can do some investigating for yourself.

Using Archie and Veronica, you can search on strings for your platform (e.g., PC, Windows, msdos, Mac, Macintosh, UNIX, unix, etc.) and

Vendor	Product Name	Additional Information
Apple Computer	MacTCP	Most broadly used Macintosh IP software 20525 Mariani Avenue, Cupertino, CA, 95014 (408) 996-1010
Beame & Whiteside	BW-TCP for DOS	DOS and Windows TCP/IP software 706 Hillsborough St, Raleigh, NC, 27603-1655 (919) 831-8989
Distinct Corp	Distinct TCP	DOS and Windows TCP/IP software PO Box 3410, Saratoga, CA, 95070-1410 (408) 741-0781
Frontier Technologies	Super-TCP	DOS and Windows IP software; add-ons 10201 Port Washington Rd, Mequon, WI, 53092 (414) 241-4555
FTP Software	PC-TCP	DOS and Windows IP software 2 High Street, North Andover, MA, 01845 (800) 282-4287
IBM	TCP/IP for DOS	DOS and Windows TCP/IP software Dept E15, PO Box 12915, Triangle Pk, NC, 27709 (800) 426-2255
Ipswitch, Inc.	Piper/IP	DOS TCP/IP software 580 Main St, Reading, MA 01867 (617) 942-0621
Lanera Corporation	TCPOpen/Standard	DOS and Windows TCP/IP software 516 Valley Way, Milpitas, CA 05035 (408) 956-8344
Netmanage, Inc.	Chameleon[†]	Windows IP Software, add-ons 20823 Stevens Crk Blvd, Cupertino, CA, 95014 (408) 973-7171
Novell, Inc.	LAN Workplace for DOS and Windows for Macintosh	DOS, Windows & Mac TCP/IP software; add-ons 2180 Fortune Drive, San Jose, CA, 95131 (408) 434-2300
Spry, Inc.	AIR for Windows Internet-in-a-Box+	DOS and Windows TCP/IP software; add-ons 316 Occidental Ave So, 2nd Fl, Seattle, WA, 98104 (206) 447-0300
SunSelect, Inc.	PC-NFS	DOS and Windows TCP/IP software; add-ons 2 Elizabeth Drive, Chelmsford, MA, 01824 (508) 442-0000

Note: [†] Indicates special Internet access product (dial-in support) available.

Table 24.3 *A Sampling of Commercial TCP/IP Providers (continued)*

Table 24.3—Continued

Vendor	Product Name	Additional Information
Turbosoft Pty Ltd	TTCP	DOS and Windows TCP/IP software 3rd Fl, 579 Harris St, Ultimo, NSW Australia 2007 +61-2-281-3155
TWG	Pathway Access	DOS, Windows, & Mac TCP/IP software; add-ons 1129 San Antonio Rd, Palo Alto, CA, 94303 (415) 962-7202
X Link Technology	PC-LINK for DOS ...for Windows	DOS and Windows TCP/IP software, add-ons 741 Ames Avenue, Milpitas, CA 95035 (408) 263-8201

Table 24.3 *A Sampling of Commercial TCP/IP Providers*

for other qualifying strings like client, tcpip, winsock, and more. Most of the press reviews are mentioned in various e-mail messages and FAQ listings, so you can track those down pretty easily.

If you have a PC running DOS or Windows, we also strongly recommend that you download a document regularly uploaded and lovingly maintained by C. J. Sacksteder at Pennsylvania State University. To obtain it, please use Anonymous FTP to ftp.cac.psu.edu, look in directory /pub/dos/info/tcpip.packages for a document named tcp-ip.ibmpc (other platform users might also find it useful because of the resources and vendors it covers). It includes a treasure trove of information and is well worth reading.

SUMMARY

In this chapter we looked at shareware/freeware and commercial providers of TCP/IP software for a number of desktop platforms. Use this information as a guide for potential sources for such packages and products, but be sure to check the Internet for the latest and greatest information on the subject before making any final selections. You never know what will pop up in the meantime!

BULLETIN BOARD SECRETS

MAKING THE MOST OF USENET

In Chapter 10 we introduced Usenet, that vast conglomeration of academic conference, research institution, and coffee shop. You are aware that Usenet offers more information than you ever knew you needed, and perhaps you've already started exploring it. This chapter gives you the next set of tools you need to deal effectively with Usenet and keep that incredible amount of data from overwhelming you. First we offer some tips on finding information on Usenet, then we go over some strategies for getting the most out of your time on-line with it.

FINDING THINGS

In our previous discussions about Usenet, we emphasized that one should post only in newsgroups relevant to the question or comment. The next question that probably comes to your mind is: How do I find out which groups are relevant? You're in the same boat as the person who suspects that the answer she needs is somewhere on Usenet, but has no idea where. This section, then, gives you some tips on finding things in the tangle of Usenet.

Finding a Newsgroup

You're wondering whether a newsgroup exists to discuss classical music. You could post a question to some randomly chosen group (news.newusers.questions is popular) and hope someone there can tell you. But this is not really the correct topic for that group, and while people there might be more tolerant of your mistake than people on, say, comp.lang.fortran, you really are better off learning how to find the answers yourself. So let's try some other avenues.

Searching Using Your Newsreader

This method is surprisingly easy. Most newsreaders have search capabilities, enabling you to search through the entire list of newsgroups at your site for a group whose name contains a string you specify. In our example, you might start by searching for the string `music`. This is awfully broad, though, and would be likely to turn up far more groups than you really want to see. Next, try searching for the string `classical`. Sure enough, there it is: rec.music.classical. Your newsreader might ask you at this point whether you want to subscribe.

This technique has some drawbacks. First, it requires that the topic string actually appears in the name of the newsgroup, which is not necessarily going to be the case. Second, your site might not have all of the newsgroups, but your newsreader can search only those that it knows about. If you can find the name of a group, you can often ask your system administrator to add it to the list of groups at your site, but if you lack the name he or she might not be able to help you much.

So we need another level of search. Most people next turn to the list of newsgroups.

Searching Through the List of Newsgroups

In our sample Internet tour in Chapter 6, we downloaded a master list of newsgroups from an ftp site and searched through the list for keywords relating to the topic we wanted to research. While this list is not absolutely exhaustive, it's pretty close. Though new groups get added every day, this file is updated often enough that you can count on it listing the group you seek, if the group exists at all.

On UNIX, the string search utility called *grep* enables you to find a string within a file. On other systems, the command may be different. Consult your system documentation or administrator.

This method of finding newsgroups beats searching through the list of newsgroups using your newsreader because, as we saw in Chapter 6, the list also contains descriptions of most newsgroups. Thus your chances of finding a matching keyword go up quite a bit when you look through this file.

Surprise! There Is a Newsgroup For These Questions

If you still haven't found a group that looks promising, post a question to the news.groups.questions group. This is a group specifically for queries about where to look for topics and is especially well suited to searches for obscure topics.

Finding the List of Newsgroups

Well, it's all very nice of us to advise you to look in the list of newsgroups for information, but it doesn't do you much good if you don't happen to have that list. Never fear, there are several places from which you can get it.

The person who maintains the list posts it to news.answers periodically (once or twice per month), so if you are reading that group regularly, you are bound to see the list. Save it to your local storage space when you see it; it is quite useful.

If you don't have time to wait until the next time the list gets posted, you can always do what we did in Chapter 6—telnet a site that carries it and download it from there. We found a copy on the machine at ftp.uu.net, in the directory networking/news/config.

Once you have a copy of the list, you may find dozens, maybe hundreds, of newsgroups that sound interesting or to which you would like to subscribe. Browsing through the list can be almost as entertaining as reading news itself. We have warned you.

Finding Information Within Newsgroups

Ah, finally. You have found the group that brings together all lovers of potato salad, and you can happily read the postings to the group for a while as you begin to develop a sense of the rhythm of the group, the local potato salad culture, if you will. You are still wondering what the best way is to store and transport potato salad for picnics, but you are in no hurry, and trust that the answer will come along if you are patient.

In fact, it probably will. Then perhaps you get a phone call—there is an emergency, and you have to bring the potato salad to the next family picnic, the day after tomorrow. You panic. Then you head for the FAQ.

Read the FAQ

Most newsgroups see certain questions over and over, so the members create a file containing those questions and their answers to which they can direct new members. These questions are called *frequently asked questions*, and the files full of wisdom are called FAQs. Not all groups have FAQs, but those that do typically post them periodically (usually once a month, sometimes twice or more). In addition, the FAQs often get posted to one of the answers groups, such as comp.answers or news.answers. On top of that, a few sites have collections of many FAQs in storage and available for downloading; one such repository is at rtfm.mit.edu.

So using ftp, you retrieve the potato salad FAQ and scan it for storage information. They do indeed discuss storage and transport, but only in terms of temperature. That is, they agree that the salad must be kept chilled. But what you really need to know is whether a metal or plastic container is better for the flavors.

Searching the Current Articles

Perhaps by some coincidence someone is discussing this very topic in the group right now. To find out, bring up the newsgroup in your newsreader and search for some keywords. Most newsreaders have features that allow you to search for strings in the subject line, keyword list, or the entire article. You use these features to look for the strings "storage," "metal," and "plastic," but to no avail.

Ask Somebody!

You've done everything you can to find out on your own, and the answer just is not out there. So you compose your query, post it, and start boiling potatoes. When you come back to the computer several hours later, you are delighted to find that someone in New Zealand has done a careful study of the merits of potato salad storage containers and has the answer you need. Relieved, you finish your cooking and go on to enjoy the family reunion.

CONTROLLING THE FLOOD

You might enjoy the sheer volume of Usenet news at first, but as you watch your social life erode, you might start wishing you had some strategies for reducing the flow. This section offers some suggestions.

Catching Up

You don't have to read every article in every group every time you bring up your newsreader. If you want to skip all the articles in the current group, use your newsreader's Catch-Up feature, which marks all the articles as already read. You won't see them again, and the next time you start up the newsreader you'll see only those articles that have arrived since you last caught up. This feature is especially useful when you get back after being away, and every group has hundreds or even thousands of unread articles.

Dropping In

Rather than subscribing to every group in which you are even marginally interested, consider unsubscribing to all but the most important ones and just dropping in on the others occasionally. You can then keep up with the current events in a few areas, without getting involved in the minute details and without having to clear all the articles by hand. Admittedly, this takes some discipline, but if the traffic gets overwhelming, this is a good way to handle it.

Killfiles

Many newsreaders allow you to create files that contain filter commands. These commands might, for instance, instruct the reader not to show you any posts that relate to a certain topic, that have a certain string in their header, or that are from a certain person. Such a file is called a *killfile*, because it allows you to kill certain topics. If an article comes along that matches a command in your killfile, the newsreader simply does not display the article for you. You are never even aware that the article existed.

Carefully written, killfiles can reduce the amount of uninteresting traffic in some newsgroups. They can also, however, prevent you from seeing topics that do interest you if the topics happen to coincide with your killfile commands. Killfiles are most commonly used to "zap" postings from certain people rather than about certain topics.

SUMMARY

In this chapter we gave you some more tools to help you get the most out of Usenet. We discussed some searching techniques to help you find the information you need, and we went over some ways to keep the amount of information down to a manageable level.

INTERNET IN THE WORKPLACE

26

WHERE TO BEGIN

Whether you're an individual trying to get a connection to the Internet from home, or a systems administrator trying to hook up a number of users, it's wise to consider how a connection is going to be used before proceeding. A number of important decisions must be made, ranging from determining an acceptable level of service and cost, to defining and assigning domain names and numeric IP addresses, to setting up and maintaining necessary local TCP/IP-based services and applications.

From a local perspective, the first question has to be: Do you need a local-area network? For small offices or individuals, the answer to that question will most often be "no," unless a network is needed for other reasons. But as soon as you have three or four computers and a desire to share printers, fax machines, and so forth, the case for a network becomes pretty strong, whether or not Internet access is part of what's going on. If Internet access is at least desirable and a network is already in place (or is going to be), you should consider running that network using TCP/IP protocols or adding TCP/IP protocols to the existing environment (TCP/IP interoperates well with other popular LAN protocols, including Novell's IPX/SPX, NetBIOS, and NetBEUI).

The next questions relate to the type and frequency of Internet access needed: How much information will the users be moving to and from the Internet? How often will they be connecting? How long will they stay on-line? The answers to these questions will help you to determine the most useful kind of connection. If there's a lot of volume (5 MB or more per day), a lot of connections (more than four or five simultaneous logins at a time), or lots of connect time (more than four hours per day) needed, you'll want to consider a dedicated telephone line at a minimum of 14.4 Kbps (with 56 Kbps a better choice). If the need is less than this, intermittent dial-up on a 14.4 Kbps modem should be satisfactory, at least until your users begin to develop a greater appetite for Internet access.

The offsetting question versus the dictates of volume, type and frequency is budget: How much can you afford to spend on a monthly connection? If your budget stops short of $100 per month, a 14.4 dedicated PPP or SLIP connection is probably as much as you can afford. Typically, higher speed connections incur the following additional charges:

- Higher monthly service charge from the telephone company for higher-bandwidth service (at least double the normal business line charge, three or four times the normal residential line charge).
- Higher connect costs from service providers (56 Kbps dedicated PPP service starts at no less than $100 a month from even the cheapest providers; some go as high as $250 a month).
- More expensive connection equipment: to lease or purchase a CSU/DSU, a V.35 modem, and a router (to link the network to the telephone connection) will run $200 a month or more (outright cost amortized over 36 months or lease costs).

Add it all up and it's not atypical to pay $500–700 per month for a dedicated, higher speed connection. The imminent arrival of ISDN in many metropolitan areas and telephone exchanges will exert downward pressure on this, though, since ISDN costs run more in the $400–500 per month, including telephone service, a dedicated IP (PPP) connection, and hardware costs.

For smaller operations using POTS and conventional modems, you should still be prepared to pay $100–200 per month, including the costs of telephone service, Internet access provider charges, and hardware amortization. For intermittent access of less than two hours a day, you can get a dial-up account (rather than a dedicated line) in the $80–100 per month range.

Planning an Installation

When planning to provide Internet access, it's important to remember that you're also forced into planning for TCP/IP deployment as well. This means that you have to grapple with a sizable list of issues, as follows:

- Establishing a fully qualified Internet name (user@domain format) for each user, especially if the user is going to use e-mail (it will also be the user's e-mail address).
- Establishing whether you'll need one or more domain names for your organization and working with your access provider (or the InterNIC) to register that name (or names).
- Unless you represent a large organization or one with significant clout, it will probably be impossible to obtain a dedicated IP address. If this proves necessary, look for a national or local access provider that belongs to the CIX (Commercial Internet eXchange) and can resell IP addresses.

In most cases, you'll have to work with your access provider to establish e-mail names within the domain or domains it offers, or to work with it to establish domains of your own. Make sure that all e-mail names are unique and as understandable as possible (for more information on this subject, please consult our companion volume *E-mail Essentials*).

Establishing the Level of Service Needed

Once you've gone through the volume, frequency, and type versus budget analysis for access, you'll have a pretty good idea of what kind of service you'll need to request from a provider, at a minimum. Make sure you have a complete understanding of the provider's intermittent dial-up versus dedicated line costs and request information on higher bandwidth dedicated lines and ISDN service as well.

If the incremental cost of going from intermittent dial-up to dedicated line is low, it might very well be worth signing up for a dedicated line, even if you don't need the extra capacity right away. Most users start out slowly and tentatively on the Internet, but an increase in appetite always comes with improved familiarity and comfort. If you plan on 20% excess capacity and that leads you into choosing a dedicated line, you won't have to change your setup as quickly as you otherwise might.

In general, when planning for Internet access (or for systems design of any kind) leaving some slack in the design to accommodate growth is a useful strategy. When reviewing service plans with Internet providers, the following subsections cover what you're likely to hear from them (in ascending order of cost and complexity).

Simple Dial-up

This scenario has your user (or users) dialing a PC to attach to a service provider strictly to emulate a terminal on that machine (all file transfers, etc., will require non-TCP/IP software to work).

For this approach, modem rates of up to 14.4 Kbps are standard from most providers now. Be sure to buy a modem that runs at 14.4 Kbps with v.32bis and v.42 protocol support (this will support effective bandwidth of up to 38.2 Kbps because of special compression and signalling technology). Make sure your provider can handle these requirements; if not, find another.

Normal prices for this level of service ranges from $20–40 dollars a month, some with unlimited access, others with access limits on connect time. Be sure to shop around for the best combination of cost and services.

Dedicated Dial-up

This scenario has a PC dialed into the service provider continuously. Normally, the machine connected to the provider will also be attached to a network, so users can run a remote control program from their networked machines and access the Internet from their own desktops. Otherwise, they simply have to walk over to that machine and move files on and off using floppies.

Normal prices for this level of access ranges from $40–80 a month, some providers will restrict the number of individual users who can share such an attachment.

Intermittent Dial-up with PPP or SLIP Support

This scenario has the modem-attached PC running TCP/IP software (rather than communications software to the host and obtaining all services from that host). Users can run multiple TCP/IP applications from their desktops and use the remote host as a gateway to the Internet, where they can attach to whatever hosts they wish (and have access to).

Most experts recommend PPP over SLIP because it imposes less communications overhead, leaving more bandwidth for communications over the narrow telephone line. Either protocol will provide direct IP attachments from the desktop to the Internet, though.

Normal prices for this level of access range from $30–50 per month, with restrictions on the number of connect hours common (expect to pay at least $1 per hour for hours used over that limit).

Dedicated Dial-up with PPP or SLIP Support

This scenario is identical to the preceding one, except that it offers a 24-hour-a-day continuous connection. Normal prices for this level of access range from $80–$150 per month, with restrictions on the number of accounts and the amount of disk space available on the local host customary.

Dedicated and Nondedicated 56Kbps Connections

This scenario requires a more expensive phone line and costlier equipment, but provides much higher bandwidth. Network connections will involve a router, with a specialized modem and telephone connection required. Expect to spend at least $400 per month on such a setup, often more.

The best justification for this type of connection is when multiple users must get simultaneous access to the Internet over the network and when an organization seeks to establish an ongoing presence on the Internet (through a dedicated FTP server, WAIS service, a WWW server, etc.).

Dedicated and Non-dedicated ISDN Connections

This scenario resembles the preceding one strongly, except that it requires ISDN specific hardware and also assumes that your local telephone company can deliver ISDN services to your premises. Expect to spend at least $400 monthly for an ISDN connection, but expect to gain more effective bandwidth from such a connection than with a 56-Kbps linkup. Otherwise the justification is the same, and the technology newer and more capable.

Individuals or small businesses with no prior equipment investment are advised to seek ISDN services first and settle for conventional 56 Kbps services only if ISDN is not available. This is true not only because ISDN offers higher bandwidth, but also because the hardware is expected to be less expensive.

Dedicated T-1 or T-3 Connections

These are the kinds of connections most service providers use to gain access to a national access provider with a link to the Internet backbone. Bandwidth for T-1 goes up to 1.544 Mbps, and for T-3 up to 45 Mbps, but it's common for most local service providers to consume one or more 64 Kbps channels from a T-1 connection.

Such service costs at least $800 per month per channel, sometimes significantly more, depending on location. Only large organizations will typically need such connections, which also require a POP (point of presence) from the access provider as well.

Asynchronous Transfer
Mode (ATM) Connections

The major long-haul and regional telecommunications companies are revamping their own services to include 155 Mbps and 622 Mbps connections for telephone service backbones. Some companies are starting to use these technologies for LAN and WAN use, and a proposed RFC for IP over ATM is working its way through the IETF at present.

Expect to see ATM-based Internet access available by the end of 1995, or some time in 1996. We have no idea what such a service will cost, but it's reasonable to assume that it will be high enough to attract only national service providers and large, multinational or multiregional organizations with tens of thousands of dollars to spend monthly on high-bandwidth Internet access costs.

Only you can decide what level of service is appropriate, of course, but knowing what's generally available and normal price ranges in the United States could help you find a good deal or pass on a poor one.

Selecting a Service Provider

There are lots of qualities to look for in a service provider. In addition to cost, you'll want to find out what kind of services the provider offers. These include human services, like technical support and consulting (should you need it), as well as the range of Internet services directly available from their local host(s). It's customary to pay more to get more, so you'd expect to pay a service provider a greater monthly fee if its host offered local Gopher, WAIS, WWW, or other sophisticated Internet applications, as well as the standard collection.

It's also worthwhile to inquire what kind of newsfeeds a service provider collects, how many days' worth of news messages it keeps online (this is sometimes called the *scroll rate* since it determines how quickly such files age off a system). The type of Internet connection it uses and its bandwidth will also be a limiting factor on your use of the system, so it's wise to inquire about that, as well.

Often a bit of local research on the Internet itself can do a world of good. Even if you have no Internet account yourself, you probably know someone who does. Using Veronica, perform a search on the string "Access Providers" or "Local Access Providers." This will very often produce a document that you can use to obtain further information about what's available by way of Internet connections in your area. Don't forget to ask around, either—whether by e-mail or word of mouth, you can learn a lot about who's worth doing business with simply by asking.

User Training

Once you've decided on the connection that's right and have mapped out addresses for your users (even if it's just yourself), it's still a good idea to bone up on Internet technology, applications, protocols, and organization before venturing forth. We like to think that this book is all you'll ever need to find your way around, but the truth is that a staggering amount of information is available for training users, both in your local bookstore and on the Internet itself.

Very often, your service provider will offer classes, either on its premises or at yours, to bring newbies gently onto the Internet. While reading materials may abound, there's no substitute for a gently guided tour from an experienced professional. Even if you can't attend a formal class or arrange one for your users, it's always a good idea to team a newcomer up with an old hand, for a bit of one-on-one demonstration and question-and-answer.

Be prepared to spend some time and devote some effort to your users; you'll be rewarded manyfold. Ignore your users at your peril though—they'll continue to pester you with questions and complaints, no matter how hard you try to avoid them. The best approach is to schedule training (or one-on-one sessions) with new users and give them a hand getting started. This will save effort and avoid having to interrupt your day to repeatedly answer common questions and will help to cement a good working relationship with your user community.

ALLOCATING RESOURCES

Exposure to the Internet creates an appetite for information. Be it a stream of news messages or the latest and greatest update of the new Windows Mosaic client, you and your users won't come back from your forays onto the Internet empty-handed. Even though what some would call treasures others would call junk, the need for additional storage space can't be overlooked. Don't expect to open up a whole new world of information without adding some additional storage space to accommodate the new arrivals such access will provoke.

Likewise, adding Internet access to an existing network can be expected to increase the traffic load on that network. It's wise to do some capacity planning and review ahead of such an introduction, to make sure that Internet traffic doesn't become the straw that breaks the network's proverbial backbone. (For more information on capacity planning and network reconfigurations, please consult our companion volume *Network Design Essentials*.)

Finally, we already alluded to the need to devote people resources to the Internet, if only to prepare users to encounter its limitless majesty (and temptations) for the first time. In addition to training, be prepared to spend more time policing your disks to flush out stale treasures and monitor the network to keep tabs on traffic loads and conditions.

All in all, adding something—anything, in fact—to an existing network will consume some degree of resources, no matter how small. As long as you understand that adding an Internet link to your network (or your desktop, for that matter) will forever change your work habits and computer usage, you can remain flexible enough to deal with those changes. Being prepared to deal with this means being ready to spend time and to learn yourself; remembering this will help you deal with the difficulties and dramas that will sometimes come up.

SECURITY RULES AND GUIDELINES

The Internet is more than the sum of its parts, and it's an entire world of information. It's also the world's largest computing community, currently peopled by millions of users, regular and occasional, according to recent estimates. Inevitably, some of these millions, however small a percentage, will be malefactors, intent on exploiting unprotected resources and taking what they can get "for free."

Opening up to the Internet, especially if your organization installs a publicly accessible server or service, means being prepared to deal with the onslaught of outsiders. It's wise to set up your network so that such servers are isolated from the rest of your resources, perhaps even to the point of installing them on a standalone network segment that can be accessed only by going through a gateway or router.

That way, you can keep the bad guys at bay and protect the private resources and information your company needs to do business, while making the publicly available stuff just that—available to the public. Be sure to discuss any public access with your access provider and consider retaining a networking consultant to help you review your plans and designs from a security standpoint before going public. It's far better to pay an expert big money to head off problems, than to spend those funds fixing them after your security's been breached. Just as the victim of a burglary is likely to be hit again, so also do successful security violations breed further attempts.

SUMMARY

Bringing the Internet into a workplace can bring with it remarkable benefits, ranging from increased access to information and software to improved communication among colleagues and peers. Such a task is not to be undertaken lightly: It demands planning and careful consideration of the type and nature of the services that will be required. It also benefits from shopping around for an access provider that can meet your particular needs. Adding Internet access also imposes training requirements to prepare you and your users to deal with this treasure trove and to protect you from the world that waits without. If you're prepared to shoulder this burden, the benefits can be tremendous. But like all expeditions, it's best pursued after forethought and planning the steps that need to be taken along the way. The Boy Scout motto "Be prepared" is worth recalling when starting down the path to the Internet.

ACCESS PROVIDERS AND MORE . . .

27

GETTING TO THE LISTS

Lots of lists of Internet access providers are available. In fact, the bulk of this chapter is the work of Peter Kaminski, who very graciously gave us permission to reproduce his famous "PDIAL" (Public Dialup Internet Access List) document.

Finding lists on the Internet is a piece of cake, if you have access to Gopher. Select the Veronica service, and supply the words *Access Provider* or you can even try *Local Access Provider* or *National Access Provider*. We had no trouble conjuring up more information that you could believe, so you should have no difficulties, either. If you have access to a nearby Jughead, this is one of those cases where acting locally on a local collection of data will really get you exactly what you want.

National and Local Providers

Broadly stated, there are two classes of Internet access providers, typically called local and national. The difference has to do with presence, or the number of locations or area codes served. It also has to do with bandwidth—most local providers consume less than a full 1.544 Mbps T-1 link; most national providers consume multiple T-1s, and some even operate private 45 Mbps T-3 links. Since at least one of these national providers is a subsidiary of U.S. Sprint (SprintLink), some of them are probably using 622 Mbps ATM connections owned by a parent company or a long-haul service provider.

The relationship between local and national providers is sometimes quite interesting. Most local providers have relationships with one or more nationals for their own Internet access, so it is not unreasonable to think of the nationals as the wholesalers of Internet access and the local providers as the retailers of the same access. Actually, part of what local providers do is divvy up the bandwidth they buy from national providers and resell it to the public.

However, this picture is complicated by two significant elements. First, many national providers also do business with individuals and organizations, meaning that they are both wholesalers and retailers. Second, many local providers also offer services via the Internet that can be consumed by anyone with access—to some degree, this means they are doing business on more than a local basis.

The real criterion in selecting a national over a local provider should be determined by a need to obtain access from outside a local area, traded off against the typically higher fees that national providers charge. If your company has an outside sales force that covers the United States or the world and they need Internet access, you will probably be better served by doing business with a national provider, who can probably provide 800 numbers or local access, no matter where a call might originate. If you are not subject to these requirements, some combination of local access with pay-as-you-go service from a national provider when you're away from home may be the best bet.

PDIAL

In this section of the chapter we reproduce a document copyrighted by Peter Kaminski. This version preserves the contents of his work exactly, with only some minor changes to formatting to keep it consistent with the rest of this book. We encourage you to read the entire thing—not only does it present a comprehensive collection of local and national Internet service providers, it also includes a compendium of resources and information about the Internet that you will have to find interesting. The document also tells you everything you need to know about it, including how to download the most recent copy, and how to be placed on automatic distribution for future versions.

THE PUBLIC DIALUP INTERNET ACCESS LIST (PDIAL)

File PDIAL015.TXT—09 December 1993
Copyright 1992–1993 Peter Kaminski, of the Information Deli. Do not modify. Freely distributable for non-commercial purposes. Please contact me if you wish to distribute commercially or in modified form.

I make no representations about the suitability or accuracy of this document for any purpose. It is provided "as is" without express or implied warranty. All information contained herein is subject to change.

Contents:

-00- Quick Start!
-01- Area Code Summary: Providers With Many Local Dialins (1-800, PDN)
-02- Area Code Summary: US/Canada Metro and Regional Dialins
-03- Area Code Summary: International Dialins
-04- Alphabetical List of Providers
-05- What *Is* The Internet?
-06- What The PDIAL Is
-07- How People Can Get The PDIAL (This List)
-08- Appendix A: Other Valuable Resources
-09- Appendix B: Finding Public Data Network (PDN) Access Numbers
-10- Providers: Get Listed in PDIAL!

-00-Quick Start!

The Internet
is a global cooperative information network which can give you instant access to millions of people and terabytes of data. Providers listed in the PDIAL provide inexpensive public access to the Internet using your regular modem and computer. [Special note: the PDIAL currently lists only providers directly connected to the Internet. Much of the Internet can still be explored through systems with only Internet e-mail and USENET netnews connections, but you need to check other BBS lists to find them.]

Get a Guide:

I highly recommend obtaining one of the many good starter or guide books to the Internet. Think of them as travel guides to a new and different country, and you wouldn't be far off. See section -08- below for more details.

Choosing a Provider:

Phone charges can dominate the cost of your access to the Internet. Check first for providers with metro or regional dialins that are a local call for you (no per-minute phone charges). If there aren't any, move on to comparing prices for PDN, 800, and direct-dial long distance charges. Make sure to compare all your options. Calling long distance out-of-state or across the country is often cheaper than calling 30 miles away.

If you're not in North America and have no local provider, you may still be able to use one of the providers listed as having PDN access. Contact the individual providers with PDN access (see listings below) to find out.

Information Changes:

The information listed in the PDIAL changes and expands rapidly. If this edition is more than 2 months old, consider obtaining a new one. You can use the Info Deli e-mail server, which will provide you with updates and other information. Choose from the commands below and just e-mail them to <info-deli-server@netcom.com>.

"Send PDIAL"—receive the current PDIAL

"Subscribe PDIAL"—receive new editions of the PDIAL automatically

"Subscribe Info-Deli-News"—news of Info Deli changes and additions

See section -07- below for more details and other ways to obtain the PDIAL.

Check it Out:

Remember, the PDIAL is only a summary listing of the resources and environment delivered by each of the various providers. Contact the providers that interest you by e-mail or voice phone and make sure you find out if they have what you need.

Then GO FOR IT! Happy 'netting!

-01- Area Code Summary: Providers With Many Local Dialins (1-800, PDN)

800
class, cns, crl, csn, dial-n-cerf-usa, hookup.net, IGC, jvnc, OARnet
PDN
delphi, holonet, hookup.net, IGC, michnet, millennium, novalink, portal
PDN
psi-world-dial, psilink, tmn, well, world

"PDN" means the provider is accessible through a public data network (check the listings below for which network); note that many PDNs listed offer access outside North America as well as within North America. Check with the provider or the PDN for more details.

"800" means the provider is accessible via a "toll-free" US phone number. The phone company will not charge for the call, but the service provider will add a surcharge to cover the cost of the 800 service. This may be more expensive than other long-distance options.

-02- Area Code Summary: US/Canada Metro and Regional Dialins

If you are not local to any of these providers, it's still likely you are able to access those providers available through a public data network (PDN). Check the section above for providers with wide area access.

201 jvnc-tiger
202 CAPCON clarknet express michnet tmn
203 jvnc-tiger
205 nuance
206 eskimo GLAIDS halcyon netcom nwnexus olympus
212 echonyc maestro mindvox panix pipeline
213 crl dial-n-cerf kaiwan netcom
214 metronet netcom
215 jvnc-tiger PREPnet
216 OARnet wariat
217 prairienet
301 CAPCON clarknet express michnet tmn
302 ssnet
303 cns csn netcom nyx

305 gate.net
310 class crl dial-n-cerf kaiwan netcom
312 InterAccess mcsnet netcom xnet
313 michnet MSen
401 anomaly ids jvnc-tiger
403 PUCnet UUNET-Canada
404 crl netcom
407 gate.net
408 a2i netcom portal
410 CAPCON clarknet express
412 PREPnet telerama
415 a2i class crl dial-n-cerf IGC netcom portal well
416 hookup.net UUNET-Canada uunorth
419 OARnet
503 agora.rain.com netcom teleport
504 sugar
508 anomaly nearnet northshore novalink
510 class crl dial-n-cerf holonet netcom
512 realtime
513 fsp OARnet
514 CAM.ORG UUNET-Canada
516 jvnc-tiger
517 michnet
519 hookup.net UUNET-Canada uunorth
602 crl Data.Basix evergreen indirect
603 MV nearnet
604 UUNET-Canada
609 jvnc-tiger
613 UUNET-Canada uunorth
614 OARnet
616 michnet
617 delphi nearnet netcom northshore novalink world
619 cg57 class crash.cts.com cyber dial-n-cerf netcom
703 CAPCON clarknet express michnet netcom tmn
704 concert Vnet
707 crl
708 InterAccess mcsnet xnet
713 blkbox nuchat sugar
714 class dial-n-cerf express kaiwan netcom
717 PREPnet
718 maestro mindvox netcom panix pipeline
719 cns csn oldcolo

804 wyvern
810 michnet MSen
814 PREPnet
815 InterAccess mcsnet xnet
817 metronet
818 class dial-n-cerf netcom
905 UUNET-Canada
906 michnet
907 alaska.edu
908 express jvnc-tiger
910 concert
916 netcom
919 concert Vnet

These are area codes local to the dialups, although some prefixes in the area codes listed may not be local to the dialups. Check your phone book or with your phone company.

-03- Area Code Summary: International Dialins

If you are not local to any of these providers, there is still a chance you are able to access those providers available through a public data network (PDN). Check section -01- above for providers with wide area access, and send e-mail to them to ask about availability.

+44	(0)81 Demon dircon ibmpcug
+49	Individual.NET
+49 23	ins
+49 069	in-rhein-main
+49 089	mucev
+61 2	connect.com.au
+61 3	connect.com.au
+301	Ariadne
+353 1	IEunet

-04-: Alphabetical List of Providers

Fees are for personal dialup accounts with outgoing Internet access; most sites have other classes of service with other rate structures as well. Most support e-mail and netnews along with the listed services.

"Long distance: provided by user" means you need to use direct dial long distance or other long distance services to connect to the provider.

<< a2i >>
name ------------→ a2i communications
dialup————————→ 408-293-9010 (v.32bis), 415-364-5652 (v.32bis), 408-293-9020
                  (PEP); login 'guest'
area codes ———→ 408, 415
local access ——→ CA: West and South SF Bay Area
long distance -→ provided by user
services ————→ shell (SunOS UNIX and MS-DOS), ftp, telnet, irc, feeds,
                  domains and host-less domains, virtual ttys, gopher
fees ————————→ $20/month or $45/3 months or $72/6 months
email ————————→ info@rahul.net
voice ————————→ 408-293-8078 voicemail
ftp more info -→ ftp.rahul.net:/pub/BLURB

<< agora.rain.com >>
name ————————→ RainDrop Laboratories
dialup ————————→ 503-293-1772 (2400) 503-293-2059 (v.32, v.32 bis) 'apply'
area codes ——→ 503
local access ——→ OR: Portland, Beaverton, Hillsboro, Forest Grove, Gresham,
                  Tigard, Lake Oswego, Oregon City, Tualatin, Wilsonville
long distance -→ provided by user
services ————→ shell, ftp, telnet, gopher, usenet
fees ————————→ $6/month (1 hr/day limit)
email ————————→ info@agora.rain.com
voice ————————→ n/a
ftp more info -→ agora.rain.com:/pub/gopher-data/agora/agora

<< alaska.edu >>
name ————————→ University Of Alaska Southeast, Tundra Services
dialup ————————→ 907-789-1314
area codes ——→ 907
local access ——→ All Alaskan sites with local UACN access—Anchorage, Barrow,
                  Fairbanks, Homer, Juneau, Keni, Ketchikan, Kodiak, Kotzebue,
                  Nome, Palmer, Sitka, Valdez
long distance -→ provided by user
services ————→ Statewide UACN Mail, Internet, USENET, gopher, Telnet, FTP
fees ————————→ $20/month for individual accounts, discounts for 25+ and 50+
                  to public, gov't and non-profit organizations.

email ─────→ JNJMB@acad1.alaska.edu
voice ─────→ 907-465-6453
fax ─────→ 907-465-6295
ftp more info ─→ n/a

<< anomaly >>
name ─────→ Anomaly - Rhode Island's Gateway To The Internet
dialup ─────→ 401-331-3706 (v.32) or 401-455-0347 (PEP)
area codes ───→ 401, 508
local access ──→ RI: Providence/Seekonk Zone
long distance ─→ provided by user
services ─────→ shell, ftp, telnet, SLIP
fees ─────→ Commercial: $125/6 months or $200/year; Educational: $75/6
                   months or $125/year
email ─────→ info@anomaly.sbs.risc.net
voice ─────→ 401-273-4669
ftp more info ─→ anomaly.sbs.risc.net:/anomaly.info/access.zip

<< Ariadne >>
name ─────→ Ariadne - Greek Academic and Research Network
dialup ─────→ +301 65-48-800 (1200 - 9600 bps)
area codes ───→ +301
local access ──→ Athens, Greece
long distance ─→ provided by user
services ─────→ e-mail, ftp, telnet, gopher, talk, pad(EuropaNet)
fees ─────→ 5900 drachmas per calendar quarter, 1 hr/day limit.
email ─────→ dialup@leon.nrcps.ariadne-t.gr
voice ─────→ +301 65-13-392
fax ─────→ +301 6532910
ftp more info ─→ n/a

<< blkbox >>
name ─────→ The Black Box
dialup ─────→ (713) 480-2686 (V32bis/V42bis)
area codes ───→ 713
local access ──→ TX: Houston
long distance ─→ provided by user
services ─────→ shell, ftp, telnet, SLIP, PPP, UUCP
fees ─────→ $21.65 per month or $108.25 for 6 months
email ─────→ info@blkbox.com
voice ─────→ (713) 480-2684
ftp more info ─→ n/a

<< CAM.ORG >>

name	——→	Communications Accessibles Montreal
dialup	——→	514-931-7178 (v.32 bis), 514-931-2333 (2400bps)
area codes	——→	514
local access	——→	QC: Montreal, Laval, South-Shore, West-Island
long distance	--→	provided by user
services	——→	shell, ftp, telnet, gopher, wais, WWW, irc, feeds, SLIP, PPP, AppleTalk, FAX gateway
fees	——→	$25/month Cdn.
email	——→	info@CAM.ORG
voice	——→	514-931-0749
ftp more info	--→	ftp.CAM.ORG

<< CAPCON >>

name	——→	CAPCON Library Network
dialup	——→	contact for number
area codes	——→	202, 301, 410, 703
local access	——→	District of Columbia, Suburban Maryland & Northern Virginia
long distance	--→	various plans available/recommended; contact for details
services	——→	menu, archie, ftp, gopher, listservs, telnet, wais, whois, full day training and 'CAPCON Connect User Manual'
fees	——→	$35 start-up + $150/yr + $24/mo for first account from an institution; $35 start-up + $90/yr + $15/mo for additional users (member rates lower); 20 hours/month included, additional hours $2/hr
email	——→	capcon@capcon.net
voice	——→	202-331-5771
fax	——→	202-797-7719
ftp more info	--→	n/a

<< cg57 >>

name	——→	E & S Systems Public Access *Nix
dialup	——→	619-278-8267 (V.32bis, TurboPEP), 619-278-8267 (V32) 619-278-9837 (PEP)
area codes	——→	619
local access	——→	CA: San Diego
long distance	--→	provided by user
services	——→	shell, ftp, irc, telnet, gopher, archie, bbs (UniBoard)
fees	——→	bbs (FREE), shell - $30/3 months, $50/6 months, $80/9 months, $100/year
email	——→	steve@cg57.esnet.com

```
voice ─────────→    619-278-4641
ftp more info ─→    n/a
```

<< clarknet >>
```
name ──────────→    Clark Internet Services, Inc. (ClarkNet)
dialup ────────→    410-730-9786, 410-995-0271, 301-596-1626, 301-854-0446,
        301-621-5216 'guest'
area codes ────→    202, 301, 410, 703
local access ──→    MD: Baltimore; DC: Washington; VA: Northern VA
long distance ─→    provided by user
services ──────→    shell, menu, ftp, telnet, irc, gopher, hytelnet, www, WAIS,
                    SLIP/PPP, ftp space, feeds (UUCP & uMDSS), dns, Clarinet
fees ──────────→    $23/month or $66/3 months or $126/6 months or $228/year
email ─────────→    info@clark.net
voice ─────────→    Call 800-735-2258 then give 410-730-9764 (MD Relay Svc)
fax ───────────→    410-730-9765
ftp more info ─→    ftp.clark.net:/pub/clarknet/fullinfo.txt
```

<< class >>
```
name ──────────→    Cooperative Library Agency for Systems and Services
dialup ────────→    contact for number; NOTE: CLASS serves libraries and informa-
                    tion distributors only
area codes ────→    310, 415, 510, 619, 714, 818, 800
local access ──→    Northern and Southern California or anywhere (800) service is
                    available
long distance ─→    800 service available at $6/hour surcharge
services ──────→    menus, mail, telnet, ftp, gopher, wais, hytelnet, archie, WWW,
                    IRC, Unix shells, SLIP, etc. Training is available.
fees ──────────→    $4.50/hour + $150/year for first account + $50/year each addi-
                    tional account + $135/year CLASS membership. Discounts
                    available for multiple memberships.
email ─────────→    class@class.org
voice ─────────→    800-488-4559
fax ───────────→    408-453-5379
ftp more info ─→    n/a
```

<< cns >>
```
name ──────────→    Community News Service
dialup ────────→    719-520-1700 id 'new', passwd 'newuser'
area codes ────→    303, 719, 800
local access ──→    CO: Colorado Springs, Denver; continental US/800
```

long distance ⟶ 800 or provided by user
services ⟶ UNIX shell, email, ftp, telnet, irc, USENET, Clarinet, gopher, Commerce Business Daily
fees ⟶ $2.75/hour; $10/month minimum + $35 signup
email ⟶ service@cscns.com
voice ⟶ 719-592-1240
ftp more info ⟶ cscns.com

<< concert >>
name ⟶ CONCERT-CONNECT
dialup ⟶ contact for number
area codes ⟶ 704, 910, 919
local access ⟶ NC: Asheville, Chapel Hill, Charlotte, Durham, Greensboro, Greenville, Raleigh, Winston-Salem, Research Triangle Park
long distance ⟶ provided by user
services ⟶ UUCP, SLIP
fees ⟶ SLIP: $150 educational/research or $180 commercial for first 60 hours/month + $300 signup
email ⟶ info@concert.net
voice ⟶ 919-248-1999
ftp more info ⟶ ftp.concert.net

<< connect.com.au >>
name ⟶ connect.com.au pty ltd
dialup ⟶ contact for number
area codes ⟶ +61 3, +61 2
local access ⟶ Australia: Melbourne, Sydney
long distance ⟶ provided by user
services ⟶ SLIP, PPP, ISDN, UUCP, ftp, telnet, NTP, FTPmail
fees ⟶ AUS$2000/year (1 hour/day), 10% discount for AUUG members; other billing negotiable
email ⟶ connect@connect.com.au
voice ⟶ +61 3 5282239
fax ⟶ +61 3 5285887
ftp more info ⟶ ftp.connect.com.au

<< crash.cts.com >>
name ⟶ CTS Network Services (CTSNET)
dialup ⟶ 619-637-3640 HST, 619-637-3660 V.32bis, 619-637-3680 PEP 'help'
area codes ⟶ 619
local access ⟶ CA: San Diego, Pt. Loma, La Jolla, La Mesa, El Cajon, Poway,

Ramona, Chula Vista, National City, Mira Mesa, Alpine, East County, new North County numbers, Escondido, Oceanside, Vista

long distance ⟶	provided by user
services ⟶	Unix shell, UUCP, Usenet newsfeeds, NNTP, Clarinet, Reuters, FTP, Telnet, SLIP, PPP, IRC, Gopher, Archie, WAIS, POPmail, UMDSS, domains, nameservice, DNS
fees ⟶	$10-$23/month flat depending on features, $15 startup, personal $20/month flat depending on features, $25 startup, commercial
email ⟶	info@crash.cts.com (server), support@crash.cts.com (human)
voice ⟶	619-637-3637
fax ⟶	619-637-3630
ftp more info ⟶	n/a

<< crl >>

name ⟶	CR Laboratories Dialup Internet Access
dialup ⟶	415-389-UNIX
area codes ⟶	213, 310, 404, 415, 510, 602, 707, 800
local access ⟶	CA: San Francisco Bay area + San Rafael, Santa Rosa, Los Angeles, Orange County; AZ: Phoenix, Scottsdale, Tempe, and Glendale; GA: Atlanta metro area; continental US/800
long distance ⟶	800 or provided by user
services ⟶	shell, ftp, telnet, feeds, SLIP, WAIS
fees ⟶	$17.50/month + $19.50 signup
email ⟶	info@crl.com
voice ⟶	415-381-2800
ftp more info ⟶	n/a

<< csn >>

name ⟶	Colorado SuperNet, Inc.
dialup ⟶	contact for number
area codes ⟶	303, 719, 800
local access ⟶	CO: Alamosa, Boulder/Denver, Colorado Springs, Durango, Fort Collins, Frisco, Glenwood Springs/Aspen, Grand Junction, Greeley, Gunnison, Pueblo, Telluride; anywhere 800 service is available
long distance ⟶	provided by user or 800
services ⟶	shell or menu, UUCP, SLIP, 56K, ISDN, T1; ftp, telnet, irc, gopher, WAIS, domains, anonymous ftp space, email-to-fax
fees ⟶	$1/hour off-peak, $3/hour peak ($250 max/month) + $20 signup, $5/hr surcharge for 800 use

email ───────→ info@csn.org
voice ───────→ 303-273-3471
fax ───────→ 303-273-3475
ftp more info ─→ csn.org:/CSN/reports/DialinInfo.txt
off-peak ───────→ midnight to 6am

<< cyber >>
name ───────→ The Cyberspace Station
dialup ───────→ 619-634-1376 'guest'
area codes ──→ 619
local access ─→ CA: San Diego
long distance ─→ provided by user
services ───────→ shell, ftp, telnet, irc
fees ───────→ $15/month + $10 startup or $60 for six months
email ───────→ help@cyber.net
voice ───────→ n/a
ftp more info ─→ n/a

<< Data.Basix >>
name ───────→ Data Basix
dialup ───────→ 602-721-5887
area codes ──→ 602
local access ─→ AZ: Tucson
long distance ─→ provided by user
services ───────→ Telnet, FTP, NEWS, UUCP; on-site assistance
fees ───────→ $25 monthly, $180 yearly; group rates available
email ───────→ info@Data.Basix.com (automated); sales@Data.Basix.com
              (human)
voice ───────→ 602-721-1988
ftp more info ─→ Data.Basix.COM:/services/dial-up.txt

<< Demon >>
name ───────→ Demon Internet Systems (DIS)
dialup ───────→ +44 (0)81 343 4848
area codes ──→ +44 (0)81
local access ─→ London, England
long distance ─→ provided by user
services ───────→ ftp, telnet, SLIP/PPP
fees ───────→ GBPounds 10.00/month; 132.50/year (inc 12.50 startup charge).
              No on-line time charges.
email ───────→ internet@demon.co.uk

voice ──────→ +44 (0)81 349 0063
ftp more info ─→ n/a

<< delphi >>
name ──────→ DELPHI
dialup ──────→ 800-365-4636 'JOINDELPHI password:INTERNETSIG'
area codes ───→ 617, PDN
local access ──→ MA: Boston; KS: Kansas City
long distance ─→ Sprintnet or Tymnet: $9/hour weekday business hours, no charge nights and weekends
services ─────→ ftp, telnet, feeds, user groups, wire services, member conferencing
fees ───────→ $10/month for 4 hours or $20/month for 20 hours + $3/month for Internet services
email ──────→ walthowe@delphi.com
voice ──────→ 800-544-4005
ftp more info ─→ n/a

<< dial-n-cerf >>
name ──────→ DIAL n' CERF or DIAL n' CERF AYC
dialup ──────→ contact for number
area codes ───→ 213, 310, 415, 510, 619, 714, 818
local access ──→ CA: Los Angeles, Oakland, San Diego, Irvine, Pasadena, Palo Alto
long distance ─→ provided by user
services ─────→ shell, menu, irc, ftp, hytelnet, gopher, WAIS, WWW, terminal service, SLIP
fees ───────→ $5/hour ($3/hour on weekend) + $20/month + $50 startup OR $250/month flat for AYC
email ──────→ help@cerf.net
voice ──────→ 800-876-2373 or 619-455-3900
ftp more info ─→ nic.cerf.net:/cerfnet/dial-n-cerf/
off-peak ─────→ Weekend: 5pm Friday to 5pm Sunday

<< dial-n-cerf-usa >>
name ──────→ DIAL n' CERF USA
dialup ──────→ contact for number
area codes ───→ 800
local access ──→ anywhere (800) service is available
long distance ─→ included
services ─────→ shell, menu, irc, ftp, hytelnet, gopher, WAIS, WWW, terminal service, SLIP

fees ⟶ $10/hour ($8/hour on weekend) + $20/month
email ⟶ help@cerf.net
voice ⟶ 800-876-2373 or 619-455-3900
ftp more info ⟶ nic.cerf.net:/cerfnet/dial-n-cerf/
off-peak ⟶ Weekend: 5pm Friday to 5pm Sunday

<< dircon >>
name ⟶ The Direct Connection
dialup ⟶ +44 (0)81 317 2222
area codes ⟶ +44 (0)81
local access ⟶ London, England
long distance ⟶ provided by user
services ⟶ shell or menu, UUCP feeds, SLIP/PPP, ftp, telnet, gopher, WAIS, Archie, personal ftp/file space, email-to-fax
fees ⟶ Subscriptions from GBPounds 10 per month, no on-line charges. GBPounds 7.50 signup fee.
email ⟶ helpdesk@dircon.co.uk
voice ⟶ +44 (0)81 317 0100
fax ⟶ +44 (0)81 317 0100
ftp more info ⟶ n/a

<< echonyc >>
name ⟶ Echo Communications
dialup ⟶ (212) 989-8411 (v.32, v.32 bis) 'newuser'
area codes ⟶ 212
local access ⟶ NY: Manhattan
long distance ⟶ provided by user
services ⟶ shell, ftp, telnet, gopher, archie, wais, SLIP/PPP
fees ⟶ Commercial: $19.95/month; students/seniors: $13.75/month
email ⟶ horn@echonyc.com
voice ⟶ 212-255-3839
ftp more info ⟶ n/a

<< eskimo >>
name ⟶ Eskimo North
dialup ⟶ 206-367-3837 300-14.4k, 206-362-6731 for 9600/14.4k, 206-742-1150 World Blazer
area codes ⟶ 206
local access ⟶ WA: Seattle, Everett
long distance ⟶ provided by user
services ⟶ shell, ftp, telnet

fees ───────→ $10/month or $96/year
email ───────→ nanook@eskimo.com
voice ───────→ 206-367-7457
ftp more info ─→ n/a

<< evergreen >>
name ───────→ Evergreen Communications
dialup ───────→ (602) 955-8444
area codes ───→ 602
local access ──→ AZ
long distance ─→ provided by user or call for additional information
services ──────→ ftp, telnet, gopher, archie, wais, www, uucp, PPP
fees ───────→ individual: $239/yr; commercial: $479/yr; special educational
                          rates
email ───────→ evergreen@libre.com
voice ───────→ 602-955-8315
fax ────────→ 602-955-5948
ftp more info ─→ n/a

<< express >>
name ───────→ Express Access - A service of Digital Express Group
dialup ───────→ 301-220-0462, 410-766-1855, 703-281-7997, 714-377-9784, 908-937-
                          9481 'new'
area codes ───→ 202, 301, 410, 703, 714, 908
local access ──→ Northern VA, Baltimore MD, Washington DC, New Brunswick
                          NJ, Orange County CA
long distance ─→ provided by user
services ──────→ shell, ftp, telnet, irc, gopher, hytelnet, www, Clarinet, SLIP/PPP,
                          archie, mailing lists, autoresponders, anonymous FTP archives
fees ───────→ $25/month or $250/year
email ───────→ info@digex.net
voice ───────→ 800-969-9090, 301-220-2020
ftp more info ─→ n/a

<< fsp >>
name ───────→ Freelance Systems Programming
dialup ───────→ (513) 258-7745 to 14.4 Kbps
area codes ───→ 513
local access ──→ OH: Dayton
long distance ─→ provided by user
services ──────→ shell, ftp, telnet, feeds, email, gopher, archie, SLIP, etc.

fees ————————→ $20 startup and $1 per hour
email ————————→ fsp@dayton.fsp.com
voice ————————→ (513) 254-7246
ftp more info ——→ n/a

<< gate.net >>
name ——————→ CyberGate, Inc
dialup ——————→ 305-425-0200
area codes ———→ 305, 407
local access ———→ South Florida, expanding in FL
long distance ——→ provided by user
services ——————→ shell, UUCP, SLIP/PPP, leased, telnet, FTP, IRC, archie, gopher,
                   etc.
fees ————————→ $17.50/mo on credit card; group discounts; SLIP/PPP:
                   $17.50/mo + $2/hr
email ————————→ info@gate.net or sales@gate.net
voice ————————→ 305-428-GATE
fax —————————→ 305-428-7977
ftp more info ——→ n/a

<< GLAIDS >>
name ——————→ GLAIDS NET (Homosexual Network)
dialup ——————→ 206-322-0621
area codes ———→ 206
local access ———→ WA: Seattle
long distance ——→ provided by user
services ——————→ BBS, Gopher, ftp, telnet
fees ————————→ $10/month. Scholarships available. Free 7 day trial. Visitors are
                   welcome.
email ————————→ tomh@glaids.wa.com
voice ————————→ 206-323-7483
ftp more info ——→ GLAIDS.wa.com

<< halcyon >>
name ——————→ Halcyon
dialup ——————→ 206-382-6245 'new', 8N1
area codes ———→ 206
local access ———→ Seattle, WA
long distance ——→ provided by user
services ——————→ shell, telnet, ftp, bbs, irc, gopher, hytelnet
fees ————————→ $200/year, or $60/quarter + $10 start-up

email ———————→ info@halcyon.com
voice ———————→ 206-955-1050
ftp more info —→ halcyon.com:/pub/waffle/info

<< holonet >>
name ———————→ HoloNet
dialup ———————→ 510-704-1058
area codes ———→ 510, PDN
local access ——→ Berkeley, CA
long distance —→ [per hour, off-peak/peak] Bay Area: $0.50/$0.95; PSINet A: $0.95/$1.95; PSINet B: $2.50/$6.00; Tymnet: $3.75/$7.50
services ———————→ ftp, telnet, irc, games
fees ———————→ $2/hour off-peak, $4/hour peak; $6/month or $60/year minimum
email ———————→ info@holonet.net
voice ———————→ 510-704-0160
ftp more info —→ holonet.net:/info/
off-peak ———————→ 5pm to 8am + weekends and holidays

<< hookup.net >>
name ———————→ HookUp Communication Corporation
dialup ———————→ contact for number
area codes ———→ 800, PDN, 416, 519
local access ——→ Ontario, Canada
long distance —→ 800 access across Canada, or discounted rates by HookUp
services ———————→ shell or menu, UUCP, SLIP, PPP, ftp, telnet, irc, gopher, domains, anonymous ftp space
fees ———————→ Cdn$14.95/mo for 5 hours; Cdn$34.95/mo for 15 hrs; Cdn$59.95/mo for 30 hrs; Cdn$300.00/yr for 50 hrs/mo; Cdn$299.00/mo for unlimited usage
email ———————→ info@hookup.net
voice ———————→ 519-747-4110
fax ———————→ 519-746-3521
ftp more info —→ n/a

<< ibmpcug >>
name ———————→ UK PC User Group
dialup ———————→ +44 (0)81 863 6646
area codes ———→ +44 (0)81
local access ——→ London, England
long distance —→ provided by user

services ———→ ftp, telnet, bbs, irc, feeds
fees ———→ GBPounds 15.50/month or 160/year + 10 startup (no time charges)
email ———→ info@ibmpcug.co.uk
voice ———→ +44 (0)81 863 6646
ftp more info –→ n/a

<< ids >>
name ———→ The IDS World Network
dialup ———→ 401-884-9002, 401-785-1067
area codes ———→ 401
local access ———→ East Greenwich, RI; northern RI
long distance –→ provided by user
services ———→ ftp, telnet, SLIP, feeds, bbs
fees ———→ $10/month or $50/half year or $100/year
email ———→ sysadmin@ids.net
voice ———→ 401-884-7856
ftp more info –→ ids.net:/ids.net

<< IEunet >>
name ———→ IEunet Ltd., Ireland's Internet Services Supplier
dialup ———→ +353 1 6790830, +353 1 6798600
area codes ———→ +353 1
local access ———→ Dublin, Ireland
long distance –→ provided by user, or supplied by IEunet
services ———→ DialIP, IPGold, EUnet Traveller, X400, X500, Gopher, WWW, FTP, FTPmail,SLIP/PPP, FTP archives
fees ———→ IEP25/month Basic
email ———→ info@ieunet.ie, info@Ireland.eu.net
voice ———→ +353 1 6790832
ftp more info –→ ftp.ieunet.ie:/pub

<< IGC >>
name ———→ Institute for Global Communications/IGC Networks (PeaceNet, EcoNet, ConflictNet, LaborNet, HomeoNet)
dialup ———→ 415-322-0284 (N-8-1), 'new'
area codes ———→ 415, 800, PDN
local access ———→ CA: Palo Alto, San Francisco
long distance –→ [per hour, off-peak/peak] SprintNet: $2/$7; 800: $11/$11
services ———→ telnet, local newsgroups for environmental, peace/social justice issues; NO ftp

fees ——————→ $10/month + $3/hr after first hour
email ——————→ support@igc.apc.org
voice ——————→ 415-442-0220
ftp more info —→ igc.apc.org:/pub

<< indirect >>
name ——————→ Internet Direct, Inc.
dialup ——————→ 602-274-9600 (Phoenix); 602-321-9600 (Tucson); 'guest'
area codes ———→ 602
local access ——→ AZ: Phoenix, Tucson
long distance —→ provided by user
services ——————→ Shell/menu, UUCP, Usenet, NNTP, FTP, Telnet, SLIP, PPP, IRC,
                  Gopher, WAIS, WWW, POP, DNS, nameservice, QWK (offline
                  readers)
fees ——————→ $20/month (personal); $30/month (business)
email ——————→ info@indirect.com (automated); support@indirect.com (human)
voice ——————→ 602-274-0100 (Phoenix), 602-324-0100 (Tucson)
ftp more info —→ n/a

<< Individual.NET >>
name ——————→ Individual Network e.V. (IN)
dialup ——————→ contact for number
area codes ———→ +49
local access ——→ Germany: Berlin, Oldenburg, Bremen, Hamburg, Krefeld, Kiel,
                  Duisburg, Darmstadt, Dortmund, Hannover, Ruhrgebiet, Bonn,
                  Magdeburg, Duesseldorf, Essen, Koeln, Paderborn, Bielefeld,
                  Aachen, Saarbruecken, Frankfurt, Braunschweig, Dresden, Ulm,
                  Erlangen, Nuernberg, Wuerzburg, Chemnitz, Muenchen,
                  Muenster, Goettingen, Wuppertal, Schleswig, Giessen, Rostock,
                  Leipzig and others
long distance —→ provided by user
services ——————→ e-mail, usenet feeds, UUCP, SLIP, ISDN, shell, ftp, telnet,
                  gopher, irc, bbs
fees ——————→ 15-30 DM/month (differs from region to region)
email ——————→ in-info@individual.net
voice ——————→ +49 2131 64190 (Andreas Baess)
fax ——————→ +49 2131 605652
ftp more info —→ ftp.fu-berlin.de:/pub/doc/IN/

<< in-rhein-main >>
name ——————→ Individual Network - Rhein-Main

dialup ————→ +49-69-39048414, +49-69-6312934 (+ others)
area codes ——→ +49 069
local access ——→ Frankfurt/Offenbach, Germany
long distance –→ provided by user
services ————→ shell (Unix), ftp, telnet, irc, gopher, uucp feeds
fees ————————→ SLIP/PPP/ISDN: 40 DM, 4 DM / Megabyte
email ——————→ info@rhein-main.de
voice ——————→ +49-69-39048413
ftp more info –→ n/a

<< ins >>
name ————————→ INS - Inter Networking Systems
dialup ————→ contact for number
area codes ——→ +49 23
local access ——→ Ruhr-Area, Germany
long distance –→ provided by user
services ————→ e-mail,uucp,usenet,slip,ppp,ISDN-TCP/IP
fees ————————→ fees for commercial institutions and any others:
                 uucp/e-mail,uucp/usenet:$60/month; ip:$290/month mini-
                 mum
email ——————→ info@ins.net
voice ——————→ +49 2305 356505
fax ——————————→ +49 2305 25411
ftp more info –→ n/a

<< InterAccess >>
name ————————→ InterAccess
dialup ————→ 708-671-0237
area codes ——→ 708, 312, 815
local access ——→ Chicagoland metropolitan area
long distance –→ provided by user
services ————→ ftp, telnet, SLIP/PPP, feeds, shell, UUCP, DNS, ftp space
fees ————————→ $23/mo shell, $26/mo SLIP/PPP, or $5/mo +$2.30/hr
email ——————→ info@interaccess.com
voice ——————→ (800) 967-1580
fax ——————————→ 708-671-0113
ftp more info –→ interaccess.com:/pub/interaccess.info

<< jvnc >>
name ————————→ The John von Neumann Computer Network - Tiger Mail &
                 Dialin' Terminal

dialup	———→	contact for number
area codes	———→	800
local access	———→	anywhere (800) service is available
long distance	—→	included
services	———→	email and newsfeed or terminal access only
fees	———→	$19/month + $10/hour + $36 startup (PC or Mac SLIP software included)
email	———→	info@jvnc.net
voice	———→	800-35-TIGER, 609-897-7300
fax	———→	609-897-7310
ftp more info	—→	n/a

<< jvnc-tiger >>

name	———→	The John von Neumann Computer Network - Dialin' Tiger
dialup	———→	contact for number
area codes	———→	201, 203, 215, 401, 516, 609, 908
local access	———→	Princeton & Newark, NJ; Philadelphia, PA; Garden City, NY; Bridgeport, New Haven, & Storrs, CT; Providence, RI
long distance	—→	provided by user
services	———→	ftp, telnet, SLIP, feeds, optional shell
fees	———→	$99/month + $99 startup (PC or Mac SLIP software included— shell is additional $21/month)
email	———→	info@jvnc.net
voice	———→	800-35-TIGER, 609-897-7300
fax	———→	609-897-7310
ftp more info	—→	n/a

<< kaiwan >>

name	———→	KAIWAN Public Access Internet Online Services
dialup	———→	714-539-5726, 310-527-7358
area codes	———→	213, 310, 714
local access	———→	CA: Los Angeles, Orange County
long distance	—→	provided by user
services	———→	shell, ftp, telnet, irc, WAIS, gopher, SLIP/PPP, ftp space, feeds, dns, 56K leasd line
fees	———→	$15.00/signup + $15.00/month or $30.00/quarter (3 month) or $11.00/month by credit card
email	———→	info@kaiwan.com
voice	———→	714-638-2139
ftp more info	—→	kaiwan.com:/pub/KAIWAN

<< maestro >>

name ————→ Maestro
dialup ————→ (212) 240-9700 'newuser'
area codes ——→ 212, 718
local access ——→ NY: New York City
long distance —→ provided by user
services ————→ shell, ftp, telnet, gopher, wais, irc, feeds, etc.
fees ————→ $15/month or $150/year
email ————→ info@maestro.com (autoreply); staff@maestro.com, rkelly@mae-
                   stro.com, ksingh@maestro.com
voice ————→ 212-240-9600
ftp more info —→ n/a

<< mcsnet >>

name ————→ MCSNet
dialup ————→ (312) 248-0900 V.32, 0970 V.32bis, 6295 (PEP), follow prompts
area codes ——→ 312, 708, 815
local access ——→ IL: Chicago
long distance —→ provided by user
services ————→ shell, ftp, telnet, feeds, email, irc, gopher, hytelnet, etc.
fees ————→ $25/month or $65/3 months untimed, $30/3 months for 15
                   hours/month
email ————→ info@genesis.mcs.com
voice ————→ (312) 248-UNIX
ftp more info —→ genesis.mcs.com:/mcsnet.info/

<< metronet >>

name ————→ Texas Metronet
dialup ————→ 214-705-2901/817-261-1127 (V.32bis),214-705-2929(PEP),'info' or
                   214-705-2917/817-261-7687 (2400) 'signup'
area codes ——→ 214, 817
local access ——→ TX: Dallas, Fort Worth
long distance —→ provided by user
services ————→ shell, ftp, telnet, SLIP, PPP, uucp feeds
fees ————→ $5-$45/month + $10-$30 startup
email ————→ info@metronet.com
voice ————→ 214-705-2900, 817-543-8756
fax ————→ 214-401-2802 (8am-5pm CST weekdays)
ftp more info —→ ftp.metronet.com:/pub/metronetinfo/

<< michnet >>

name ————→ Merit Network, Inc.—MichNet project

dialup ———→   contact for number or telnet hermes.merit.edu and type 'help'
at 'Which host?' prompt
area codes ——→   202, 301, 313, 517, 616, 703, 810, 906, PDN
local access ——→   Michigan; Boston, MA; Wash. DC
long distance —→   SprintNet, Autonet, Michigan Bell packet-switch network
services ———→   telnet, SLIP, PPP, outbound SprintNet, Autonet and Ann Arbor
dialout
fees ————→ $35/month + $40 signup ($10/month for K-12 & libraries in
Michigan)
email ————→   info@merit.edu
voice ————→   313-764-9430
ftp more info —→   nic.merit.edu:/

<< millennium >>
name ————→   Millennium Online
dialup ————→   contact for numbers
area codes ——→   PDN
local access ——→   PDN private numbers available
long distance —→   PDN
services ———→   shell, ftp, telnet, irc, feeds, gopher, graphical bbs
(interface required)
fees ————→ $10 monthly/.10 per minute domestic .30 internationally
email ————→   jjablow@mill.com
voice ————→   800-736-0122
ftp more info —→   n/a

<< mindvox >>
name ————→   MindVOX
dialup ————→   212-989-4141 'mindvox' 'guest'
area codes ——→   212, 718
local access ——→   NY: New York City
long distance —→   provided by user
services ———→   conferencing system ftp, telnet, irc, gopher, hytelnet, Archives,
BBS
fees ————→ $15-$20/month. No startup.
email ————→   info@phantom.com
voice ————→   212-989-2418
ftp more info —→   n/a

<< MSen >>
name ————→   MSen
dialup ————→   contact for number

area codes ———→ 313, 810
local access ———→ All of SE Michigan (313, 810)
long distance —→ provided by user
services ————→ shell, WAIS, gopher, telnet, ftp, SLIP, PPP, IRC, WWW, Picospan
BBS, ftp space
fees ——————→ $20/month; $20 startup
email —————→ info@msen.com
voice —————→ 313-998-4562
fax ———————→ 313-998-4563
ftp more info —→ ftp.msen.com:/pub/vendor/msen

<< mucev >>
name ————→ muc.de e.V.
dialup ————→ contact for numbers
area codes ———→ +49 089
local access ——→ Munich/Bavaria, Germany
long distance —→ provided by user
services ————→ mail, news, ftp, telnet, irc, gopher, SLIP/PPP/UUCP
fees ——————→ From DM 20.— (Mail only) up to DM 65.— (Full Account with
PPP)
email —————→ postmaster@muc.de
voice —————→
ftp more info —→ ftp.muc.de:public/info/muc-info.*

<< MV >>
name ————→ MV Communications, Inc.
dialup ————→ contact for numbers
area codes ———→ 603
local access ——→ Many NH communities
long distance —→ provided by user
services ————→ shell, ftp, telnet, gopher, SLIP, email, feeds, dns, archives, etc.
fees ——————→ $5.00/mo minimum + variable hourly rates. See schedule.
email —————→ info@mv.com
voice —————→ 603-429-2223
ftp more info —→ ftp.mv.com:/pub/mv

<< nearnet >>
name ————→ NEARnet
dialup ————→ contact for numbers
area codes ———→ 508, 603, 617
local access ——→ Boston, MA; Nashua, NH

long distance —→	provided by user
services ———→	SLIP, email, feeds, dns
fees ———→	$250/month
email ———→	nearnet-join@nic.near.net
voice ———→	617-873-8730
ftp more info —→	nic.near.net:/docs

<< netcom >>

name ———→	Netcom Online Communication Services
dialup ———→	206-547-5992, 214-753-0045, 303-758-0101, 310-842-8835, 312-380-0340, 404-303-9765, 408-241-9760, 408-459-9851, 415-328-9940, 415-985-5650, 503-626-6833, 510-274-2900, 510-426-6610, 510-865-9004, 617-237-8600, 619-234-0524, 703-255-5951, 714-708-3800, 818-585-3400, 916-965-1371
area codes ———→	206, 213, 214, 303, 310, 312, 404, 408, 415, 503, 510, 617, 619, 703, 714, 718, 818, 916
local access ———→	CA: Alameda, Irvine, Los Angeles, Palo Alto, Pasadena, Sacramento, San Diego, San Francisco, San Jose, Santa Cruz, Walnut Creek; CO: Denver; DC: Washington; GA: Atlanta; IL: Chicago; MA: Boston; OR: Portland; TX: Dallas; WA: Seattle
long distance —→	provided by user
services ———→	shell, ftp, telnet, irc, WAIS, gopher, SLIP/PPP, ftp space, feeds, dns
fees ———→	$19.50/month + $20.00 signup
email ———→	info@netcom.com
voice ———→	408-554-8649, 800-501-8649
fax ———→	408-241-9145
ftp more info —→	ftp.netcom.com:/pub/netcom/

<< northshore >>

name ———→	North Shore Access
dialup ———→	617-593-4557 (v.32bis, v.32, PEP) 'new'
area codes ———→	617, 508
local access ———→	MA: Wakefield, Lynnfield, Lynn, Saugus, Revere, Peabody, Salem, Marblehead, Swampscott
long distance —→	provided by user
services ———→	shell (SunOS UNIX), ftp, telnet, archie, gopher, wais, www, UUCP feeds
fees ———→	$9/month includes 10 hours connect, $1/hr thereafter, higher volume discount plans also available
email ———→	info@northshore.ecosoft.com

voice ⟶ 617-593-3110 voicemail
ftp more info ⟶ northshore.ecosoft.com:/pub/flyer

<< novalink >>
name ⟶ NovaLink
dialup ⟶ (800) 937-7644 'new' or 'info', 508-754-4009 2400, 14400
area codes ⟶ 508, 617, PDN
local access ⟶ MA: Worcester, Cambridge, Marlboro, Boston
long distance ⟶ CPS: $1.80/hour 2400, 9600; SprintNet $1.80/hour nights and weekends
services ⟶ ftp, telnet, gopher, shell, irc, XWindows, feeds, adult, user groups, FAX, Legends of Future Past
fees ⟶ $12.95 sign-up (refundable and includes 2 hours), + $9.95/mo (includes 5 daytime hours) + $1.80/hr
email ⟶ info@novalink.com
voice ⟶ 800-274-2814
ftp more info ⟶ ftp.novalink.com:/info

<< nuance >>
name ⟶ Nuance Network Services
dialup ⟶ contact for number
area codes ⟶ 205
local access ⟶ AL: Huntsville
long distance ⟶ provided by user
services ⟶ shell (Unix SVR4.2), ftp, telnet, gopher, SLIP, PPP, ISDN
fees ⟶ personal $25/mo + $35 start-up, corporate: call for options
email ⟶ staff@nuance.com
voice ⟶ 205-533-4296 voice/recording
ftp more info ⟶ ftp.nuance.com:/pub/NNS-INFO

<< nuchat >>
name ⟶ South Coast Computing Services, Inc.
dialup ⟶ (713) 661-8593 (v.32) - (713) 661-8595 (v.32bis)
area codes ⟶ 713
local access ⟶ TX: Houston metro area
long distance ⟶ provided by user
services ⟶ shell, ftp, telnet, gopher, Usenet, UUCP feeds, SLIP, dedicated lines, domain name service, FULL time tech support
fees ⟶ dialup - $3/hour, UUCP - $1.50/hour or $100/month unlimited, dedicated - $120, unlimited access
email ⟶ info@sccsi.com

voice ————→ 713-661-3301
ftp more info ––→ sccsi.com:/pub/communications/*

<< nwnexus >>
name ————→ Northwest Nexus Inc.
dialup ————→ contact for numbers
area codes ——→ 206
local access ——→ WA: Seattle
long distance ––→ provided by user
services ————→ UUCP, SLIP, PPP, feeds, dns
fees ————→ $10/month for first 10 hours + $3/hr; $20 start-up
email ————→ info@nwnexus.wa.com
voice ————→ 206-455-3505
ftp more info ––→ nwnexus.wa.com:/NWNEXUS.info.txt

<< nyx >>
name ————→ Nyx, the Spirit of the Night; Free public internet access provided by the University of Denver's Math & Computer Science
Department
dialup ————→ 303-871-3324
area codes ——→ 303
local access ——→ CO: Boulder/Denver
long distance ––→ provided by user
services ————→ shell or menu; semi-anonymous accounts; ftp, news, mail
fees ————→ none; donations are accepted but not requested
email ————→ aburt@nyx.cs.du.edu
voice ————→ login to find current list of volunteer 'voice' helpers
ftp more info ––→ n/a

<< OARnet >>
name ————→ OARnet
dialup ————→ send e-mail to nic@oar.net
area codes ——→ 614, 513, 419, 216, 800
local access ——→ OH: Columbus, Cincinnati, Cleveland, Dayton
long distance ––→ 800 service
services ————→ email, ftp, telnet, newsfeed
fees ————→ $4.00/hr to $330.00/month; call for code or send email
email ————→ nic@oar.net
voice ————→ 614-292-8100
fax ————→ 614-292-7168
ftp more info ––→ n/a

<< oldcolo >>

name ——————→	Old Colorado City Communications
dialup ——————→	719-632-4111 'newuser'
area codes ——→	719
local access ——→	CO: Colorado Springs
long distance —→	provided by user
services ——————→	shell, ftp, telnet, AKCS, home of the NAPLPS conference
fees ——————————→	$25/month
email ——————————→	dave@oldcolo.com / thefox@oldcolo.com
voice ——————————→	719-632-4848, 719-593-7575 or 719-636-2040
fax ——————————————→	719-593-7521
ftp more info —→	n/a

<< olympus >>

name ——————→	Olympus - The Olympic Peninsula's Gateway To The Internet
dialup ——————→	contact voice number below
area codes ——→	206
local access ——→	WA:Olympic Peninsula/Eastern Jefferson County
long distance —→	provided by user
services ——————→	shell, ftp, telnet, pine, hytelnet
fees ——————————→	$25/month + $10 startup
email ——————————→	info@pt.olympus.net
voice ——————————→	206-385-0464
ftp more info —→	n/a

<< panix >>

name ——————→	PANIX Public Access Unix
dialup ——————→	212-787-3100 'newuser'
area codes ——→	212, 718
local access ——→	New York City, NY
long distance —→	provided by user
services ——————→	shell, ftp, telnet, gopher, wais, irc, feeds
fees ——————————→	$19/month or $208/year + $40 signup
email ——————————→	alexis@panix.com, jsb@panix.com
voice ——————————→	212-877-4854 [Alexis Rosen], 212-691-1526 [Jim Baumbach]
ftp more info —→	n/a

<< pipeline >>

name ——————→	The Pipeline
dialup ——————→	212-267-8606 'guest'
area codes ——→	212, 718

```
local access    ──→   NY: New York City
long distance   ──→   provided by user
services        ──→   Windows interface or shell/menu; all IP services
fees            ──→   $15/mo. (inc. 5 hrs) or $20/20 hrs or $35 unlimited
email           ──→   info@pipeline.com, staff@pipeline.com
voice           ──→   212-267-3636
ftp more info   ──→   n/a
```

```
<< portal >>
name            ──→   The Portal System
dialup          ──→   408-973-8091 high-speed, 408-725-0561 2400bps; 'info'
area codes      ──→   408, 415, PDN
local access    ──→   CA: Cupertino, Mountain View, San Jose
long distance   ──→   SprintNet: $2.50/hour off-peak, $7-$10/hour peak; Tymnet:
                      $2.50/hour off-peak, $13/hour peak
services        ──→   shell, ftp, telnet, IRC, UUCP, feeds, bbs
fees            ──→   $19.95/month + $19.95 signup
email           ──→   cs@cup.portal.com, info@portal.com
voice           ──→   408-973-9111
ftp more info   ──→   n/a
off-peak        ──→   6pm to 7am + weekends and holidays
```

```
<< prairienet >>
name            ──→   Prairienet Freenet
dialup          ──→   (217) 255-9000 'visitor'
area codes      ──→   217
local access    ──→   IL: Champaign-Urbana
long distance   ──→   provided by user
services        ──→   telnet, ftp, gopher, IRC, etc.
fees            ──→   Free for Illinois residents, $25/year for non-residents
email           ──→   jayg@uiuc.edu
voice           ──→   217-244-1962
ftp more info   ──→   n/a
```

```
<< PREPnet >>
name            ──→   PREPnet
dialup          ──→   contact for numbers
area codes      ──→   215, 412, 717, 814
local access    ──→   PA: Philadelphia, Pittsburgh, Harrisburg
long distance   ──→   provided by user
services        ──→   SLIP, terminal service, telnet, ftp
```

fees ———————→ $1,000/year membership. Equipment-$325 onetime fee plus $40/month

email ———————→ prepnet@cmu.edu

voice ———————→ 412-268-7870

fax ———————→ 412-268-7875

ftp more info —→ ftp.prepnet.com:/prepnet/general/

<< psilink >>

name ———————→ PSILink - Personal Internet Access

dialup ———————→ North America: send email to classa-na-numbers@psi.com and classb-na-numbers@psi.com; Rest of World: send email to classb-row-numbers@psi.com

area codes ———→ PDN

local access -----→

long distance —→ [per hour, off-peak/peak] PSINet A: included; PSINet B: $6/$2.50; PSINet B international: $18/$18

services ————→ email and newsfeed, ftp

fees ———————→ 2400: $19/month; 9600: $29/month (PSILink software included)

email ———————→ all-info@psi.com, psilink-info@psi.com

voice ———————→ 703-620-6651

fax ———————→ 703-620-4586

ftp more info —→ ftp.psi.com:/

<< psi-world-dial >>

name ———————→ PSI's World-Dial Service

dialup ———————→ send email to numbers-info@psi.com

area codes ———→ PDN

local access -----→

long distance —→ [per hour, off-peak/peak] V.22bis: $1.25/$2.75; V.32: $3.00/$4.50; 14.4K: $4.00/$6.50

services ————→ telnet, rlogin, tn3270, XRemote

fees ———————→ $9/month minimum + $19 startup

email ———————→ all-info@psi.com, world-dial-info@psi.com

voice ———————→ 703-620-6651

fax ———————→ 703-620-4586

ftp more info —→ ftp.psi.com:/

off-peak ————→ 8pm to 8am + weekends and holidays

<< PUCnet >>

name ———————→ PUCnet Computer Connections

dialup ———————→ 403-484-5640 (v.32 bis) 'guest'

area codes ———→ 403
local access ———→ AB: Edmonton and surrounding communities in the Extended Flat Rate Calling Area
long distance ——→ provided by user
services ————→ shell, menu, ftp, telnet, archie, gopher, feeds, USENET
fees —————→ Cdn$25/month (20 hours connect time) + Cdn$6.25/hr (ftp & telnet only) + $10 signup
email ————→ info@PUCnet.com (Mail responder) or pwilson@PUCnet.com
voice ————→ 403-448-1901
fax —————→ 403-484-7103
ftp more info —→ n/a

<< realtime >>
name ————→ RealTime Communications
dialup ————→ 512-459-4391 'new'
area codes ———→ 512
local access ——→ TX: Austin
long distance ——→ provided by user
services ————→ shell, ftp, telnet, irc, gopher, feeds, SLIP, UUCP
fees —————→ $80/half-year. Monthly and quarterly rates available.
email ————→ hosts@bga.com
voice ————→ 512-451-0046 (11am-6pm Central Time, weekdays)
fax —————→ 512-459-3858
ftp more info —→ n/a

<< ssnet >>
name ————→ Systems Solutions
dialup ————→ contact for info
area codes ———→ 302
local access ——→ Wilminton, Delaware
long distance ——→ provided by user
services ————→ shell, UUCP, SLIP, PPP, ftp, telnet, irc, gopher, archie, mud, etc.
fees —————→ full service $25/month $20/startup; personal slip/ppp $25/month + $2/hour, $20/startup; dedicated slip/ppp $150/month, $450/startup
email ————→ sharris@marlin.ssnet.com
voice ————→ (302) 378-1386, (800) 331-1386
ftp more info —→ n/a

<< sugar >>
name ————→ NeoSoft's Sugar Land Unix

```
dialup        ———→  713-684-5900
area codes    ———→  504, 713
local access  ———→  TX: Houston metro area; LA: New Orleans
long distance ——→  provided by user
services      ———→  bbs, shell, ftp, telnet, irc, feeds, UUCP
fees          ———→  $29.95/month
email         ———→  info@NeoSoft.com
voice         ———→  713-438-4964
ftp more info ——→  n/a
```

<< teleport >>
```
name          ———→  Teleport
dialup        ———→  503-220-0636 (2400) 503-220-1016 (v.32, v.32 bis) 'new'
area codes    ———→  503
local access  ———→  OR: Portland, Beaverton, Hillsboro, Forest Grove, Gresham,
                    Tigard, Lake Oswego, Oregon City, Tualatin, Wilsonville
long distance ——→  provided by user
services      ———→  shell, ftp, telnet, gopher, usenet, ppp, WAIS, irc, feeds, dns
fees          ———→  $10/month (1 hr/day limit)
email         ———→  info@teleport.com
voice         ———→  503-223-4245
ftp more info ——→  teleport.com:/about
```

<< telerama >>
```
name          ———→  Telerama Public Access Internet
dialup        ———→  412-481-5302 'new' (2400)
area codes    ———→  412
local access  ———→  PA: Pittsburgh
long distance ——→  provided by user
services      ———→  telnet, ftp, irc, gopher, ClariNet/Usenet, shell/menu, uucp
fees          ———→  66 cents/hour 2400bps; $1.32/hour 14.4K bps; $6 min/month
email         ———→  info@telerama.pgh.pa.us
voice         ———→  412-481-3505
ftp more info ——→  telerama.pgh.pa.us:/info/general.info
```

<< tmn >>
```
name          ———→  The Meta Network
dialup        ———→  contact for numbers
area codes    ———→  703, 202, 301, PDN
local access  ———→  Washington, DC metro area
```

long distance —→   SprintNet: $6.75/hr; FTS-2000; Acunet
services ———→   Caucus conferencing, email, shell, ftp, telnet, bbs, feeds
fees ————→ $20/month + $15 signup/first month
email ————→   info@tmn.com
voice ————→   703-243-6622
ftp more info —→   n/a

<< UUNET-Canada >>
name ———→   UUNET Canada, Inc.
dialup ———→   contact for numbers
area codes ——→   416, 905, 519, 613, 514, 604, 403
local access —→   ON: Toronto, Ottawa, Kitchener/Waterloo, London, Hamilton,
                 QC: Montreal,   AB: Calgary,   BC: Vancouver
long distance —→   provided by user
services ———→   terminal access to telnet only, UUCP (e-mail/news), SLIP/PPP,
                 shared or dedicated basis, from v.32bis to 56k+
fees ————→   (All Cdn$ + GST) TAC: $6/hr, UUCP: $20/mo + $6/hr,
                 IP/UUCP: $50/mo + $6/hr, ask for prices on other services
email ————→   info@uunet.ca
voice ————→   416-368-6621
fax ————→   416-368-1350
ftp more info —→   ftp.uunet.ca

<< uunorth >>
name ———→   UUnorth
dialup ———→   contact for numbers
area codes ——→   416, 519, 613
local access —→   ON: Toronto
long distance —→   provided by user
services ———→   shell, ftp, telnet, gopher, feeds, IRC, feeds, SLIP, PPP
fees ————→   (All Cdn$ + GST) $20 startup + $25 for 20 hours off-peak +
                 $1.25/hr OR $40 for 40 hours up to 5/day + $2/hr OR $3/hr
email ————→   uunorth@uunorth.north.net
voice ————→   416-225-8649
fax ————→   416-225-0525
ftp more info —→   n/a

<< Vnet >>
name ———→   Vnet Internet Access, Inc.
dialup ———→   704-347-8839, 919-406-1544, 919-851-1526 'new'

area codes ⟶ 704, 919

local access ⟶ NC: Charlotte, RTP, Raleigh, Durham, Chappel Hill. Winston Salem/Greensboro

long distance ⟶ Available for $3.95 per hour through Global Access. Contact Vnet offices for more information.

services ⟶ shell, ftp, telnet, hytelnet, irc, gopher, WWW, wais, usenet, clarinet, NNTP, DNS, SLIP/PPP, UUCP, POPmail

fees ⟶ $25/month individual. $12.50 a month for telnet-in-only. SLIP/PPP/UUCP starting at $25/month.

email ⟶ info@char.vnet.net

voice ⟶ 704-374-0779

ftp more info ⟶ n/a

<< well >>

name ⟶ The Whole Earth 'Lectronic Link

dialup ⟶ 415-332-6106 'newuser'

area codes ⟶ 415, PDN

local access ⟶ Sausalito, CA

long distance ⟶ Compuserve Packet Network: $4/hour

services ⟶ shell, ftp, telnet, bbs

fees ⟶ $15.00/month + $2.00/hr

email ⟶ info@well.sf.ca.us

voice ⟶ 415-332-4335

ftp more info ⟶ n/a

<< wariat >>

name ⟶ APK- Public Access UNI* Site

dialup ⟶ 216-481-9436 (V.32bis, SuperPEP on separate rotary)

area codes ⟶ 216

local access ⟶ OH: Cleveland

long distance ⟶ provided by user

services ⟶ shell, ftp, telnet, archie, irc, gopher, feeds, BBS(Uniboard1.10)

fees ⟶ $15/20 hours, $35/monthly, $20 signup

email ⟶ zbig@wariat.org

voice ⟶ 216-481-9428

ftp more info ⟶ n/a

<< world >>

name ⟶ The World

dialup ⟶ 617-739-9753 'new'

```
area codes ──→  617, PDN
local access ──→  Boston, MA
long distance ──→  Compuserve Packet Network: $5.60/hour
services ──→  shell, ftp, telnet, irc
fees ──→  $5.00/month + $2.00/hr or $20/month for 20 hours
email ──→  office@world.std.com
voice ──→  617-739-0202
ftp more info ──→  world.std.com:/world-info/description
```

<< wyvern >>
```
name ──→  Wyvern Technologies, Inc.
dialup ──→  (804) 627-1828 Norfolk, (804) 886-0662 (Peninsula)
area codes ──→  804
local access ──→  VA: Norfolk, Virginia Beach, Portsmouth, Chesapeake, Newport
                  News, Hampton, Williamsburg
long distance ──→  provided by user
services ──→  shell, menu, ftp, telnet, uucp feeds, irc, archie, gopher, UPI
              news, email, dns, archives
fees ──→  $15/month or $144/year, $10 startup
email ──→  system@wyvern.com
voice ──→  804-622-4289
fax ──→  804-622-7158
ftp more info ──→  n/a
```

<< xnet >>
```
name ──→  XNet Information Systems
dialup ──→  (708) 983-6435 V.32bis and TurboPEP
area codes ──→  312, 708, 815
local access ──→  IL: Chicago, Naperville, Hoffman Estates
long distance ──→  provided by user
services ──→  shell, telnet, hytelnet, ftp, irc, gopher, www, wais, SLIP/PPP,
              dns, uucp feeds, bbs
fees ──→  $45/3 months or $75/6 months
email ──→  info@xnet.com
voice ──→  (708) 983-6064
ftp more info ──→  ftp.xnet.com:/xnet.info/
```

-05- What *Is* The Internet?

The Internet is a global cooperative network of university, corporate, government, and private computers, all communicating with each other by means of something called TCP/IP (Transmission Control Protocol/Internet Protocol). Computers directly on the Internet can exchange data quickly and easily with any other computer on the Internet to download files, send e-mail, provide remote logins, etc.

Users can download files from publicly accessible archive sites ("anonymous FTP"); login into remote computers (telnet or rlogin); chat in real-time with other users around the world (Internet Relay Chat); or use the newest information retrieval tools to find a staggering variety of information (Wide Area Information Servers, Gopher, World Wide Web).

Computers directly on the Internet also exchange e-mail directly and very quickly; e-mail is usually delivered in seconds between Internet sites.

Sometimes the Internet is confused with other related networks or types of networking.

First, there are other ways to be "connected to the Internet" without being directly connected as a TCP/IP node. Some computers connect via UUCP or other means at regular intervals to an Internet site to exchange e-mail and USENET newsgroups, for instance. Such a site can provide e-mail (though not as quickly as a directly connected systems) and USENET access, but not Internet downloads, remote logins, etc.

"e-mail" (or "Internet e-mail", "netmail") can be exchanged with a wide variety of systems connected directly and indirectly to the Internet. The e-mail may travel solely over the Internet, or it may traverse other networks and systems.

"USENET" is the collection of computers all over the world that exchange USENET news—thousands of "newsgroups" (like forums, or echos) on a wide range of topics. The newsgroup articles are distributed all over the world to USENET sites that wish to carry them (sometimes over the Internet, sometimes not), where people read and respond to them.

The "NSFNET" is one of the backbones of the Internet in the US. It is funded by the NSF, which restricts traffic over the NSFNET to "open research and education in and among US research and instructional institutions, plus research arms of for-profit firms when engaged in open scholarly communication and research." Your Internet provider can give you more details about acceptable use, and alternatives should you need to use the Internet in other ways.

-06- What The PDIAL Is

This is the PDIAL, the Public Dialup Internet Access List.

It is a list of Internet service providers offering public access dialins and outgoing Internet access (ftp, telnet, etc.). Most of them provide e-mail and USENET news and other services as well.

If one of these systems is not accessible to you and you need e-mail or USENET access, but *don't* need ftp or telnet, you have many more public access systems from which to choose. Public access systems without ftp or telnet are *not* listed in this list, however. See the nixpub (alt.bbs, comp.misc) list and other BBS lists.

Some of these providers offer time-shared access to a shell or BBS program on a computer connected directly to the Internet, through which you can FTP or telnet to other systems on the Internet. Usually other services are provided as well. Generally, you need only a modem and terminal or terminal emulator to access these systems. Check for "shell", "bbs", or "menu" on the "services" line.

Other providers connect you directly to the Internet via SLIP or PPP when you dial in. For these you need a computer system capable of running the software to interface with the Internet, e.g., a Unix machine, PC, or Mac. Check for "SLIP", or "PPP" on the services line.

While I have included all sites for which I have complete information, this list is surely incomplete. If you have any additions or corrections please send them to me at one of the addresses listed in section -10-.

-07- How People Can Get The PDIAL (This List)

Email:
From the Information Deli archive server (most up-to-date):

To receive the current edition of the PDIAL, send e-mail containing the phrase "Send PDIAL" to "info-deli-server@netcom.com".

To be put on a list of people who receive future editions as they are published, send e-mail containing the phrase "Subscribe PDIAL" to "info-deli-server@netcom.com".

To receive both the most recent and future editions, send both messages.

From time to time, I'll also be sending out news and happenings that relate to the PDIAL or The Information Deli. To receive the Info Deli News automatically, send e-mail containing the phrase "Subscribe Info-Deli-News" to "info-deli-server@netcom.com".
From the news.answers FAQ archive:

Send e-mail with the message "send usenet/news.answers/pdial" to"mail-server@rtfm.mit.edu". For help, send the message "help" to "mail-server@rtfm.mit.edu".

Usenet:
The PDIAL list is posted semi-regularly to alt.internet.access.wanted, alt.bbs.lists, alt.online-service, ba.internet, and news.answers.

FTP Archive Sites (PDIAL and other useful information):
Information Deli FTP site:
    ftp.netcom.com:/pub/info-deli/public-access/pdial [192.100.81.100]

As Part of a Collection of Public Access Lists:
VFL.Paramax.COM:/pub/pubnet/pdial [128.126.220.104] (used to be GVL.Unisys.COM)
    From the Merit Network Information Center Internet information archive: nic.merit.edu:/internet/providers/pdial [35.1.1.48]

As Part of an Internet Access Compilation File:
liberty.uc.wlu.edu:/pub/lawlib/internet.access [137.113.10.35]
    As part of the news.answers FAQ archive:
rtfm.mit.edu:/pub/usenet/news.answers/pdial [18.70.0.209]

-08- Appendix A: Other Valuable Resources

InterNIC Internet Help Desk
The US National Science Foundation has funded Information, Registration, and Directory services for the Internet, and they are avail-

able to all Internet users. The most useful branch for PDIAL readers is Information Services, which provides all sorts of information to help Internet users. Contact Information Services by:

voice: 800-444-4345 (US)
voice: +1 (619) 455-4600
fax: +1 (619) 455-4640
e-mail: mailserv@is.internic.net, put "SEND HELP" in body
e-mail: info@internic.net
gopher: gopher gopher.internic.net / telnet gopher.internic.net
ftp: is.internic.net
postal: InterNIC Information Services
General Atomics
PO Box 85608
San Diego, CA 92186-9784 USA

Internet Guide Books

Connecting To The Internet; Susan Estrada; O'Reilly & Associates; ISBN 1-56592-061-9 (A how-to on selecting the right IP provider, from dialup to dedicated.)

A DOS User's Guide to the Internet—E-mail, Netnews and File Transfer with UUCP; James Gardner; MKS; ISBN 0-13-106873-3 ("Internet" in the title is misleading—covers UUCP connections only.)

The Electronic Traveller—Exploring Alternative Online Systems; Elizabeth Powell Crowe; Windcrest/McGraw-Hill; ISBN 0-8306-4498-9. (A good tour of various personal IP and other types of providers, but some data is seriously out of date.)

Internet Basics; Steve Lambert, Walt How; Random House; ISBN 0-679-75023-1

The Internet Companion; Tracy LaQuey, Jeanne C. Ryer; Addison-Wesley; ISBN 0-201-62224-6

The Internet Companion Plus; Tracy LaQuey, Jeanne C. Ryer; Addison-Wesley; ISBN 0-201-62719-1

The Internet Complete Reference; Harley Hahn, Rick Stout; Osborne; ISBN 0-07-881980-6

The Internet Directory; Eric Brawn; Fawcett Columbine; ISBN 0-449-90898-4 (Phone book style listing of resources.)

The Internet for Dummies; John R. Levine, Carol Baroudi; IDG Books Worldwide; ISBN 1-56884-024-1 (Lots of useful information, but much of it is intermediate level, not "dummy".)

Internet: Getting Started; April Marine, Susan Kirkpatrick, Vivian Neou, Carol Ward; PTR Prentice Hall; ISBN 0-13-289596-X

The Internet Guide for New Users; Daniel P. Dern; McGraw-Hill; ISBN 0-07-016511-4 (Good, very thorough guide for new users.)

The Internet Navigator; Paul Glister; John Wiley & Sons; ISBN 0-471-59782-1 (Good, comprehensive guide for new users.)

The Internet Roadmap; Bennet Falk; Sybex; ISBN 0-7821-1365-6

Internet Starter Kit for the Macintosh With Disk; Adam C. Engst; Hayden Books; ISBN 1-568300646

The Mac Internet Tour Guide; Michael Fraase; Ventana Press; ISBN 1-56604-062-0

Navigating the Internet; Richard J. Smith, Mark Gibbs; SAMS Publishing; ISBN 0-672-30362-0

Welcome to . . . Internet—From Mystery to Mastery; Tom Badgett, Corey Sandler; MIS:Press; ISBN 1-55828-308-0

The Whole Internet User's Guide & Catalog; Ed Krol; O'Reilly & Associates; ISBN 1-56592-025-2 (Good all around guide.)

Zen & the Art of the Internet: A Beginner's Guide; Brendan P. Kehoe; PTR Prentice Hall; ISBN 0-13-010778-6

Other BBS/Internet Provider Lists

FSLIST—The Forgotten Site List. USENET: alt.internet.access.wanted; ftp: freedom.nmsu.edu:/pub/docs/fslist/ or login.qc.ca:/pub/fslist/

nixpub—public access Unixes. USENET: comp.bbs.mis, alt.bbs; e-mail: to <mail-server@bts.com>, body containing "get PUB nixpub.long"; ftp: VFL.Paramax.COM:/pub/pubnetc/nixpub.long

-09- Appendix B: Finding Public Data Network (PDN) Access Numbers

Here's how to get local access numbers or information for the various PDNs. Generally, you can contact the site you're calling for help, too.

IMPORTANT NOTE: Unless noted otherwise, set your modem to 7E1 (7 data bits, even parity, 1 stop bit) when dialing to look up access numbers by modem as instructed below.

BT Tymnet
For information and local access numbers, call 800-937-2862 (voice) or 215-666-1770 (voice).

To look up access numbers by modem, dial a local access number, hit <cr> and 'a', and enter "information" at the "please log in:" prompt.

Compuserve Packet Network

You do NOT have to be a Compuserve member to use the CPN to dial other services.

For information and local access numbers, call 800-848-8199 (voice).

To look up access numbers by modem, dial a local access number, hit <cr> and enter "PHONES" at the "Host Name:" prompt.

PSINet

For information, call 800-82PSI82 (voice) or 703-620-6651 (voice), or send e-mail to "all-info@psi.com". For a list of local access numbers send e-mail to "numbers-info@psi.com".

-10- Providers: Get Listed in PDIAL!

New Submission/Correction Procedures:

The PDIAL will be undergoing expansion in both breadth (how many and what kinds of public access providers) and depth (how much information is carried for each provider). To collect the data, I will be e-mailing a questionnaire to providers already on the PDIAL, and to any providers who wish to be added. Corrections can also be submitted via update questionnaires.

To be listed in the PDIAL, retrieve the PDIAL questionnaire by sending e-mail to <info-deli-server@netcom.com> containing the command "Send PDIAL-Q". The questionnaire will not be available until 15 Dec 1993, but requests received before then will be queued and honored when it is available.

Peter Kaminski / The Information Deli
kaminski@netcom.com (preferred)
71053.2155@compuserve.com

PUBLICATIONS

While there are lots of computer trade publications that regularly cover the Internet, at present we are aware of only one regular Internet-focused publication. Consequently, we include a list of potentially useful publications that will mention the Internet from time to time (nearly every issue) as well as the sole Internet magazine, *Internet World*.

Computer Shopper is published 12 times a year by Coastal Associates, a division of Ziff Communications Company. The address is One Park Avenue, New York, NY, 10016, and its subscription department can be reached at (800) 274-6384 (inside the United States) or at (303) 447-9330 (outside the United States). The magazine costs $29.97 inside the United States, and an additional $39 for postage outside the United States. *Computer Shopper* is primarily a PC-focused advertising supplement—a normal issue looks like an oversized phone book—but it includes ads and contact information for hundreds of mail-order dealers who carry networking equipment and software. It also includes comprehensive and regular listings of BBS services nationwide, which can often provide low-budget access to Internet e-mail, Usenet, and a variety of newsfeeds.

Computerworld is published 53 times a year by IDG Publications, P.O. Box 9171, 375 Cochituate Road, Framingham, MA, 01701-9171, and can be reached at (800) 669-1002 for subscriptions, (508) 879-0700 for editorial information. The magazine costs $48 inside the United States, and between $95 and $295 outside the country, depending on exact location. *Computerworld* covers the computer industry in general, but gives networking issues good coverage as well. It's a good counterpoint to the Ziff-Davis *PC Week*, in that its focus includes coverage of non-PC systems as well.

Infoworld is published 51 times a year by Infoworld Publishing Company, a subsidiary of IDG, at 155 Bovet Road, San Mateo, CA, 94402, and can be reached at (415) 572-7341. The magazine is free to qualified subscribers, but otherwise costs $130 inside the United States, and $145 in Canada (other subscription costs available upon request). *Infoworld* covers the computer industry in general, but gives networking issues good coverage as well. It also publishes Rich Tennant's cartoons in every issue (our personal favorite nerdy form of entertainment).

Internet World is published 10 times a year (monthly, except for July/August and November/December) by Mecklermedia Corporation, 11 Ferry Lane West, Westport, CT, 06880, and can be reached at (203) 226-6967. Its Internet e-mail address is meckler@jvnc.net. Subscriptions cost $29 annually in the United States (£29 in the U.K); add $18 for subscriptions in Canada, and Central and South America (please call for rates elsewhere). Internet World covers only the Internet including news, features on software and resources, and a series of topical columns. An excellent guide to new and familiar resources.

LAN: The Network Solutions Magazine is published monthly by Miller Freeman, 600 Harrison Street, San Francisco, CA, 94107, who can be reached at (415) 905-2200. An annual subscription costs $19.97. This magazine provides coverage on a broad range of networking topics, including technology overviews, user tutorials, and product reviews. For an excellent source of network product and vendor information, be sure to check out its annual *Buyers Guide* (published in September of each year).

LAN Times is published 25 times a year by McGraw-Hill, Inc., 1221 Avenue of the Americas, New York, NY, 10020, who can be reached at (415) 513-6800. The magazine is free to qualified subscribers. *LAN Times* also provides coverage on a broad range of networking topics, including technology overviews, network industry news, product reviews, and includes editorials from networking industry leaders and personalities. For an excellent source of network product and vendor information, be sure to check out its annual *Buyers Directory* (published in August of each year).

Networking Management is published 12 times a year by PenWell Publishing Company, 1421 South Sheridan, Tulsa, OK, 74112, who can be reached at (918) 831-9424 (subscriptions) or (508) 692-0700 (editorial inquiries). The magazine is free to qualified subscribers, and costs $42 inside the United States, and $65 outside the country, for nonqualified subscribers. *Networking Management* provides coverage on a broad range of network management topics, including technology overviews, network industry news, and standards information.

Network World is published 51 times a year by IDG Publications, 161 Worcester Road, Framingham, MA, 01701-9172, and can be reached at (508) 875-6400. The magazine is free to qualified subscribers, and costs $95 inside the United States, and between $95 and $245 outside the country, depending on exact location, for nonqualified subscribers. *Network World* provides weekly coverage on a broad range of network management topics, including technology overviews, network industry news, and offers special departments for enterprise internets, local networks, global services, and client-server applications.

Open Systems Today is published 28 times a year by CMP Publications, Inc., 600 Community Drive, Manhasset, NY, 11030-3875, (708) 647-6834 (subscription) . The magazine is free to qualified subscribers, and costs $79 inside the United States and Canada, and between $179 and $200 outside the country, depending on exact location, for non-qualified subscribers, per year. *OST* provides semi-monthly coverage on a broad range of computer industry topics, including technology overviews, and industry news, and offers special departments on networking, that is primarily focused at the open systems side of the computer industry, with a strong emphasis on UNIX. It offers a valuable complement to most of the other magazines mentioned here, which devote most of their networking coverage to PC-related topics.

PC Week is published 51 times a year by Ziff-Davis Publishing Company, a division of Ziff Communications Company, One Park Avenue, New York, NY, 10016, (609) 786-8230 (subscriptions). The magazine is free to qualified subscribers, and costs $160 inside the United States, and between $200 and $350 outside the country, depending on exact location, for nonqualified subscribers, per year. *PC Week* provides weekly coverage on a broad range of computer industry topics, including technology overviews, industry news, and offers special departments on networking. It also publishes a weekly network-focused supplement, called *PCWeek Netweek*, that will be shipped to readers who express interest in networking.

INTERNET IN THE REAL WORLD

IV

OVERVIEW

In the first three sections of the book we gave you all the background you need to to surf the Internet on your own. In this section we peel pack the top of the Internet and let you look inside the operations of a couple of Internet service providers.

Here, we look at two different Internet service providers, with different philosophies, services, and equipment, but with the same basic goal: to participate in the growing marketplace that Internet services and access represent. We include a recent startup as our example of a smaller operation and a former Bulletin Board System (BBS) provider as an example of a medium-sized one.

We hoped to include a national Internet service provider as an example of a large operation, but all of them were too busy to talk about their operations! While this kept us from learning some no-doubt interesting details of operations on such a scale, it is also a profound testimony to the vigorous growth and activity in this marketplace. We called them, they just wouldn't call us (back, that is).

From BBS to Internet—
All in a Day's Work!

To begin with, we visit the operations of Real/Time Communications, a sizable local operator in Austin, Texas. RTC supports a good-sized user community that ranges from 3,000 to 4,500 users in any given month, which consists of an eclectic mix of students from the University of Texas, businesses, professionals, software developers, and techno-junkies of all kinds. RTC's roots were in the Bulletin Board System business, giving it a predilection for PC-based computing services that it has pushed to the limits of that technology. As we take you on a tour of the facilities, the network, and the service offerings, you will be amazed at what it has been able to accomplish in the two years it has been in business!

A Startup, but No Upstart

Zilker Internet Park is a smaller operation, but one with a compelling pedigree. Although the company has only been in operation since the beginning of 1994, its principals include Internet luminaries John S. Quarterman and Smoot Carl-Mitchell, both of whom have authored numerous books on the Internet. These gentlemen also teach Internet-related seminars at NetWorld+Interop, the preeminent networking industry professional meeting and trade show. Therefore, it should come as no surprise that Zilker offers an extremely broad range of Internet services and a sophisticated array of connection and use options. In Chapter 29 we investigate their operations more thoroughly.

28

REAL/TIME
COMMUNICATIONS

THE ORGANIZATION

In this chapter we look at a medium-sized Internet service provider, one with 130-odd incoming telephone lines and a collection of seven servers or so.

Real/Time Communications (a dba for a company by the name of Bob Gustwick & Associates), is located at 6721 North Lamar Boulevard, Austin, Texas, 78752, and occupies about a third of the ground floor in a large two-story building that is home to a variety of businesses. Real/Time Communications (which we abbreviate as RTC from now on) is in only one business: that of providing Internet access to businesses and individuals who want to plug into the information superhighway.

RTC has been in business in one form or fashion since 1988, when it began its life as a provider of a bulletin board system (BBS) to the Austin community. Since then, the BBS marketplace has grown up and has taken RTC along with it. Although the company is no longer BBS-based, it exudes the kind of bare-bones, can-do attitude that typically accompanies most operations that have had to bring themselves up by their bootstraps, with funding supplied by internal growth. Put another way, there isn't a lot of fancy furniture or artwork on the walls and the entire operation is straining against the limits of its space, its systems, and its people.

If this sounds critical, it doesn't do justice to the burgeoning demand that RTC and many other Internet access providers are experiencing. The reason the company is straining at its seams is not because of poor planning or management, but because it's racing like mad to accommodate a growing market for its services and resources.

RTC's History

Although RTC's operation stretches back into the mid-1980s, it wasn't really until early 1993 that the company began its odyssey onto the Internet. At that point, George Wenzel, the company's principal manager, began to refocus its business on the Internet and away from its traditional BBS roots.

What possible advantages could these roots have provided? Since most BBS systems are built around connecting large groups of users via telephone into a computer, the convergence with their Internet business is at least 50%. According to George, most of what he knows about modems, telephony, and computers was learned as a self-taught electrical engineer and computer programmer, during the course of his involvement with several BBS systems during the 1980s. Likewise, a stint as a programmer and hardware designer for Gary Kildall of Digital Research, Inc., stood him in good stead as he had reason to explore the limits of PC technology from both an operating system and a hardware perspective.

RTC's foray into Internet technology mixed the strange and the familiar. George made a conscious decision to base the operation around affordable commodity PCs and related hardware, but also decided to invest considerable time and effort into learning UNIX. As the operating system of choice in the Internet community, this was a wise decision, but it involved climbing a serious learning curve. Because the Berkeley Software Distribution, Inc., version of UNIX was available for Intel PCs at a reasonable price and included access to the operating system's source code, George elected to use an environment where he and his fellow programmers on RTC's staff could augment or enhance the software when and if it was necessary.

"Given that UNIX serial communications were designed as a point-to-point link between pairs of computers," opines George, "and not as a way to link dozens of dial-in links to a single machine, we had to make some changes in order to get the best use out of our systems." What resulted from these efforts is a growing and successful business, with a sizable user community, as shown in the network diagram in

Figure 28.1 in the next section. Before we examine the current layout, let's continue to trace RTC's evolution from BBS operator to Internet access provider.

Jumping onto the Internet

RTC's Internet connection began at the beginning of 1993, with a single 14.4 kilobaud connection to Alternet using SLIP as the access protocol. In a matter of a few months, the number of users outstripped the capacity of this relatively narrow pipe to the Internet, and RTC's number of phone lines began to grow steadily along with it.

Starting with 8 phone lines and modems and a single terminal server, at the beginning of that year, by mid-year RTC was using three PCs as host machines and an equal number of terminal servers, for a total of 48 phone lines. At the year's end, this number had doubled across the board. By the time we visited with it in July 1994, it had 130-odd phone lines installed, with six PCs acting as terminal servers and six additional PCs acting in a number of different service capacities (all of the servers, terminal and otherwise, are running BSDI UNIX).

During the same time frame, RTC's user community grew from around 300 users to its current level of nearly 2,000 active users, along with a transient user population nearly half again as large. "While coping with explosive growth has been a real stretch," says George with a grin, "these are the kinds of problems that businesses want to have. We may struggle from time to time, but we're grateful to our users for keeping our business growing and prospering."

At the same time, though, it is clear that RTC is trying to minimize overhead and control costs in whatever ways it can. George backs this observation up with one of his own: "I know what my competitors charge, and what services they offer. Right now, I'm making money as a service provider—I don't know too many other companies that can make the same claim." Later on, when we examine RTC's marketing strategies and its user community, some of the reasons for its success should become evident. But first, let's take a look at the layout.

THE NETWORK LAYOUT

As you can see in Figure 28.1, the RTC network is built around an Ethernet backbone that links the 12 PC servers, their T-1 based Internet

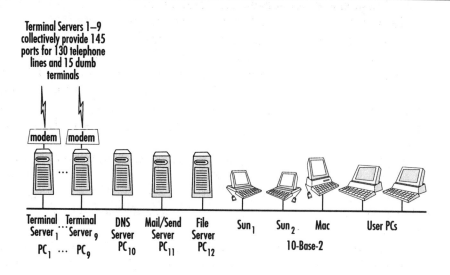

Figure 28.1 *RTC's Present Network Layout*

connection (via a Cisco router) and by extension, the nine terminal servers that gather in the phone lines. The network also features a couple of older Sun 3XX class machines, which RTC uses for training and development. While the diagram may look orderly and simple, it is important to visualize 130-odd telephone lines coming out of a couple of punchdown blocks and feeding into an equal number of U.S. Robotics 14.4 modems. RTC's machine room is a classic example of controlled chaos: All the lines are out in the open, well-labeled and carefully routed, but this is clearly an environment that is growing and changing a lot. Put in other terms: Easy access clearly outweighs aesthetics.

In this environment, the important functions are supplied by the four major types of hardware elements in use, and the network acts as the highway where incoming traffic is directed to one of the UNIX hosts and as the conduit for traffic on its way to and from the Internet link.

The Servers

RTC has chosen to keep its server configurations as similar as different times of purchase will allow. Today, the standard platform is a 486/66 DX2 processor, with ISA bus, 32 MB RAM per machine, and at least 1

GB of disk space per server. The total storage capacity at RTC is 12 GB, reflecting that several machines now sport multiple 2 GB drives.

RTC's staff tries to keep storage consumption below 80% of capacity, to provide speedy disk access. The staff also performs regular backups, consisting of nightly incrementals, with full backups over the weekend. "Since RTC never goes off-line," says George, "backup is a challenge, but that's why we have more servers than we really need, so we can shift users off systems being backed up, and then redistribute the load as the available pool of servers changes."

Of the seven servers in use, four act as terminal servers, providing Telnet, FTP, and other TCP/IP application support. The other three supply a Usenet database, e-mail services (both on one machine), a dedicated user file server, and a dedicated domain name server (DNS server).

For easy management of individual servers, RTC has installed two keyboard switches; each of these devices lets a single keyboard and monitor control half of the servers (6 per unit). "We felt it was critical to be able to get to each system from a single location," explains George, "rather than having to jump from machine to machine." Given the somewhat cozy quarters in their machine room, this looks like a very good investment indeed.

The Modems

RTC uses the same principal of similarity when it comes to modems: All of them are identical U.S. Robotics 14.4 units. "We tried to get the best performance for our money," says George, "and we've found these modems to offer a good combination of value and features at a very affordable price." He goes on to admit that buying in bulk also leads to some "nice discounts" as well.

RTC uses steel shelving with built-on power strips that span the entire length of the shelves, along with an ingenious racking system to accommodate its modems' external power supplies and cords. The firm also labels all of its RJ-11 and RJ-45 telephone cables, for easy identification and replacement. When asked about the stock of spares he keeps on hand, George jokes: "Let's just say we'd have to lose a lot of our modems before I'd have to go out and buy any."

Given Austin's proclivity to thunderstorms and power fluctuations, George's desire to keep lots of spares on hand makes good sense. So also do the uninterruptible power supplies that support the servers, terminal servers, network hub, and Cisco router.

The Terminal Servers

RTC uses multiple 8- and 16-port RISCOM boards in six of its PCs to act as terminal servers. While this job is not terribly exciting, these machines supply the network connections for dial-in and dedicated line users. None of these machines has more than five of the boards connected, for a maximum of 40 serial ports per machine (the average is actually close to 22 ports per machine). They just sit there all day long, providing users with the dial-up and dedicated lines that they need.

The Network

RTC uses 10Base2 as its Ethernet topology. RTC makes its own cables and adds network capacity on an as-needed basis. Because the building has a suspended ceiling, the cables are routed in through the overhead and dropped down behind the four computers attached outside the machine room. One of RTC's terminal servers also supplies connections for over a dozen old-fashioned terminals in the classroom and at several employees' desks.

The Router

RTC is using a Cisco GS3000 router, to connect its Ethernet to a V.35 modem, which in turn is connected to a CSU/DSU for the T-1 link that ties it into the Internet. RTC uses US Sprint to provide its carrier service to Alternet, which supplies its ultimate link into the Internet environment. Of the 1.544 Mbps available on a T-1 channel, RTC is currently using (and paying for) 256 Kbps (four 64 Kbps channels), with plans to expand to 768 Kbps in the near future, when they will be adding eight ISDN lines (each of which consumes 64 Kbps).

THE STAFF

Currently, RTC employs a staff of seven, of which four work full-time, and the remainder part-time. Of these seven, five have some kind of system management responsibilities that range from providing user support to managing the huge collection of software and other information continually flowing through RTC.

While the workload is such that RTC cannot support its employees investigating the Internet on company time, the policy is to make its systems freely available to them and to encourage feedback from the user base. "Our employees are always online, whether they're working or not," says George. "Many of them are still young enough that they can function better on computing than on sleep." This has fostered a workplace of well-informed, enthusiastic staff that obviously brings personal as well as professional commitments to their work.

Even though the majority of RTC's staff is under 35, all of them have at least 10 years' computing experience; some have significantly more. It is obviously a group of passionate computer fiends, whose focus is on providing the best bang for its user community's bucks.

THE USER COMMUNITY

George claims that, in large part, RTC still serves the same community as it did when doing business as a BBS supplier. "It's just that the user base has grown up a little," he jokes. Upon closer examination, the RTC user community is indeed an interesting mix:

- Nearly half the users are students or recent graduates from the nearby University of Texas (size of student body: approximately 45,000).
- The other half of the users are a combination of high-tech professionals, small to medium-sized businesses, and organizations looking for a presence on the Internet.
- About 1,500 "transient users"—mostly students—come and go on the system from month to month.
- Usenet access, e-mail, and IRC are by far the most popular applications, with IRC the clear favorite among the students, and e-mail and Usenet among the others.
- Usage stays very steady all day long and well into the night: the students take over when the professionals leave off.
- Businesses are coming on-line in increasing number, primarily to communicate among themselves, with multisite bookstores, computer outlets, media companies, and law offices in the vanguard of this movement.
- The UNIX development community, long a mainstay of the Internet, is quite active through bga.com as well.

It's hard to fathom that a group this large and varied can find itself a home on a collection of PCs running UNIX, but therein lies the strange magic of the Internet.

RTC's Services and Offerings

The clearest impetus for purchasing Internet access through RTC is price: A mere $20 dollars monthly will buy unlimited access to RTC's computers, with no time limits. Add SLIP at no additional charge; dedicated SLIP lines at speeds of up to 56 Kbps are only somewhat higher. George promises that ISDN support, when it arrives later this year, will also be "competitively priced." Based on its current prices, we believe him! Currently, RTC plans to add 24 ISDN ports before the year's end.

What does this money buy RTC's user community? First and foremost, RTC supports all of the Internet software supplied with the BDSI operating system. To get an idea of what this represents, try Anonymous FTP (or use Archie) to get to the server named freebsd.cdrom.com, where much of the same software resides. It includes all of the basic TCP/IP applications, plus most of the navigation tools we covered in Part II of this book. It also includes all of the English-language Usenet newsfeeds as well. A quick look will show you there is no shortage of material on the various RTC servers.

RTC also offers training classes in its facilities, taught by members of the staff and affiliate organizations. Classes like Introduction to the Internet and UNIX Basics are very popular with the business community. RTC will also handle the details of InterNIC address registration for companies seeking a presence on the Internet and will install and maintain servers at client sites or will operate servers for such clients at its own location. Currently RTC has helped over 20 companies establish such a presence and is seeing the demand for WWW page definition and both free and for-a-fee FTP archives are growing substantially.

RTC's goals are to help its user community get the best value from the Internet and to assist them in making the process as painless as possible. As one of the larger local providers in the Austin area, this thriving organization appears to be well-launched toward these goals. "The truth is," says George, "is that commercial use of the Internet is really just starting. By helping companies get involved and begin to use the Internet effectively, there's nowhere for RTC to go but up." We can only add "and out," simply to accommodate the growth that the whole Internet access industry is currently experiencing!

CONTACT INFORMATION

Real/Time Communications
6721 North Lamar Boulevard
Austin, Texas, 78752
Voice Line: (512) 451-0046
Dial in at (512) 459-0604 (8 data bits, 1 stop bit, no parity)
Domain name bga.com; dynamic address assignment precludes IP address provision
Login as "new" (omit quotation marks); no password required
Complete new user questionnaire
Free access for first two weeks
Rates:
$20/month; $45/quarter; $80/6 months (includes SLIP)

ZILKER
INTERNET
PARK

29

ABOUT THE ORGANIZATION

This case study is of a fairly small Internet service provider, one that services a user community of about 350 individuals and businesses. This operation is run by Zilker Internet Park, which is devoted to providing state-of-the-art Internet services and access in Austin, Texas.

Zilker Internet Park is located at 1106 Clayton Lane, Suite 500W, Austin, Texas, 78723, in a large professional office building on a major thoroughfare. Zilker also happens to be the name of a popular public park in Austin, much beloved by the town's residents. Even so, we refer to the company as *Zilker* for the rest of this chapter, hoping that local readers will be able to tell the difference between this company and the place!

Zilker has been in operation since the beginning of 1994. In seven months that have elapsed, the company has grown to support a user community of nearly 350 and currently supports 32 incoming phone lines, with 16 more on order (along with eight ISDN lines) at the time we visited their operation.

THE ZILKER STAFF

At present the company is run by three principals and also employs four others, two full-time and two part-time. The principals are

- Smoot Carl-Mitchell, a former University of Texas computer science instructor and system administrator, as well as a former city councilman. Smoot has been active on the Internet for over 10 years. Together with Quarterman, he is the author of two books on the subject, a regular consultant to academia and industry, and a regular instructor at the NetWorld+Interop tutorials worldwide.
- John S. Quarterman is a well-known Internet luminary, author of the acclaimed book *The Matrix*, coauthor of two additional titles on the Internet (with Carl-Mitchell), and has written numerous titles on other computing subjects. He too, works as a consultant and instructor on Internet-related topics, as well as writing ceaselessly in that subject area.
- Dinah McNutt is a mechanical engineer by training and an acknowledged expert on UNIX systems administration. She contributed the impetus to form Zilker and runs the system side of things for the company. She, too, has written frequently for publications that include *Unix Today*, *Unix Review* (where she is a featured columnist), and *Byte* magazine.

The other members of the staff include two full-time system administrators who double as technical support for customers, with a colleague working part-time on an evening shift. All of these individuals are extremely knowledgeable about the system and the Internet, making one of Zilker's strongest draws to customers an excellent reputation for technical support.

THE NETWORK LAYOUT

Figure 29.1 shows a simplified diagram of the Zilker network. The main ingredients are as follows:

- The Sun Classic, which acts as the primary Zilker host machine
- The Morningstar router, which connects Zilker to the Internet through PSI, Inc.

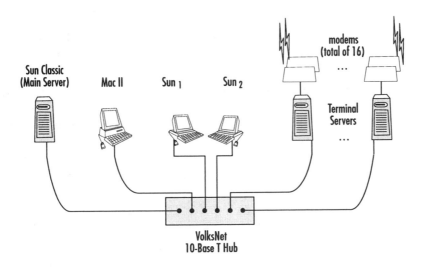

Figure 29.1 *The Zilker Internet Park Network*

- A 10BaseT network, with an 8-port Volksnet hub
- Two 16-port terminal servers, which attach the modems (and incoming telephone lines) to the local network for host access

The Server

Zilker uses a 50 MHz Sun Classic, with 48 MB of RAM, and 4.5 GB of disk space, as its primary network server (through a fallback arrangement with a sister company, Zilker also has access to a backup server should the need for one ever arise). The system is installed on a desktop in the system administration office—while it looks pretty unprepossessing, it provides effective service for the current customer base.

The system is backed up onto a Sun-labeled high capacity tape backup unit, with nightly incrementals and full system backups on a weekly basis. The system is further protected by an uninterruptible power supply, along with built-in line conditioning capabilities. In our interview, McNutt made it clear that Zilker's most important goal is to provide reliable, easy-to-use services to its customers, so they can access the Internet any time they need to.

The Router

Zilker uses a Morningstar router, with a single V.35 modem and an Ethernet port to bridge its connection with PSI for Internet access to its Ethernet LAN. The router is provided as a part of the access service through PSI, and the systems administrators tout its reliability and constant uptime. "The best thing about it is that you never notice that it's there," says Charles Malone, Zilker's chief on-site administrator and head of technical support. "We like systems that work that way," he continues.

The Network

In addition to the Sun server, two terminal servers (to be discussed), and the router, Zilker also has a PC, a Macintosh, and a Sun workstation for its staff to use. All of these devices are interconnected via a single 8-port Volksnet 10BaseT hub. Zilker uses prefab cables, connected through a premises wiring system. As networks go, this is simple, clean and elegant: Networking doesn't get much easier than this!

The Terminal Servers and Modems

Zilker operates two standalone 16-port terminal servers to bring its incoming phone lines onto the network. Between the two punchdown blocks installed by Southwestern Bell and these terminal servers, Zilker uses a battery of U.S. Robotics 14.4 modems to supply the intervening link. Like the folks at RTC, it has found these modems to be cheap, reliable, and efficient.

The terminal servers include one Lantronix and one Specialix units, each with 16 RS-232 ports, where the digital side of the modems plug in. These units include built-in Telnet support, which offloads some processing from the Sun server and lets users coming in on PPP or SLIP connections go directly to the Internet without having to login to the Zilker server (whose domain name is zilker.net).

ZILKER'S SERVICE OFFERINGS

Among the many enlightened attitudes we encountered at Zilker, there is a customer-first, technology-second approach to running the business. McNutt was clear on two points during our interview: Zilker encourages all of its technical staff to explore the Internet, but customers with problems always come ahead of everything else, no matter how interesting those explorations might be. This has led to a problem-solving attitude among the Zilker staff and has also brought lots of interesting applications and services onto the Zilker server.

Zilker is pretty much alone, of all the smaller service providers we contacted, in offering local servers for Archie, Gopher, WWW, WAIS, and the first one to offer Alex, we encountered. Alex is a way of mapping FTP access to remote file systems through NFS, so that users can explore remote FTP archives just by working through what appears to be a directory tree that's purely local to the zilker.net file system.

Zilker also takes direction from its customers and has recently upgraded its account options to include unlimited monthly dial-in and unlimited monthly PPP services, in addition to basic account offerings. "We try to go out and find the programs and services our customers want," says McNutt, "and so far, they've been really good about giving us lots of feedback."

Of course, keeping Internet heavies like Quarterman and Carl-Mitchell around also guarantees that the latest and greatest toys and tools will probably show up at Zilker as well. "John [Quarterman] was the source for bringing Alex into Zilker," says McNutt. Apparently, all the senior staff members take a very hands-on approach to the business, with regular involvement in software selection, system management, and company policy.

But what really sets Zilker apart is its support-oriented attitude. The company offers client software packages (and usage credits) to customers when they first sign up for service and provides ample technical support to get those users on-line as well. It has also recently installed a menu system on the server to insulate novice users from the "harsh reality of UNIX," as McNutt somewhat jokingly put it. "We want our users using the Internet, not figuring out how to run the system that gets them to it." The staff at Zilker has taken considerable pains to make this wish a reality.

ZILKER'S FUTURE PLANS

Like most other organizations involved with computers and telephony, Zilker is investigating ISDN, which recently became available in the Austin area. McNutt is currently in the process of ordering and experimenting with ISDN equipment, so that Zilker can understand what it's like to be an end-user, as well as a service provider.

The attitude at Zilker is something like this: Unless it understands what its users have to go through to get connected, it cannot help them use new services. And since ISDN offers considerably higher bandwidth and capability, it is keen to make this service available, especially to business customers who want to leverage a presence on the Internet.

Consequently, Zilker is planning on adding eight ISDN ports in the near future and offering them to its customers for both dedicated and nondedicated use. Carl-Mitchell voices the excitement of the staff about this service as he says, "We think ISDN is going to make a whole new class of applications possible for the Internet, and we want to be in on this right from the start." Research and development on WWW programming and services is already underway at Zilker (Quarterman and Carl-Mitchell are also at work on a book on the subject), and it foresees the need for animated and voice services via the Internet as well. Future plans also include for-a-fee and free WAIS servers, and Mosaic server access.

For as far ahead as can be seen, though, Zilker's main focus will continue to be the professionals and businesses that sign up for its services, whether using POTS (plain old telephone system) or new technologies like ISDN. Given its broad range of services and capabilities and the can-do attitude for its customers, we can see nothing but success for Zilker as the Internet beats its way to front and back doors all over America, and the world!

CONTACT INFORMATION

Zilker Internet Park
1106 Clayton Lane, Suite 500W
Austin, TX 78723
Voice: (512) 206-3850
Dial in at 512-206-3854 (8 data bits, 1 stop bit, no parity)

Login as "new" (omit quotes, no password needed); fill out on-line application

Rates:
Dial-in: $20/month (20 hours of access time, $1/hr thereafter; 10 MB disk space, $0.10/MB/month thereafter)
$50/month unlimited access; disk charges remain the same
PPP: $30 month (20 hours of access time, $1.50/hr thereafter; disk charges same)
$80/month unlimited access; disk charges same
SLIP: $30 month (20 hours of access time, $1.50/hr thereafter; disk charges same)
$80/month unlimited access; disk charges same
UUCP: $50/month flat fee for UUCP connection. Price includes registration of an Internet domain and running two domain servers for MX records and mail forwarding. Support for user's end UUCP connection available at consulting rates
ISDN: $150/month plus a one time ($75 startup fee); includes dedicated 64 Kpbs ISDN line (Can run PPP/SLIP/TCP over connection)

Special for-a-fee software offers for PPP users, including Eudora, TCP/IP software, Gopher client, etc., for Macintosh and PC users.

ZILKER PUBLICATIONS

Quarterman, John S., *The Matrix: Computer Networks and Conferencing Systems Worldwide*, Digital Press, Bedford, MA, 1990. List price: $49.95.
Quarterman, John S., and Smoot Carl-Mitchell, *Practical Internetworking with TCP/IP and UNIX*, Addison-Wesley, Reading, MA, 1993. List price: $45.45.
Carl-Mitchell, Smoot, and John S. Quarterman: *The Internet Connection: System Connectivity and Configuration*, Addison-Wesley, Reading, MA, 1994. List price: $45.45.

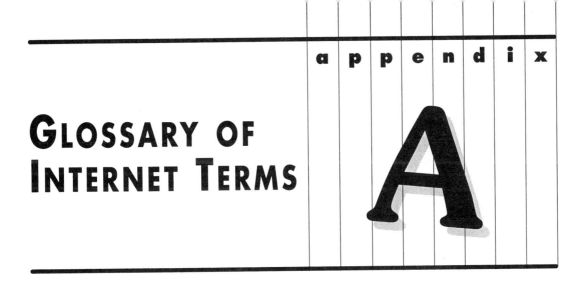

Glossary of Internet Terms

14.4 kbps: (and other typical modem speeds): The rated speed at which a modem can send bit patterns across the line (14.4 kbps = 14,400 bps). Other common modem speeds include 300, 1200, 2400, 9600, and 19,200 bps. In general, faster is better when it comes to modems. (*See also* bps, kbps)

3270: A model number for a family of IBM computer terminals; one of the most common of mainframe terminal types.

address resolution: Conversion of a logical IP address into its corresponding MAC-layer (physical) address.

acronym: An abbreviation formed by taking the first letter of each word of the phrase you want to abbreviate. Since e-mail terminology is loaded with long wordy phrases, it's also loaded with acronyms. Some technologists talk about TLAs, which stands for three-letter acronyms, as essential for legitimacy among nerds!

anonymous: When applied to FTP or Telnet, means being able to log in to and use those services on remote systems without possessing an individual account and password. With Anonymous FTP, the account is usually anonymous and the password is one's e-mail name; with Telnet, the account depends on the service requested (e.g., Archie, WAIS).

ANSI: American National Standards Institute; one of the primary standards-setting bodies for computer technology in the United States.

Archie: A program that catalogs files on over a thousand Anonymous FTP servers worldwide and lets users search against this database using interactive queries, e-mail, or through other programs like Gopher.

archives: A place where obsolete or unused records are stored; in computerese, a place where backed-up files are kept.

ARP: Address Resolution Protocol; the IP protocol that handles conversion of numeric IP addresses into MAC-layer equivalents (limited to network topologies that support hardware broadcast—i.e., to bus and equivalent topologies).

ARPA: Advanced Research Projects Administration. ARPA was a branch of the Department of Defense that funds advanced research in communications and computing and funded development of ARPANET (*see later*). In the 1980s this agency was renamed Defense ARPA, to make its roots clearer.

ARPANET: A packet-switched network developed in the 1970s, ARPANET is the granddaddy of the Internet (and was decommissioned in 1990).

article: A posting in a Usenet newsgroup; every article typically occupies its own separate file.

ASCII: Computer acronym for "American Standard Code for Information Interchange;" an eight-bit code for data transfer that was adopted by ANSI to ensure compatibility among data types.

ATM: Asynchronous transfer mode, a high-speed, high-bandwidth cell relay technology currently in use for telecommunications backbones (at speeds of 622 Mbps over fiber-optic links) and in limited LAN use (at speeds of 622 and155 Mbps, with other variants also available). ATM is expected to become a major high-bandwidth long-haul technology as fiber-optic services proliferate.

AUP: Acceptable use policy, the official policy statement governing use of a network (as with the NSFnet) and the type of traffic permitted

backbone: A high-speed link that ties multiple networks together. For the Internet, its backbone is operated by ANS (the conglomerate consisting of AT&T, General Atomics, and Network Solutions founded to form the InterNIC) as a collection of T-3 links; other parts of the Internet use T-3 or T-1 links for their backbones.

bandwidth: A measure of the capacity of any type of transmission medium; computer networks and telephone links (a.k.a. asynchronous connections) are typically measured in bits per second—bps). Most network links are measured in megabits per second (Mbps) or gigabits per second (Gbps); most telephone links are measured in kilobits per second (kbps) or Mbps.

baud: A unit of signalling speed defined as cycles per second. This equals bits per second (bps) only if one bit is transmitted per cycle. Bps is more accurate for rating modem speed, but baud is more commonly used when discussing modems.

BBS: Bulletin board system, a computer-operated dial-in service that typically supports file uploads and downloads, and that often offers electronic mail services. BBSs may be either private or public.

BCNU: E-mail acronym for "be seeing you."

bit: The smallest unit of computer information—a 1 or a 0—as represented in binary (Base 2) form.

BITNET: Because It's Time NETwork, a network that uses IBM RJE protocols as well as TCP/IP founded as an extension to the ARPANET in the early 1980s.

BOF: Birds of a feather. Informal discussion groups, typically focused on a particular topic or subject area. Sometimes used as a way to bring together interested parties at meetings and conferences (on-line or off-line).

BootP, BOOTP: The internet bootstrap protocol, BootP allows a client to discover its IP address, and obtain startup information (including operating system code download) from a designated BootP server.

bounce: E-mail will sometimes be returned because of delivery problems (bad address, unreachable network, etc.), including diagnostic error messages. When this happens, the messages is said to have "bounced."

bps: Bits per second; a measure of the number of ones and zeros that a computer or telephone connection can handle in one second.

broadcast: A packet delivery system, where a copy of a packet is automatically sent to all hosts attached to a single physical cable segment on the network (e.g., Ethernet).

BSD: Berkeley Software Distribution, used to describe a version of the UNIX operating system compiled and distributed at University of California at Berkeley (now handled by a separate commercial spinoff).

byte: Eight bits of computer data; kilobyte (1,024 or 210 bytes), megabyte (1,048,576 or 220 bytes), and gigabyte (230 bytes) are common measures of computer capacity.

CCITT: Consultative Committee for International Telegraphy and Telephony; a group within the International Telecommunications Union (ITU) that defines telecommunications standards.

client: A PC when it is in the position of requesting a service from a network server, also an e-mail user or his or her workstation can be called an *e-mail client*.

client-server model: A way of describing network services that assumes that an exchange between computers casts one machine in the role of a client, which requests services and handles end-user interaction, and the other in the role of a server, which responds to requests and handles back-end services.

CompuServe: A very large bulletin board. This is a great source of information in many topics; nearly all computer equipment and software vendors maintain forums here.

connectionless: A mode of intercommunications where information passes from sender to receiver without establishing a connection between the two.

connection oriented: A mode of intercommunications that proceeds through three well-defined phases: (1) connection establishment; (2) data transfer; and (3) teardown, or connection release. During phase 2 the connection that is established is often referred to as a *virtual circuit*.

daemon: A process that runs continuously in the background on a network host, ready to handle connection requests for a particular service (e.g., Telnet, FTP, and many other IP applications rely on daemons to field and respond to connection requests).

data link layer: The OSI layer responsible for data transfer across a single physical connection, or series of bridged connections, between a sender and a receiver.

desktop: Shorthand for desktop computer.

desktop computer: A computer used by an individual user, most commonly a personal computer (PC) or a workstation.

distribution list: A named list of recipients for an e-mail message (synonym: mailing list).

DNS: Domain Name Service is a distributed name/address database used on the Internet and in other private TCP/IP-based networking and e-mail environments.

domain: In the Internet world, a domain is part of a naming hierarchy. Syntactically, an Internet domain name consists of a sequence of names separated by periods (as discussed in explaining Internet addresses in Chapter 3). In the OSI world, a domain is generally used as an administrative partition of a complex distributed address space.

DOS: Disk Operating System. DOS is synonymous with the operating system used for IBM PCs and clones controlled by Microsoft (flavors of this particular DOS include Microsoft's MS-DOS, IBM's PC-DOS, and Novell DOS, formerly known as DR-DOS).

e-mail: Shorthand for electronic mail, e-mail refers to any of a number of software systems that let multiple users exchange messages electronically via some kind of connection (LAN, WAN, asynchronous, or otherwise).

EBCDIC: Computer acronym for extended binary coded decimal interchange code, an IBM data encoding format (similar to ASCII in intent, but different in actual physical format).

EFF: Electronic Frontier Foundation, an organization founded to guide the development of electronic communications into a livable human community, most of whose publicity has emerged from its interest in defending the privacy of electronic communications.

EGP: Exterior gateway protocol, a routing protocol used by gateways on an IP-based internetwork. EGP is used in the Internet core system, but will be replaced by a next-generation routing protocol the Border Gateway Protocol (BGP) before the year 2000.

electronic mail: See e-mail.

envelope: The "wrapper" that goes around data being sent over a network (synonymous with packet or datagram in this context) or around a message being sent by e-mail (synonymous with message header in this context).

Ethernet: A very common network technology; inexpensive to install but its age is showing, primarily in its speed limitations. Faster than ARCnet, though.

FAQ: Frequently asked questions list. One of the most common and informative types of documents posted on the Internet, a FAQ contains answers to the most frequently asked questions relating to the particular topic area. These are almost always worth reading.

FDDI: Fiber distributed data interface, the fastest of the four major network technologies (the others are ARCnet, Ethernet, and Token-Ring), and also the most expensive.

flame: A strong, sometimes inflammatory opinion on a particular subject, usually in the form of an e-mail message. When one flame leads to another, and so on, the result is sometimes called a *flame war*.

fragmentation: The process in which an IP datagram is subdivided into data frames for shipment over a network medium (this job is handled at the network layer in the OSI reference model).

frame: The unit of transmission at the data-link layer, consisting of an address header followed by a packet of data.

FTP: File transfer protocol, the Internet protocol and application that provides reliable file transfer between two hosts.

FWIW: The e-mail acronym "for what it's worth."

FYI: The e-mail acronym "for your information."

gateway: Generally, a gateway is a special-purpose software program that knows how to move information from one kind of system to another; originally, a gateway was used as an Internet term for what we now call a *router*; that is, a computer that could transfer messages between two disjoint administrative domains.

Gopher: A program/protocol developed at the University of Minnesota, Gopher provides for unified, menu-driven presentation of a variety of Internet services, including WAIS, Telnet, and FTP. Veronica supplies a search tool for navigating the global collection of Gopher servers, known as *Gopherspace*.

ground address: The address on earth, used to situate someone on the planet, but most often used to send snail mail.

header: Control information at the beginning of a message, segment, datagram, packet, or block of data (the address on what we also call an envelope).

host: Synonymous with computer, usually a mainframe or a minicomputer that provides ("host") services for other users on PCs or terminals.

host based mail: Any electronic mail system that runs on a minicomputer or mainframe.

IAB: Internet Architecture Board (formerly known as the Internet Activities Board), the governing body that oversees the definition and development of the Internet protocols and related services and applications.

ICMP: Internet control message protocol, an error-reporting and traffic management protocol that occupies the network layer in the TCP/IP protocol suite. ICMP is used among hosts and gateways to report problems and to suggest routes.

IETF: Internet Engineering Task Force, the technical group within the IAB that is responsible for meeting current engineering needs on the Internet and has custody over RFC content and related standards status.

IGP: Interior gateway protocol, a routing protocol used to exchange information between collaborating routers on the Internet, both RIP and OSPF are examples of IGPs.

IM(H)O: The e-mail acronym for "in my (humble) opinion" (the parentheses around humble mean it's optional, so you could write IMO or IMHO).

image: In this book, the term *image* is used to refer to a complex type of computer data that represents a high-resolution picture, or image, of some document or other visual data. For example, image data for a signature card in a bank lets a teller look at a customer's signature at his or her terminal without having to retrieve the signature card from a paper filing system.

Internet: The name for a worldwide, TCP/IP-based networked computing community with over 2 million users worldwide that links government, business, industry, and education together. Sometimes also called *the Internet*.

internetwork: A network of networks; an internetwork is therefore a collection of individual media segments linked together by special equipment built for that purpose (e.g., bridges and routers are types of internetworking equipment).

IP: An acronym for Internet protocol, this protocol name actually acts as shorthand for TCP/IP, which is the name of the protocol suite used on the Internet and consists of a collection of protocols and related networking applications including e-mail.

IP-connectivity: The ability to internetwork with an IP-based network.

IRTF: Internet Research Task Force, one of the two major task forces within the IAB, the IRTF is responsible for research into and further development of the TCP/IP protocol suite and related services and applications.

ISDN: Integrated services digital network. A high-bandwidth communications service, ISDN combines voice and digital services over a single medium, enabling telephone lines to handle both on a single physical wire. ISDN is a subset of the CCITT broadband ISDN (B-ISDN) standard.

ISO: International Standards Organization, an international standards group for networking and communications, and defining body for the OSI

(Open Standards Interconnect) suite of networking protocols and standards.

Jughead: A deliberately restricted implementation of Veronica, Jughead searches only Gopher menus for a specific subset of Gopherspace, as defined by the Jughead server's administrator (usually used to provide lookup for purely local information).

kbps: Kilobits per second (kilo is a special binary counting prefix for computers and amounts to 210 or 1,024).

kill file: The file or files that define topics, e-mail addresses, and threads you wish to block Usenet articles about (in other words, the stuff you want to ignore).

LAN: Local area network, supplied by many types of networking technology used to allow computers to communicate within a more-or-less confined geographical area (usually 2-4 square miles or less).

local application: An application that runs purely on a desktop machine, be it a PC or a workstation, without involving the network in any way, shape, or form.

login/logon: Login is the activity required to establish a working connection to a network and the resources it provides; a logon is the set of keystrokes or information that must be provided to make a successful login.

logout/logoff: Logout is the activity required to break a working connection to a network; a logoff is the set of keystrokes or other information that must be provided to log out successfully from a network.

lpd, lpr, lpq: Line printer daemon, line printer remote, line printer queue. The lpd acts to service remote print requests over the network from TCP/IP users; lpr is used to send such print commands; lpq lets remote print queues be managed by end-users.

machine: PC, computer, workstation.

Macintosh: Apple's Motorola-based microprocessor machines; Macintoshes are popular in today's marketplace because they are graphically organized, easy to use, and provide a broad array of software and capabilities.

mail server: A PC, workstation, or other computer that stores and forwards electronic mail messages on behalf of senders and receivers (see also post office).

mailing list: A named list of recipients for an e-mail message (synonym: distribution list).

mainframe: A large, expensive computer—typically, made by IBM—that is invariably managed by a dedicated information systems staff.

Mbps: The computer acronym for Megabits per second (Mega is a special binary counting prefix for computer terms that means 220 or 1,048,476).

megabyte (MB): The term for 1,048,476 bytes, commonly used as a measure for memory or disk capacity.

memory address: A specific collection of computer storage elements can be located only by its address; the memory address of a datum typically acts as the sender or recipient address when that datum is in use by the computer's central processing unit (CPU).

message: A formatted collection of electronic information built for use in a particular electronic mail application; also the unit of transmission in a transport protocol (for instance a TCP segment can be called a *message*).

message database: The set of messages maintained by a particular messaging application or on a specific messaging server is called a *message database*. In most cases, it consists of all unread messages, saved messages, templates, and other e-mail documents that users and administrators have decided to keep on-line.

MH: See Rand Message Handling System.

MHS: The e-mail acronym for message handling system; the context is important to this term, because Novell MHS is completely different from OSI MHS, even though the acronym is the same in both cases. If the context isn't clear, the most commonly used MHS is Novell's, but the most commonly referred to is OSI's.

modem: Modem is actually an acronym, standing for modulator/demodulator, and refers to the kinds of equipment used to translate (modulate and demodulate) digital computer signals into analog telephone signals. Simply put, modems let computer "talk" on the telephone.

MS Windows: See Windows.

MS-DOS: See DOS.

MTU: Maximum transmission unit, the largest chunk of data that can be sent over a given physical medium. TCP/IP negotiates the MTU for datagrams as a part of the connection establishment process.

multicast: A special form of broadcast delivery where copies of a packet are delivered only to a subset of all possible addresses.

multitasking: This refers to the apparent or actual ability of a computer to handle more than one activity at a time; multitasking is important because it lets a computer communicate over the network or the telephone at the same time it does other things.

name resolution: The process of mapping a fully qualified Internet name (name@domain format) into its corresponding address.

NetBIOS: Network Basic Input Output System, a standard protocol interface for IBM PC networks and those using compatible systems (originally developed as a part of IBM's PC-LAN networking environment).

network: A collection of computers linked together to share resources, including devices and information.

Network layer: That layer in the OSI Reference Model responsible for routing, switching, and ultimately for message delivery across a network.

NFS: Network file system, a distributed file system developed by Sun Microsystems that lets users access remote file systems as an apparent extension of their local file system.

NIC: Network information center; originally, ARPANET had a single NIC, located at SRI International, then later run by the Defense Data Network. Today the worldwide Internet is administered by a conglomerate formed by AT&T, General Atomics, and Network Solutions through an agency called the InterNIC, but many organizations and internets also operate their own NICs.

network interface card: Sometimes abbreviated as NIC, a network interface card provides the link between a computer and the networking technology and topology it wishes to use.

network operating system: The software that runs on your network server and moderates the clients' access to the server resources.

NIC: See network interface card.

NNTP: Network news transfer protocol, allows news servers to exchange messages and news readers to obtain and post messages across an IP-based network.

node: A computer on an internetwork is called a *node* (taken from graph theory, where a node occurs when two or more line segments meet).

notification: A message sent to a designated recipient to indicate that a specific event has occurred; the most common usage of the term is to indicate successful delivery of an e-mail message, but all kinds of other notifications are routinely issued by messaging software, including appointment reminders, meeting information, and so on.

off-line: In an environment where a computer can participate on a network or take part in a telephonic connection, a computer that isn't participating is said to be off-line. Off-line also means that a device is unavailable (e.g., a printer or other peripheral device can also be off-line).

on-line: The opposite of off-line; that is, on-line means that a computer or device is participating on a network, part of an active telephone connection or available to prospective users.

operating system: The software that runs in your PC, whether you are on a network or not, and manages access to such resources in the PC as your PC's diskettes, hard drive, and memory.

OS: An acronym (*see operating system*).

OSI: Computer acronym for open systems interconnect, a collection of networking and communications standards defined and managed by the International Standards Organization (ISO).

OSI reference model: The seven-layer model for network communications explained in Chapter 3 that some say is the most meaningful contribution ever to come out of OSI technology.

OSPF: Open shortest path first, a routing protocol used as an interior gateway protocol (IGP) on the Internet, OSPF is a next-generation replacement for RIP.

OTOH: The e-mail acronym for "on the other hand."

packet: The unit of data passed across the interface between the data link layer and the network layer. For TCP/IP a packet may be a complete or partial IP datagram.

PC: The computer acronym for personal computer, PC usually refers to an IBM-PC or its clone equivalent, even though any microprocessor-based computer that sits on a user's desktop could rightfully be called a *personal computer*.

physical layer: The OSI reference model layer that provides the means to activate and use physical connections for signal transmission across a network medium.

PING: Packet internet groper, an Internet application used to test reachability of a destination (works by sending an ICMP echo request to the destination; a response indicates reachability, response delay provides a measure of roundtrip time that can be a useful measure of network performance and quality).

POP: (1) Point of presence, a site where telecommunications equipment is stored, typically including digital leased lines and multiprotocol routers, where a national access provider or telecommunications company interfaces with a local access provider or an organization large enough to need a sizable pipe into the Internet.

(2) Post office protocol, a protocol designed to let individual user hosts read e-mail from a server. The most recent (and most commonly used) version is POP3.

port: The logical network communications channel established on a host to receive or set up a particular connection. When a daemon for a service establishes a connection it reserves a unique port address for that connection's use for as long as the connection persists. Daemons work by listening for requests on preassigned port IDs, known as *well-known port addresses* (Telnet, FTP, etc. all have such well-known addresses for their daemons to listen on).

POTS: Plain Old Telephone System. An acronym for the kind of telephone service most people have at home.

PPP: Point-to-Point Protocol. The successor to SLIP, PPP provides router-to-router and host-to-network connections over synchronous and asynchronous circuits; because it has lower overhead and better service than SLIP, we recommend it for setting up telephone based IP connections.

presentation layer: The OSI reference model layer that handles formatting of data for delivery to applications for incoming data and encodes outgoing data in a generic format suitable for network transport.

protocol: A set of networking rules. Unless they share a protocol, two computers cannot talk to one another.

protocol set: A collection of protocols that provide network access for users and applications. AppleTalk and TCP/IP are two common protocol suite examples.

protocol suite: The same as protocol set, except that the suite is usually a complete collection of all the protocols of a particular type, whereas a set might only include some, but not all, of those protocols.

queue: A computer data structure that lets items be stored in the order of arrival (first-in, first-out); a queue is the computerized equivalent of standing in line and works to let users issue requests for service that will be handled in the order they are received (like for printing or faxing).

RAM: The computer acronym for random access memory, high-speed data storage in a computer. Usually anything stored in here vanishes when you turn off the computer.

Rand Message Handling System: The addressing scheme developed at Rand Corp., on which Internet addressing was based (sometimes abbreviated as RMHS).

RARP: Reverse address resolution protocol, the TCP/IP protocol that lets a (typically diskless) node discover its Internet address at startup. RARP maps a physical, MAC-layer address to a corresponding IP address.

real-time systems: Computer systems designed to react to service demands or reported events as quickly as possible; the term *real time* means that the system is expected to react to demands immediately, if not sooner.

RFC: The computer acronym for "request for comment," a document controlled by the Internet Architecture Board (IAB), the governing body for the TCP/IP protocol suite (all TCP/IP protocols, interfaces, and applications are governed by related RFCs).

RIP: Routing internet protocol, an interior gateway protocol (IGP) supplied as the original Internet routing protocol in BSD UNIX.

ROTFL: The e-mail acronym for "rolling on the floor laughing."

router: An internetworking device capable of decoding network addresses and forwarding packets to the destination network or at least to another router that is "closer" to the destination.

RTFM: The computer acronym for "read the friendly manual!"

r-utils: Remote utilities (including rexec, rsh, rlogin). A set of remote utilities that would let users execute commands across the network, the r-utils were introduced as a part of BSD UNIX.

scheduling: A type of message-based application that coordinates the schedules of individual group members.

segment: The unit of end-to-end data transmission in the TCP protocol, consisting of a TCP header followed by application data. A segment will be fragmented and then encapsulated in IP datagrams at the network layer in the TCP/IP stack.

server: A PC or other computer whose function is to provide access to network resources.

session: The set of communications that occur while a connection between hosts is established; also, the name of the OSI reference model layer at which session creation, maintenance, and teardown is handled.

SIG: Special interest group, a collection of individuals who share a common interest; many professional societies (e.g., Association for Computing Machinery) organize themselves into SIGs.

SLIP: Serial line interface protocol, the Internet protocol used to run IP over serial lines, like telephone connections or RS-232 serial links, used to interconnect two systems (now being replaced by PPP).

smiley: A special sequence of ASCII characters designed to look like a particular facial expression and to signify the emotion that such an expression denotes (e.g., ":)" is a basic smiley face and indicates a cheerful grin).

SMTP: The e-mail acronym for simple mail transfer protocol, SMTP is the basic TCP/IP e-mail application.

SNADS: The e-mail acronym for IBM's systems network architecture distribution services, which provides a generalized architecture for asynchronous distribution services that are used to implement office information architectures and a comprehensive document interchange architecture for exchanging documents among systems.

snail mail: A euphemism for regular mail delivery, emphasizing its speed relative to electronic mail.

SNMP: Simple network management protocol, the network management protocol in the TCP/IP protocol suite.

stack (a.k.a. protocol stack): This refers to the various layers in typical protocol suites, often as organized by the OSI reference model.

standard: A set of guidelines and rules, as stated by some standards-setting body (an official standard) or some vendor (a de facto standard).

store-and-forward systems: A software system that can retain incoming information and forward outgoing information to the designated system (a good behavior description for how e-mail servers work).

sysop: The computerese abbreviation for system operator, the individual responsible for monitoring one or more message forums on a BBS system.

TCP: Transmission control protocol, a reliable, connection-oriented protocol that contributed its name to the overall TCP/IP protocol suite, TCP is one of the important transport protocols in that environment.

telex: A text-based asynchronous data transfer system similar to, but older than, facsimile systems. Telexes are most popular in Europe and use teletype equipment over phone lines to transfer text messages at a relatively low expense.

Telnet: The terminal emulation protocol/application in the TCP/IP suite, Telnet allows users on one host to log in to a remote host across the network.

terminal: A display device for a computer system—usually a cathode-ray terminal (CRT), most often with an attached keyboard, that has little or no local processing power (which is why terminals are often called *dumb terminals*). Most minicomputer and mainframe systems originally used terminals as their only devices for human interaction (today, PCs can act like, or emulate terminals, in addition to performing other tasks).

terminal server: A device that can handle multiple RS-232 connections and provide links to a network interface, terminal servers are typically used to attach multiple dumb terminals or multiple telephone lines to a host (or a network of hosts).

TFTP: Trivial file transfer protocol, a simple file transfer protocol built on UDP, generally used only when you've already telnetted to another host and realize you need to transfer a file from your local machine to that machine.

tn3270, tn5250: Both 3270 and 5250 refer to specific models of IBM terminals; the *tn* stands for Telnet; both are acronyms for specific implementations of Telnet that can emulate those particular IBM terminals.

transport layer: The layer in the OSI reference model that handles data transfer between systems.

UDP: User datagram protocol, an Internet transport protocol, UDP uses IP, but operates in a connectionless mode (that is, it provides for exchange of datagrams without acknowledgment or guaranteed delivery).

UNIX: The name of a specific type of computer operating system, originated at Bell Labs in the 1970s. Because it is widely taught in colleges and universities worldwide, UNIX is one of the most familiar OSs in the computing community.

Usenet: A BBS accessed via the Internet, Usenet may be the most active BBS in the world today.

user ID: The abbreviation for user identifier, a unique name or bit string that identifies a system user to a particular software system.

UUCP: UNIX-to-UNIX copy program, a protocol used to exchange information between trusted UNIX hosts (i.e., security arrangement are predetermined). UUCP is the protocol used for exchange of information on Usenet.

Veronica: A program that searches Gopher menu entries to match user-supplied search strings, Veronica can search all menu entries or menu directory entries only.

virtual circuit: A connection established between two application programs over the network, works very much like a telephone call (involves connection setup, maintenance, and teardown).

WAIS: Wide Area Information Service, a collection of programs that implement a specific protocol for information retrieval, able to index large-scale collections of data around the Internet, WAIS provides content-oriented query services to users with WAIS client capability. Available both in free and for-a-fee implementations, WAIS is one of the most powerful Internet search tools available.

WAN: The computer acronym for wide area network, a network whose span exceeds 2-4 square miles, that usually depends on some kind of specialized high-speed access technology, or that uses a high-bandwidth asynchronous connection between individual LANs.

Windows: Microsoft Corporation's graphical user interface software, MS-Windows is on of the best-selling PC software systems in the world.

workgroup: A collection of individuals who work together and are interconnected via a network of computers.

workstation: A desktop computer, usually a more powerful machine than an ordinary IBM-PC or clone, often with a high-speed reduced instruction set computer (RISC) processor, often running UNIX as its OS.

WWW: World Wide Web, a hypertext Internet service developed at CERN in Switzerland, WWW is emerging as another powerful content-oriented search and information retrieval mechanism.

X.400: The ISO standard governing e-mail systems, X.400 describes message formats, protocols, and message exchange technologies.

X.500: The ISO standard governing synchronization of multiple directory service environments, X.500 describes name and address requirements and defines a method to map between multiple directory services.

YMMV: The e-mail acronym for "your mileage may vary"; indicates that individual experiences may not live up to the claims made for a particular system feature or function.

INDEX

10Base2, 340
10BaseT, 347–348
14.4 kbps, 353
3270, 353

A

Academic Periodical Index, 94
Acceptable Use Policy (AUP), 29–31, 86–87, 324–325, 354
Acronyms, 62, 353, 367
Acunet, 321
Address resolution, 353
Address Resolution Protocol (ARP), 49, 354, 365
Addresses
    Class A IP address, 42
    Class B IP address, 42
    Class C IP address, 40, 42
Advanced Research Projects Administration (ARPA), 13, 17–19, 21, 24, 354
Advisories, 242–243
ALOHAnet, 19, 24, 33
AlterNet, 28
America Online, 28, 117, 123
American National Standards Institute (ANSI), 353–354
Amiga, 128
Animation, 108
Anonymous FTP
    servers, 183, 353
    sites, 200–201
AppleTalk, 296, 364
Archie, 199–209, 354
    command switches, 205
    e-mail alternative, 208

    interactive commands, 207
    master servers, 204
Archive, 174–176, 200, 326
ARCnet, 48, 357
Ariadne, 293, 295
ARPANET, 354
Article, 354
ASCII, 354
Assigned Numbers Authority, 41
Asynchronous Transfer Mode (ATM), 49, 108, 110, 282, 288, 354
Autologout, 207–208
Autonet, 311
Autoreply, 123–124, 310
Autoresponders, 303

B

Backbone, 30–31, 354
Bandwidth, 107, 282, 354
Baud, 355
BBN, 19
Berkeley Software Distribution (BSD), 26, 121, 355, 365
BITNET, 19–20, 66, 142–144, 355
    mailing lists, 144
Bolt, Beranek & Newman, 21, 23, 48
Bombing, 124
Bookmark, 209
BootP, 355
Bootstrap, 355
Border Gateway Protocol (BGP), 53, 357
Bounce, 355
Broadband Integrated Services Digital Network (B-ISDN), 359

Broadcast, 355
Browsing, 273
BSD, 26, 121, 355, 365
BT Tymnet, 328
Bulletin Board System (BBS), 289, 304, 311–312, 322,
     325, 328, 330, 335–337, 341, 355, 366–367

C

CAPCON, 291–292, 296
Carnegie-Mellon University (CMU), 19
CCITT, 356, 359
CDT, 130
CERFnet, 20, 28–29, 66
CERN, 20, 368
Character-mode, 189, 257
Checksum, 53
ClariNet, 320
ClarkNet, 297
Clarkson Packet Driver, 264, 267
Class A IP Address, 42
Class B IP Address, 42
Class C IP Address, 40, 42
Client–server, 185, 194, 202, 331, 356
CMU, 19
Commercial Internet Exchange (CIX), 28, 30, 87, 109,
     279
Common Interactive Abbreviations (CIA), 245
Compressed PC Formats, 175
Compression, 173, 175–176
CompuServe, 20, 28, 82, 117, 123, 127, 356
Conference, 19, 23
Conferencing Systems, 351
Configuration, 189, 351
ConflictNet, 306
Connection oriented, 356
Connectionless, 50, 356
Consultative Committee on Telephony & Telegraphy
     (CCITT), 356, 359
Copy Files Using FTP, 169
CSNET, 20
CSU/DSU, 78, 278, 340
CTSNET, 298
CyberGate, 304
Cyberspace, 300

D

Daemon, 150, 356
Data Collection, 201
Data Grade, 110
Data Link, 358
Data Link Layer, 37, 356
Data Link Protocols, 48
Database management system (DBMS), 202–203
Datagram, 52
Debug, 168
Decompress, 176
Decompression Tools, 175
Dedicated, 79, 83, 280–282

Defense Advanced Research Projects Administration
     (DARPA), 19, 24, 26
Defense Information Services Agency (DISA), 19
Delphi, 123
Department of Defense (DoD), 13, 17, 19–21, 23, 35, 63,
     68, 354
Department of Energy, 27
Dewey Decimal System, 232
Dial-in, 351
Dial-up, 80, 82, 280–281
Directory, 20, 65, 163, 169, 176, 250, 327, 331
Distribution list, 356
Domain name, 149, 177, 182, 192
Domain Name Service (DNS), 45, 55, 66, 264, 299,
     307–308, 314, 322, 339, 356
Domains, 43, 357
DOS-based, 134
Download, 69, 81
Dynamic Link Library (DLL), 261

E

E-mail, 19, 23, 28–30, 34, 43–45, 56, 64–65, 67, 71–77,
     82–83, 86–87, 89, 91–93, 95, 101–103, 110, 113–114,
     117–125, 129, 132, 138, 141–146, 149, 151–152, 165,
     169, 173, 177–182, 185, 192, 207–208, 245–249,
     251–253, 263, 269, 279, 283, 289–290, 293, 295,
     307–308, 315, 321, 324–330, 339, 341, 353–354,
     356–366, 368
   harassing, 124
   mail bombing, 124
   mail headers, 119
   managing addresses, 247, 249, 251, 253
E-mail-to-fax, 299, 302
EBCDIC, 58, 357
EcoNet, 306
Electronic Frontier Foundation (EFF), 69, 357
Emulator, 325
Encoding, 79, 173, 179–180, 357
End-to-end, 365
ENIAC, 14
Envelope, 357
Ethernet, 357
Eudora, 178, 351
EUnet, 306
EuropaNet, 295
European Ecomonic Community (EEC), 27
Exterior Gateway Protocol (EGP), 53–54, 357

F

Fax, 118, 249, 277, 295–300, 302–305, 307–310, 312–316,
     318–319, 321, 323, 327
Fiber Distributed Data Interface (FDDI), 48, 108, 357
FidoNet, 20
File Transfer Protocol (FTP), 54, 58–60, 64, 67, 69, 95,
     113–115, 158–159, 161–169, 171–175, 177–183,
     185–186, 190, 199–203, 207–208, 211, 262, 266–269,
     281, 294, 299–300, 303–304, 306–307, 324–326, 339,
     342, 349, 353–354, 356, 358, 364, 367

archive sites, 326
by-mail, 178
commands, 166–168
Find, 130, 235, 249
Finding
compression, 175
information within newsgroups, 273
people, 247
Public Data Network, 289, 328
things, 271
Finger, 55–56, 152, 249–250, 265
Flame, 103, 138, 358
Folklore, 237, 239
Forged messages, 125
Forgotten site list, 328
Forward, 17, 153, 179, 366
Fragmentation, 50, 358
Frame, 49, 108–110, 171, 337, 358
Freedom of Information Act, 243
Freenet, 317
Freeware, 262–263, 267
Frequently-Asked-Questions (FAQs), 135–138, 143, 158,
178, 195, 209, 235, 258, 269, 274, 326, 357

G

Gateway, 358
General Atomics, 20, 28–29, 62, 327, 354, 362
General posting tips, 137
Glossary, 353–367
GNU (not Unix), 176
Gopher, 20, 28, 69, 83, 100, 113, 115, 186, 191, 193–197,
199–200, 209–211, 231–234, 241–242, 244–245, 252,
255–260, 266, 283, 287, 299, 304, 306–307, 324, 349,
351, 354, 358, 360, 368
attractions, 260
client, 194
GopherSpace, 258
attractions, 259
Government documents, 241, 243, 245
Ground address, 358

H

Handbook of Computer Communications Standards,
68
Header, 358
HoloNet, 305
HomeoNet, 306
Homosexual Network, 304
HookUp, 305
Host, 40, 187, 249, 329, 358
Host-to-host, 21–22
Host-to-network, 364
Hostname, 207, 249
Hpack, 176
Hyperlinked, 116
Hypermedia, 108
Hypertext, 368

I

IANA, 41
IBM PC, 26, 258, 362
IEunet, 293, 306
IGC, 291–292, 306
Image, 359
Indexing problem, 231
Integrated Services Digital Network (ISDN), 108,
278–279, 281–282, 298–299, 307–308, 314, 340, 342,
345, 350–351, 359
Interactive Archie commands, 207
Interior Gateway Protocol (IGP), 359, 363, 365
Intermittent dial-up, 280
Internet Activities Board (IAB), 41–43, 49, 62, 66, 88,
358–359, 365
Internet Architecture Board (IAB), 41–43, 49, 62, 66, 88,
358–359, 365
Internet Control Message Protocol (ICMP), 51, 55,
358–359, 363
Internet e-mail, 74, 117–119, 121, 123, 125, 327
Internet Engineering Task Force (IETF), 49, 62–64, 282,
359
Internet guide books, 327
Internet Network Information Center (InterNIC), 20,
29, 41–42, 62, 65–66, 209–210, 279, 326–327, 342,
354, 362
Internet provider lists, 328
Internet Research Task Force (IRTF), 62, 359
InternetsSociety, 20, 88
Internet timeline, 19–20, 33–34
Internetworked Packet Exchange (IPX), 277
Internetworking, 19, 68, 351
Interop, 346
IP Address
address layout, 39
applications, 54
basics, 35
Class A, 42
Class B, 42
Class C, 40, 42
resources, 68
routing protocols, 53
software, 261, 263, 265, 267–269
standards, 64
IRC, IRCii, 147, 154–159, 178, 266, 297, 299, 304, 307,
312, 317, 321, 341
client, 155
commands, 156–157
ISDN-TCP, 308
ISO, 36, 359, 363, 368

J

Jughead, 211, 260, 287, 360
JUNET, 20

K

killfile, 276, 360

L

LaborNet, 306
Law of Net Conservation, 256
Legal issues, 138
Library of Congress, 185, 244
Lincoln Laboratories, 23
Line interface unit, 78
Line printer services, 60
List of lists, 143–144
List of newsgroups, 143, 272–273
Listname-request, 145
listserv, 19, 142–144
Local access provider, 287
Local application, 360
Local-area network (LAN), 26, 83, 86, 117, 121, 261, 264, 268, 277, 282, 330–331, 348, 354, 357, 360
Login, 250, 343, 351, 360
Logout, 360
lpd, lpr, lpq, 360

M

Mac file compression formats, 176
Mac SLIP, 309
Mac TCP, 268–269
Mac Tools, 129
Macro, 168
Mail bombing, 124
Mail headers, 119
Mail-news, 121
Mail-server, 183, 251–252, 326, 328, 360
Mailbox, 92, 101–103, 145
Mailing lists, 141–145, 235, 360
    cautions, 145
MCI Mail, 123
MCSNet, 310
Memory address, 361
Merit Network, 66, 310, 326
Merit Network Information Center Internet, 326
Message, 361
Message database, 361
Message-based, 365
Messaging, 43, 102, 361, 363
Meta network, 320
Metacharacter, 167
Metronet, 310
MichNet, 310
Microsoft Corporation, 368
Minicomputer, 266, 358, 367
Minitel, 20
Modem, 78, 361
Mosaic, 20, 267, 284, 350
Moving files, 114
MS-DOS, 121, 294, 357, 361
MS-Windows, 368
MTU, 361
multicast, 361
Multipurpose Internet Mail Extensions (MIME), 121
Multisession, 191

N

Name resolution, 362
National Center for Supercomputing Applications (NCSA), 267
National Research And Education Network (NREN), 20, 32
National Science Foundation (NSF), 19–20, 29, 31, 87, 324
    NSFnet, 66, 354
Navigator, 115, 328
NEARnet, 312
Negative acknowledgement (NAK), 52
NeoSoft, 319–320
NetBIOS Enhanced User Interface (NetBEUI), 277
Netnews, 327
Network Basic Input Output System (NetBIOS), 264, 277, 362
Network Control Protocol (NCP), 19, 21, 24–25
Network Driver Interface Specification (NDIS), 264
Network File System (NFS), 61, 266, 349, 362
    NFSNET, 27
Network Information Center (NIC), 362
Network Information Services (NIS), 45
Network interface card, 362
Network layer, 37
Network News Transport Protocol (NTP or NNTP), 266, 298–299, 307, 322, 362
Network operating system, 362
News On-line, 260
News Services, 244
Newsfeed, 309, 315, 318
Newsgroup, 142, 272–273
Newsreader, 272
Newuser, 157–158, 297, 302, 310, 316, 322
Nexus, 315
Nickname, 156
Nondedicated, 350
North American Free Trade Agreement (NAFTA), 244
Notification, 362
NovaLink, 314
Novell, 264, 267–268, 277, 357, 361
NWNEXUS, 315
Nynex, 109
NYSERNet, 209

O

OARnet, 291–292, 315
Off-line, 101, 134, 363
    readers, 134
On-line, 363
Open Data-Link Interface (ODI), 264
Open Systems Interconnect (OSI), 36, 38, 45–46, 48, 56–57, 356–359, 361–364, 366–367
    reference model, 36, 362, 363
Owner-mail-server, 252
Ownership, 2

P

Package, 120
Packet, 19, 322–323, 329, 363
Packet network, 19, 322–323, 329
Packet-switched data networks (PDNs), 289–291, 293, 301, 305–306, 311, 314, 317–318, 320, 322–323, 328
PacTel, 109
PANIX Public Access Unix, 316
Password, 95, 163, 165, 169, 186
PeaceNet, 306
Performance Systems International, 28
Phone Lines, 78
Phone number, 249
Physical layer, 363
PING, 51, 55, 265, 363
PKZip, 176
Plain old telephone system (POTS), 278, 350, 364
Point-to-point protocol (PPP), 49, 77, 80, 82–83, 134, 195, 264, 278, 280–281, 295–300, 302–315, 319, 321–323, 325, 348–349, 351, 364, 366
Port, 364
Post office parallel (POP), 266, 282, 307, 364
    POPmail, 299, 322
PostScript, 64–65, 69, 158
Prairienet, 317
PREPnet, 291–293, 317
Presentation layer, 38, 364
Principle of locality, 255
Principle of polite usage, 256
Principle of similarity, 256
Privacy, 92
Prodigy, 82, 117
Protocol standards, 64, 68
Protocols, 47–48, 53, 62, 364
    set, 364
    suite, 364
PSILink, 318
PSINet, 305, 318, 329
Public-access, 326
Public-domain, 200, 203, 259, 262
PUCnet, 292, 318–319

Q

Queue, 364

R

R-Utils, 58, 365
Radio-based, 24
RAND Corporation, 23
RAND Message Handling System (RMHS), 365
Real-time systems, 365
Reply, 145
Request for comment (RFC), 64–66, 159, 164, 166, 260, 264, 282, 359, 365
    obtaining, 64
    ordering, 65
Retrieving, 95

Reverse address resolution protocol (RARP), 49, 264, 365
RIP, 365
RJ-11, 339
RJ-45, 339
Router, 340, 348, 365
Router-to-router, 364
RS-232, 348, 366–367

S

Script, 178–179
Search, 196, 203, 207, 209, 233, 256, 258
    methods, 203
    techniques, 233, 256
Security, 285
Segment, 365
Send, 65, 120, 245, 251, 290, 325–326, 329
Serial, 366
Serial Line Interface Protocol (SLIP), 49, 77, 80, 82–83, 134, 195, 264, 278, 280–281, 295–315, 317, 319, 321–323, 325, 337, 342–343, 348, 351, 364, 366
Server, 162, 169, 176, 183, 196, 204, 347, 365
Session, 38, 365
Session Layer, 38
Shareware, 262, 267
Simple Mail Transfer Protocol (SMTP), 43, 56, 264, 366
Simple Network Management Protocol (SNMP), 56–57, 266, 366
Smiley, 104, 148, 366
SNADS, 366
Snail mail, 366
Special interest group (SIG), 366
SprintLink, 30, 288
SprintNet, 306, 311, 314, 317, 321
Sputnik, 19
SPX, 277
Standard level definition, 63
Standards, 36, 64, 68, 353, 359–360, 363
Standards-making, 62
Stanford Research Institute (SRI), 19, 21–22, 362
    SRI International, 362
Store-and-forward systems, 366
StuffIT, 176
Supercomputer, 115
Superhighway, 2, 32, 66, 335
SuperNet, 299
SuperPEP, 322
Switched Multimegabit Data Service (SMDS), 49
Sysop, 366

T

T-1s, 287
T-3, 66, 282, 287, 354
Tagged image file format (TIFF), 129
Tape, 174
tar-z, 176
Tarfiles, 174
Telecommunications, 356

Telenet, 23
Telephony, 356
Telex, 367
Telnet, 19, 58–60, 64, 113, 115, 149, 164, 171, 182,
    185–192, 202–203, 208, 244, 262, 264, 266–267, 294,
    299–300, 307, 339, 348, 353, 356, 358, 364, 367
    commands, 189–190
Terminal emulation, 59
Terminal servers, 340, 348, 367
Terminate-and-stay-resident (TSR), 261
TeX, 69
TFTP, 367
THEORYNET, 19, 23
Thunderstorms, 339
Time-division multiplexing, 16
Time-sharing, 26
Timeout, 52
tn3270, tn5250, 367
Token-ring, 48, 108, 264, 357
Transmission Control Protocol (TCP), 19–20, 23–27,
    35–36, 38–42, 44–56, 58–68, 72, 83, 162, 164,
    171–172, 185, 188, 190, 202, 256–257, 261–269, 277,
    279–281, 324, 339, 342, 351, 355–356, 358–361,
    363–367
Transport layer, 38, 367
TurboPEP, 296, 323
Tymnet, 301, 305, 317, 328

U
U.S. Sprint, 288
UDP, 52–53, 59, 61, 367
Unacceptable uses, 31
Unarchive, 174
Uncompress, 95, 174–175
Uninterruptible power supply (UPS), 339, 347
UNIX, 20, 297, 299, 308, 314, 316, 319, 325, 346, 367
    basics, 342
UNIX-to-UNIX CoPy (UUCP), 19–20, 295, 297–300, 302,
    304–305, 307–308, 312–315, 317, 319–322, 324, 327,
    351, 368
Usenet basics, 128
User Datagram Protocol (UDP), 52–53, 59, 61, 367
Usergroups, 128
Userid, 123, 208, 367
Username, 43, 149, 153, 208
uudecode, 179–182
uuencode, 179–180, 182
uunet, 321

V
V32, 296

V32bis, 295
V42bis, 295
Variables, 207
Veronica, 113, 199–200, 208–211, 368
Virtual circuit, 368
Virus, 239
Vnet, 292–293, 321–322
Voicemail, 294, 314
Volksnet, 347–348
Volumes, 68
VT100, 189, 265
VT52, 265

W
WAN, 282, 357, 368
Whatis, 203
Whois, 250–252, 265
    servers, 251
Wide Area Information Service (WAIS), 20, 28, 64–65,
    67, 194, 196, 209, 231–234, 259, 266, 281, 283, 297,
    299, 301–302, 307, 309, 312–313, 320, 349–350, 353,
    358, 368
WinSock, 267, 269
Wireless, 111
Wiring, 29, 348
World Wide Web (WWW), 20, 69, 73, 83, 100, 113, 116,
    209, 231–232, 259, 266, 281, 283, 296–297, 301,
    306–307, 312, 322, 324, 342, 349–350, 368
World-dial service, 318
Worms, 239

X
X-Windows, 171
X400, 306, 368
X500, 306, 368
XNet, 323
XRemote, 318

Y
ytalk, 153

Z
zmodem, 82

INTERACTIVE ARCHIE COMMANDS

Command	Explanation
Program Control Commands	
quit	end Archie session and exit program
Help/Information Commands	
help ?	show list of commands
help *command*	show help information for command
manpage	show Archie manual page
servers	show list of Archie servers
Search Commands	
find *string*	search FTP database for *string*
whatis *string*	search whatis database for *string*
mail	ship results of last search to mailto address
Variable Settings	
show	shows values for all definable *variables*
show *variable*	show setting for *variable*
Settable Variables	*usage: set variable from list below*
autologout	idle time before autologout in minutes
mailto	Internet e-mail address to which one ships search results
maxhits	maximum matches, total, returned

Command	Explanation
maxmatch	maximum filename repetitions allowed
output_format	can be terse, verbose, or machine-readable
pager	use UNIX less command to control screen enter unset pager to turn off
search	—establish search behavior for pattern matching —similar to non-interactive, with values of: **exact**: match pattern exactly **sub**: search for any string containing pattern **subcase**: any string but distinguish upper/lower case **regex**: search for regular expression **exact_sub**=e, then sub; **exact_subcase**=e, then subcase **exact_regex**=e, then regex
sortby	none, filename, hostname, size, time **r** in front (e.g. **rsize**) reverses sort order
status	display status line during search (completion time info) enter **unset status** to turn off

UNIX COMMANDS

Command	Explanation
!! or r	Repeat last command
Backspace, Ctrl+h	Backspace
cat *filename*	Read a text file
cd	Change to home directory
cd ..	Change directory back one level
cd / *directory name*	Change directory
cp *filename*	Copy a file
cp *filename directory name*	Copy a file to another directory
^c, q	Cancel an operation
^d, logout, exit	Log out
^q	Resume display
^s	Stop display
^u	Clear command line
grep "*text*" *filename*	Search for text in file
ls	List directory contents
ls -a	List include hidden files
ls -l	List full information
ls -x	List in wide format
man *command*	Read online help for a command
more *filename*	Read a text file page by page
mv *filename directory name*	move a file
passwd	Change password
pwd	Print working directory
rm *filename*	Delete a file
rmdir *directory name*	Remove directory

TELNET COMMANDS

Command	Explanation
close	close current connection
display	display operating parameters
mode	try to enter line-by-line or character-at-a-time mode
open	connect to a site
quit	exit telnet
send	transmit special characters ('send ?' for more)
set	set operating parameters ('set ?' for more)
status	print status information
toggle	toggle operating parameters ('toggle ?' for more)
^z	suspend telnet
help, ?	print help information

INTERACTIVE ABBREVIATIONS

BCNU	be seeing you	IM(H)O	in my humble opinion
BRB	be right back	JAM	just a minute
BTW	by the way	OBTW	oh, by the way
BYE?	is this goodbye?	OTOH	on the other hand
CUL	see you later	ROTFL	rolling on the floor laughing
DWIM	do what I mean (not what I say)	*CAPS*	indicates emphasis
FWIW	for what it's worth	:-)	smiley, happy face
<G>	grin (to indicate humor)	;-)	wink (tongue in cheek)
GA	go ahead, type away (I'll wait until you're done)		

FTP Commands

File System Control Commands

Command	Explanation
cd	change remote working directory
cdup	change remote working directory to parent directory
delete	delete remote file
dir	list contents of remote directory
lcd	change local working directory
ls	list contents of remote directory
mdelete	delete multiple files
mdir	list contents of multiple remote directories
mkdir	make directory on the remote machine
mls	nlist contents of multiple remote directories
pwd	print working directory on remote machine
rename	rename file
rmdir	remove directory on the remote machine

File Transfer Management Commands

Command	Explanation
ascii	set ascii transfer type
binary	set binary transfer type
case	toggle mget upper/lower case id mapping
cr	toggle carriage return stripping on ascii gets
form	set file transfer format
glob	toggle metacharacter expansion of local file names
hash	toggle printing '#' for each buffer transferred
mode	set file transfer mode
nmap	set templates for default file name mapping
ntrans	set translation table for default file name mapping
runique	toggle store unique for local files
sendport	toggle use of PORT cmd for each data connection
struct	set file transfer structure
sunique	toggle store unique on remote machine
tenex	set tenex file transfer type
type	set file transfer type

Anonymous FTP

acctname=anonymous; password = your e-mail name

File Transfer Control Commands

Command	Explanation
append	append to a file
mget	get multiple files
mput	send multiple files
put	send one file
recv	receive file
send	send one file
get	file transfer control; receive file

Program Management Commands

Command	Explanation
!	escape to the shell
$	execute macro
?	print local help information
account	send account command to remote server
bell	beep when command completed
bye	terminate ftp session and exit
close	terminate ftp session
debug	toggle/set debugging mode
disconnect	terminate ftp session
help	print local help information
macdef	define a macro
open	connect to remote ftp
prompt	interactive prompting on multiple commands
proxy	issue command on alternate connection
quit	terminate ftp session and exit
quote	send arbitrary ftp command
remotehelp	get help from remote server
reset	clear queued command replies
status	show current status
trace	toggle packet tracing
user	send new user information
verbose	toggle verbose mode

WAIS Commands

Command	Explanation	Command	Explanation
j, ^N	Move Down one item (arrow keys work too)	=	Deselect all sources (when selecting sources)
k, ^P	Move Up one item (arrow keys work too)	d	Deselect current source (when selecting sources)
J	Move Down one screen	|	Pipe current item into a unix command
K	Move Up one screen	u	Use this item, add it to the list of sources
R	Show relevant documents		
S	Save current item to a file	v	View current item information
m	Mail current item to an address	r	Make current item a relevant document
##	Position to item number ##	s	Specify new sources to search
/sss	Position to item beginning sss	w	Make another search with new keywords
<space>	Display current item (when selecting items)	o	Set and shows WAIS options
<return>	Display current item (when selecting items)	h	Show this help display
<space>, <period>	Select current source (when selecting sources)	H	Display program history
		q	Leave this program

Talk Keyboard Shortcuts

Keystrokes	Explanation
Backspace	Back up and erase one (character) space
^H	Same as Backspace
^W	Back up and erase one word
^U	Back up and erase entire line
^X	Use instead of ^U on some systems
^L	Redisplays entire talk screen